Infrastructures
of Apocalypse

Infrastructures of Apocalypse

*American Literature
and the Nuclear Complex*

Jessica Hurley

.

University of Minnesota Press
Minneapolis
London

Portions of chapter 4 were previously published as "Impossible Futures: Fictions of Risk in the *Longue Durée*," *American Literature* 89, no. 4 (2017): 761–79; reprinted by permission of Duke University Press. Portions of the Coda were previously published as "Complicity, for the Time Being: Nuclear Entanglements from Atoms for Peace to Fukushima," in "Complicity in Post-1945 Literature: Theory, Politics, Aesthetics," ed. Adam Kelly and Will Norman, special issue of *Comparative Literature Studies* 56, no. 4 (2019): 750–68; reprinted by permission of The Pennsylvania State University Press.

Published by the University of Minnesota Press
111 Third Avenue South, Suite 290
Minneapolis, MN 55401-2520
http://www.upress.umn.edu

Printed on acid-free paper

The University of Minnesota is an equal-opportunity educator and employer.

Library of Congress Cataloging-in-Publication Data
Names: Hurley, Jessica, author.
Title: Infrastructures of apocalypse : American literature and the nuclear complex / Jessica Hurley.
Description: Minneapolis : University of Minnesota Press, 2020. | Includes bibliographical references and index.
Identifiers: LCCN 2020020417 (print) | ISBN 978-1-5179-0873-7 (hc) | ISBN 978-1-5179-0874-4 (pb)
Subjects: LCSH: Nuclear warfare in literature. | American literature—20th century—History and criticism. | American literature—Minority authors—History and criticism. | Apocalyptic literature—History and criticism. | End of the world in literature. | Minorities in literature. | Nuclear warfare and literature.
Classification: LCC PS228.N83 G55 2020 (print) | DDC 810.9/38—dc23
LC record available at https://lccn.loc.gov/2020020417

UMP KEP

Contents

Introduction
End Times

All things pass, but the poor remain. We are the people
of the Apokalis. Tomorrow there will be more of us.

—Indra Sinha, *Animal's People*

IN LYDIA MILLET'S 2005 novel *Oh Pure and Radiant Heart,* three of the scientists at the core of the atom bomb's genesis pass out of time at the moment of the first nuclear detonation in 1945 and wink back into it in 2002: Robert Oppenheimer and Enrico Fermi in Santa Fe and Leo Szilard under a cafeteria table at the University of Chicago, rib-kicked by a startled freshman. The detonation, Millet reminds us early in the narrative, held the potential to destroy the world in an instant, and no one knew that it wouldn't; Fermi, the joker, invited bets "against first the destruction of all human life and second just that of human life in New Mexico."[1] *Oh Pure and Radiant Heart,* however, constructs a different kind of apocalypse narrative around the atom bomb. When Oppenheimer visits the Bradbury Science Museum in Los Alamos, he finds in the endless video loops of the Trinity test an unexpected record of loss: he registers not the mushroom cloud but the emptiness around it, "sucking a vacuum on the ground, blistering a hole in the sky. It was vengeance on them all: it was the unspeakable and the divine. It had taken everything" (26). For Oppenheimer, "everything" means the life that he had the second before the explosion: the wife now long dead, the children grown up and finished even with their mourning of him. As the novel progresses, however, both the group of resurrected scientists and the flat narrative voice that provides paragraphs of historical information come to a different understanding of how a handful of dust, unspeakable and divine, might take "everything."

The scientists are horrified, it turns out, neither by the drama of the mushroom cloud nor by the specter of nuclear war that hangs over us but rather by the everyday world that the nuclear complex and the logics that produced it have in turn produced. The "sterile and terrible future" (28) that Oppenheimer now occupies is not one of *Planet of the Apes*–style ruins or *Children of Men*–style irradiated populations unable to reproduce but the one that we live in, that we think of as nonapocalyptic, as everyday life. Oppenheimer cannot bear this "poor sad world," a world "conquered" by cars, a "world . . . grown old" in environmental degradation and whose guiding desire is to build ever-more-perfect mechanisms for its own destruction (120, 121, 126). The unfocalized narrator, something like the voice of history, both describes and enacts at the end of the novel the brutal facticity of the world that the atom bomb has made:

> Between the invention of nuclear weapons and the turn of the twenty-first century the U.S. spent over five trillion dollars building and maintaining its nuclear arsenal—about one-tenth of the country's total spending since 1940. In America, annual spending on past and present military activities exceeds spending on all other categories of human need; approximately eighty percent of the national debt is estimated to have been created by military expenditures.
>
> The so-called "military–industrial complex" about which Eisenhower warned is thus, in a sense, the single largest consumer of the country's resources. It might fairly be seen as the prime mover of the U.S. government. (482)

Oppenheimer's emotive language contrasts with the affectless presentation of fact, but both representations have the same outcome: they defamiliarize the present, estranging us from the everyday world that we inhabit in the idea that it is nonnuclear and nonapocalyptic and revealing the most quotidian elements of our daily lives—the highways, the air travel, the industrially produced food, the toxic environments, the daily roster of species extinction—to be saturated with nuclear logics, an apocalypse in progress. "[*Oppenheimer*] *once told me he did not think the end would come from bombs because there was not time. He thought it would come earlier than that, from all the changing of the world and the destruction of it. He said to me once: it is the mind that made the bombs that is killing the world. For that purpose the bombs are not needed"* (487, emphasis original). It is not the annihilating bomb that will cut off time; the bomb is not where the end of history resides. The bomb is too slow for that, and its infrastructure is too fast; there is neither world enough for nuclear war nor time.

By repositioning the locus of nuclear apocalypse from atomic bombs to nuclear infrastructures, *Oh Pure and Radiant Heart* articulates a critical yet often unrecognized theme in the American cultural imaginary after 1945. While many in the United States understood the arrival of atomic weaponry through the lens of what historian of science Gabrielle Hecht has called "nuclear exceptionalism," experiencing it as an absolute novelty and historical rupture, subaltern writers, thinkers, and activists immediately connected the new technology to existing forms of historical and structural violence: "the atom," Langston Hughes wrote in 1945, "belongs to white folks."[2] In novels and films, stories and plays, a diverse array of authors utilized the emplotted worlds of narrative fiction to interrogate the racist, sexist, colonial, and homophobic logics that structured nuclear infrastructures, connecting antinuclear perspectives with liberatory movements for civil rights, AIDS justice, and decolonization. At the same time, as this study will show, they used fiction to repurpose the apocalyptic emplotments of the nuclear age for liberatory purposes, deploying the futureless horizon imposed on them by nuclear infrastructures to interrupt the normative time of social reproduction that reproduces the future in the image of the present.

Infrastructures of Apocalypse takes as its object of study the world that *Oh Pure and Radiant Heart* describes: a world remade in 1945 in the nuclear image and maintained every day since in the ongoing commitment of the United States to nurturing nuclear technology at the expense of any other interest: national, human, nonhuman animal, or environmental. The book argues that American literature has responded to the atom bomb not only as an unthinkable paradox or a future threat but also as a new national infrastructure that has determined the flow of resources and risks across the twentieth and twenty-first centuries. Moving beyond current critical understandings of atomic destruction as an exceptional event, this book analyses the apocalyptic force of nuclear technology as it manifests in the most mundane environments of everyday life. In so doing, it delineates a new literary history of post-1945 America, expanding the archive of atomic literature to include a wide variety of authors who have written against the nuclear–military–industrial complex from within the communities that are most vulnerable to its infrastructural violence, from James Baldwin's critique of the racialized urban spaces of civil defense to Leslie Marmon Silko's analysis of nuclear waste as a colonial weapon.

Through its foregrounding of analyses of the nuclear complex from below, *Infrastructures of Apocalypse* develops a new theorization of apocalypse in twentieth- and twenty-first-century literature and culture. When I began this project, it was to address a simple but urgent question: what does apocalypse *do* for people whose futures are already impossibly threatened or foreclosed? The etymology of apocalypse has traditionally allowed for two interpretations of its meaning: ending and revelation. Drawing on the texts in this archive, texts that position the consequences of an apocalyptic future not in that future but in the present, *Infrastructures of Apocalypse* offers a third term through which we might understand what apocalypse *does*: transfiguration. By radically changing the imagined future, apocalypse allows for different realities to become imaginable in the present. The writers in this project, bound to damaged and damaging futures by the nuclear complex as it intersects with the other histories of damage left in the wake of modernity, use apocalypse to transfigure the present: to see the other possibilities that reside in it and to couple those possibilities to their own pasts and their own futures, constructing not only a transfigured instant but wholly transfigured timelines, worlds with a solidity of their own. As contemporary thought begins to reckon with the foreclosure of its own futures by environmental and social crisis, *Infrastructures of Apocalypse* animates futurelessness as a starting point for thought rather than its end, as a place for struggle and resistance and somehow, impossibly, for hope.

From the Nuclear Sublime to the Nuclear Mundane

During the Cold War, the looming threat of World War III kept the eyes of much of the world fixed on the threat of the future explosion, the mushroom cloud over the New York skyline that signals the end of the world. For this reason, even post–Cold War accounts of the nuclear condition tend to think of the atom bomb as the one that, at least after its Japanese debut, never went off. Looking out over an artwork made from decommissioned fighter planes, Nick, the protagonist of Don DeLillo's Cold War retrospective *Underworld* (1997), contemplates the science of nuclear fission before remembering that "the bombs were not released. . . . The missiles remained in the rotary launchers. The men came back and the cities were not destroyed."[3] Nick's conceptualization of the almost ontologically undetonated atom bomb is widely shared in literary and cultural studies, which largely focus on the future nuclear apocalypse to the exclusion of all other nuclear realities. Daniel Cordle's *States of Suspense: The Nuclear Age, Postmodernism, and United States Fiction and Prose* (2008) and Daniel Grausam's *On Endings: American Postmodern Fiction and the Cold War* (2011) offer the most productive attempts to historicize American literature after 1945 in the context of the nuclear age, reading canonical works by Thomas Pynchon, Richard Powers, and Don DeLillo as articulations of the anxieties around world making, endings, and the archive circulating in the shadow of nuclear annihilation. For these critics, as for most scholars working in the intersections of literature and the nuclear, the atomic crisis is defined by its pure textuality, its absence from the material world.[4] *States of Suspense,* Cordle writes in his introduction, "is a book about things that did not happen, and the cultural consequences of their not happening," while Grausam argues that the historiographic crisis registered in postmodern aesthetics is a response to the nuclear weapons that "made newly possible—at least in the imagination—an ending . . . so final that it would preclude any position from which it could retrospectively be represented."[5] In such interpretations, literature registers the nuclear age as a crisis of narrative, a textual imprint of a textual technology whose apocalyptic violence exists only in the imagined future while the present is marked only by a damaging anticipation of disaster, the psychic wound of a bombing that might take place any second but that hasn't, so far, not yet, not here.

In fact, the United States has detonated 942 atomic bombs within the continental United States since 1945. The total number of bombings by the United States worldwide is 1,149: an average of two nuclear tests per month between the Trinity test in 1945 and the Divider test in

1992. Here, now, taking place in the present and yet strangely invisible both in and after their moment, these attacks go by the name of tests and thus are rendered acceptable, compartmentalized into a different category than "disasters," "crises," or "acts of war." Indeed, as Rebecca Solnit has argued, such a categorization arises from a profound misunderstanding of both the nature of nuclear weapons and the scientific culture that produced them. There is no partial test of an atom bomb; there are no laboratory conditions: "a test is controlled and contained, a preliminary to the thing itself, and though these nuclear bombs weren't being dropped on cities or strategic centers, they were full-scale explosions in the real world, with all the attendant effects."[6] These full-scale explosions have been devastating: each detonation has been larger than those at Hiroshima and Nagasaki; each detonation has released, on average, as much radiation as the 1986 meltdown at Chernobyl. A recent statistical analysis suggests that atmospheric nuclear testing in the United States killed between 145,300 and 429,400 Americans between 1952 and 1988, and the damage continues.[7] "From a human-environmental point of view," Barbara Rose Johnston writes, "nuclear war began with the first use of radiogenic materials for military purposes, and the assault on the world's environment and its peoples has continued ever since."[8]

Given these historical realities, why is it so plausible for both characters and readers to imagine atomic weapons as having refrained from unleashing their violence and to see the potential violence as inhering only in nuclear bombs and not in their surrounding infrastructures? The answer to this question lies at the intersection of historical fact and critical heuristic. Historically, the realities of the ongoing violence of the nuclear complex have indeed been hard to see. This is not, however, because all infrastructures are inherently invisible, as much of the scholarship in the recent "infrastructural turn" in the humanities has argued, but because the nuclear complex has made itself into what Michelle Murphy calls a "domain of imperceptibility" that renders elements of the material world invisible, unnoticed, or incomprehensible.[9] Such domains are neither natural nor inevitable but are hot spots of political contestation; the fact that the damage caused by long-term exposure to low doses of radiation seems unknowable to us is not because there is no way to establish knowledge about it but because for decades the state-sponsored corporations and government agencies that could monitor doses and health impacts and generate such knowledge have refused to do so.[10] The nuclear complex is a domain of imperceptibility that makes certain aspects of itself hypervisible in specific forms; the imbrication of "nuclear violence" with "mushroom cloud" was produced by the extensive infrastructures of technological reproduction that surrounded each nuclear detonation (Operation Crossroads at Bikini Atoll has been described as "the most photographed event in history," captured in 1.5 million feet of film and more than a million photographs).[11] Meanwhile all other aspects of the nuclear complex are rendered invisible through overlapping regimes of secrecy, misinformation, and bureaucratic boringness designed to deflect attention. Many nuclear complex fictions are thus dramas of perception in which characters come to realize that indirect violence is being done to them; in Mike Nichols's biographical *Silkwood* (1983), for example, the narrative development is structured not around the direct violence of Karen Silkwood's mysterious death in a car crash but around her slow realization that lax safety standards at the Kerr-McGee plant are habitually exposing workers to harmful levels of radiation.[12]

Conceptually, meanwhile, the fields of Cold War and nuclear literary studies have been organized around two "charismatic megaconcepts": the textuality of the bomb and the nuclear sublime.[13] The origin of the bomb's textuality, an organizing concept for both Cordle and Grausam, can be traced to an influential essay by Jacques Derrida, published in the 1984 issue of *diacritics* that launched the field of nuclear criticism. In "No Apocalypse, Not Now (Full Speed Ahead, Seven Missiles, Seven Missives)," Derrida defines the atom bomb as "fabulously textual."[14] For Derrida, nuclear war can only be a referent: since it has yet to take place, it exists only in the form of the language that circulates around it. Literary criticism has unsurprisingly been drawn to the idea of the nuclear weapon as fabulously textual, as with this descriptor Derrida opens up a field usually claimed by politics or science as an area desperately in need of the kinds of analysis that scholars of literature are trained to provide.

Unlike most of his critical heirs, however, Derrida insists equally on the concrete materiality of the bomb's paratextual infrastructures. The world-ending nuclear war may be a fable, but if that fable is purely textual, then its effects are not: "it is the war (in other words the fable)," Derrida writes, "that triggers this fabulous war effort, this senseless capitalization of sophisticated weaponry . . . this crazy precipitation which, through techno-science, through all the techno-scientific inventiveness that it motivates, structures not only the army, diplomacy, politics, but the whole of the human *socius* today, everything that is named by the old words culture, civilization."[15] The fictionality of the bomb exists only in a dialectical relationship with the technical and social infrastructures that produce it and that it in turn produces.[16] As Millet suggests in her alternation of fictional representation and the description of historical realities in *Oh Pure and Radiant Heart,* there can be no nuclear fiction without nuclear fact.

Derrida's insistence on atomic weaponry's power to structure material realities has not had the same kind of influence on nuclear criticism as has his theory of the bomb's textuality. Instead, nuclear criticism has both theorized and been held somewhat captive by the operations of what Frances Ferguson has called the "nuclear sublime." Ferguson coined the term in the same 1984 issue of *diacritics* to describe the epistemological challenge posed by the threat of atomic annihilation. Here "the notion of the sublime is continuous with the notion of nuclear holocaust: to think the sublime would be to think the unthinkable and to exist in one's own nonexistence."[17] The nuclear bomb as the limit point of thinkability has been a recurring trope in both literary criticism and other forms of discourse surrounding the bomb; the phrase "thinking the unthinkable" comes from Herman Kahn's famous book of the same name that stemmed from the RAND Corporation's nuclear war games, and the atom bomb shows up as a paradigmatic example in David Nye's influential account of the "technological sublime."[18] As I have argued, however, when we speak of the nuclear as an always-absent referent, as that which we cannot think, we limit our object of study to the bomb itself, and then only to its imagined futures: the mushroom clouds that we imagine blooming across the continents and destroying life on this planet.[19] At the same time, the operations of the sublime itself challenge our capacity to challenge it: as Ferguson writes in her gloss of Edmund Burke, "we love the beautiful as what submits to us, while we fear the sublime as what we must submit to" (6). The nuclear sublime is an aesthetic quality inherent in the mushroom cloud and amplified by its mass mediation that inculcates submission in its viewers: the nuclear sublime as embodied in the mushroom cloud is designed to reduce the capacity for critical thought and induce habits of submission to the nuclear complex for which the mushroom cloud serves as both metonym and disguise.

It is for this reason that I propose a third heuristic through which to approach the nuclear age: the *nuclear mundane*. The nuclear mundane approaches the nuclear age with an eye for its material realities, focusing on the environmental, infrastructural, bodily, and social impacts of nuclear technologies and the politics that prioritize them. Working in conversation with the recent critical turn by literature scholars like Elizabeth DeLoughrey and Molly Wallace toward a more materialist and ecocritical nuclear criticism, it is attentive to moments where nuclear infrastructures intersect with structures of power, making visible things like the co-constitution of nuclear technologies and compulsory heterosexuality in the mid-century lesbian novels *The Price of Salt* (1952) and *Rubyfruit Jungle* (1973), where the men who figure the marriage plot that the protagonists are trying to escape are both students of nuclear engineering.[20] By only ascribing nuclearity to the bomb, nuclear criticism risks being blinded to the negotiations of power, wealth, status, and vulnerability that are constantly in play around nuclear and contestably nuclear things, from bodies and rocks to highways and international treaties.[21] When the sublime teaches us to submit and the bomb blinds us to all that we are submitting to, we find ourselves unable to gain critical purchase on the multiscalar infrastructures of the nuclear age. By redefining the nuclear object as continuous with a set of militarized infrastructures rather than as their exceptional end point, the nuclear mundane makes the nuclear visible both in its extent and reach into every aspect of everyday life and in its contestability, as something that can be named and challenged.

The infrastructural perspective of the nuclear mundane turns our attention from the psychic damage of future wars to the material and cultural impact of militarization after 1945.[22] When President Eisenhower coined the phrase "military–industrial complex" in his 1961 Farewell Address to the Nation, he warned that the "total influence" of the new confluence of corporate and military structures would be "economic, political, even spiritual," affecting "the very structure of our society."[23] This "total influence" is what we now call militarization: "the contradictory and tense social process by which civil society organizes itself for the production of violence."[24] Militarization involves obvious structural transformations, such as increased military spending, the transfer of public and private land to the military, and an increased share of the labor force being dedicated to military purposes; for these changes to seem acceptable to the public, it also requires that the public change—or be induced to change—their perspective about what percentage of national resources should be dedicated to the production of violence. Violence is therefore glorified and prioritized in the culture and politics of militarized societies, as we see today in everything from the immense popularity of movies that aestheticize war to the absolute rejection of gun control legislation in U.S. politics. In addition, militarization impacts the nature of social hierarchies of race, class, gender, sexuality, disability, indigeneity, and citizenship, redefining the boundaries of "acceptable" masculinity and femininity, for example, such that to be masculine comes to involve a willingness to become soldierly and to be feminine means to raise soldierly sons from within a traditional home.[25] As a total system in the Maussian sense, militarization produces, at every scale, what C. Wright Mills called in 1956 the "military definition of world reality."[26]

It is certainly the case that militarization did not begin in the United States with the arrival of the military–industrial complex; "a nation made by war, the U.S. was birthed not just by the Revolution of 1776, but also by wars against Native Americans and the violence required to capture and enslave many millions of African people."[27] The arrival of nuclear weapons onto the military scene did, however, change the nature of militarization after 1945. Catherine Lutz refers to historically specific organizations of violence as "modes of warfare," arguing that with the invention of nuclear weapons, the United States transitioned from the industrial mode of warfare that had characterized the two world wars to a new, nuclear mode of warfare. This new technopolitical regime had different requirements and imposed different obligations than did the earlier industrial mode of warfare. Where industrial warfare required large amounts of manpower for manufacturing and soldiering and was therefore required to offer increased financial and social compensation to a large number of men (and sometimes women) of all races (though unevenly), the nuclear mode of warfare requires a much smaller number of highly trained, mostly white-collar workers, resulting in the centralization of power and resources to a much smaller, whiter, and more masculine workforce in the nuclear age. The nuclear mode of warfare also changed infrastructures around human knowledge, directing state financial resources toward specific fields (engineering, physics, psychology, area studies) as well as producing entirely new ones (earth sciences, climatology, oceanography, ecology, computing) and, by requiring security clearances to work on federally funded projects, restricting access to those fields and resources to those whose citizenship, race, gender, sexuality, disability, or political orientation would not give the FBI pause. Finally, the nuclear mode of warfare at least partly undoes the distinction between civilian and soldier, since the entire nation is vulnerable to atomic attack. As a result, the home front—and especially the city—began to be seen as a battlefield, producing new national infrastructures such as the highway system and the suburb as well as the redistribution of manufacturing bases to mostly white, mostly nonunion areas in the South and West, radically altering the geographies of race in the United States.[28]

The nuclear mundane thus asks us to combine an environmental and infrastructural perspective on the nuclear age with an intersectional understanding of how those environments and infrastructures have been structured by, and in turn continue to structure, existing distributions of power along axes of race, class, gender, sexuality, ability, and indigeneity (which, following Caroline Levine, we might also define as infrastructural inasmuch as they "[impose] order on social relations").[29] Infrastructure, social theorist Lauren Berlant has argued, is not an object or a set of objects but rather a set of relations in movement: "structure," Berlant writes, "is not what we usually call it, an intractable principle of continuity across time and space, but is really a convergence of force and value in patterns of movement that's only solid when seen from a distance. . . . Thus, I am redefining 'structure' here as that which organizes transformation and 'infrastructure' as that which binds us to the world in movement and keeps the world practically bound to itself."[30] Nuclear infrastructures are envirotechno-social systems that keep disparate elements in mobile relation to each other. America's first plutonium processing plant at the Hanford site in Washington State showcases such a system: the technological infrastructure of the reactors is an envirotechnical system in which the Columbia River is an integral part of the infrastructure as it flows through the Site and serves as coolant for the reactors. At the same time, the Site is a sociotechnical system whose ongoing work is enabled by racially structured federal subsidies that allow white

blue-collar workers to live a white-collar lifestyle and keep them segregated from Black and Latinx workers, making white workers more
likely to accept the bodily harm that they risk by working at the Site.[31]
Settler colonialism forms an equally important part of the Site's infrastructural relations; the first uranium ore to be processed at the Site in
1944 was mined by Indigenous workers on Navajo land in the United
States and in what was then the Belgian Congo, and the ongoing
cleanup of the Site since its closure in 1986 was mandated by treaty obligations to the Umatilla, Nez Perce, and Yakama tribes on whose sovereign land the reactors were built (I discuss this further in chapter 4).

To look at nuclear infrastructures within existing patterns of structural violence is thus to follow Gregory Bateson's assertion in *Steps to
an Ecology of Mind* that "what can be studied is always a relationship or
an infinite regress of relationships. Never a 'thing.'"[32] Relational infrastructures allow for domination, as when the government employed
the potent combination of eminent domain and settler-colonial white
supremacy to claim the Hanford site land, but they also allow for resistance, as when the Umatilla, Nez Perce, and Yakama nations used
those same legal infrastructures to mandate the site's remediation—as
well as for unpredictable outcomes in even the most tightly structured
infrastructures, as when the wind patterns that planners had thought
would be a helpful environmental buffer between the reactors and the
populace turned out to be depositing concentrated amounts of radioactive particles in built-up areas.

Berlant's definition of infrastructure as relations in movement, beyond Benson's more static model of relationships, also suggests the
importance of narrative for our representations, understanding, and
analysis of the nuclear mundane. The infrastructural perspective of
the nuclear mundane requires that we see objects in four dimensions:
as networked with other agential objects in three-dimensional spatial relationships structured by racism and other socially structuring
principles but also as having what Matthew Eatough calls "infrastructure's temporal dimension" constituted by both the historical forces
that produce the infrastructure and the disposition of the infrastructure itself to produce specific outcomes.[33] The title of this book, *Infrastructures of Apocalypse,* attempts to capture something of the mutually
constitutive relationship between infrastructure and narrative form in
the nuclear age. Nuclear apocalypse, often imagined as coming sud-

denly and out of nowhere, in fact requires a planetary infrastructure to bring it about and a deep and ongoing commitment to maintaining its possibility; it is unique among potential apocalypses in that, as anthropologist Joseph Masco writes, "to prevent an apocalypse the governmental apparatus has prepared so meticulously to achieve it."[34] At the same time, the infrastructures of the nuclear complex that compose this preparation are themselves the product of apocalyptic narrative forms that have long defined U.S. understandings of its geopolitical situation (as I discuss in greater depth in chapter 2). The consensus fictions through which reality becomes shared are key determinants for what infrastructures get built and how, meaning that temporality itself gains an infrastructural function; narratives of nuclear apocalypse centered on America's cities produced the highway system in the 1950s, whereas in the 1980s, new narratives of nuclear winter produced a massive nuclear freeze movement that accelerated arms control treaties and the reduction of nuclear stockpiles.[35] Narrative forms, then, are themselves infrastructural forces that determine the movement of resources. During the Cold War, the narrative form of apocalypse motivates the reshaping of the environment while the structural form of racial hierarchy shapes the environment that will be produced; apocalypse gets the suburb built, but anti-Blackness determines who will live there.

Infrastructure is thus produced by narrative forms, and at the same time it also establishes—at least partially—the kinds of narratives that can play out within its space. The narrative component of infrastructure is what architect Keller Easterling describes as its *disposition*. Easterling insists that the "meaning" of infrastructure cannot be captured simply by describing the network of objects of which it consists. Rather, infrastructure always has a futurological dimension because a part of what defines it is its disposition, an "agency or capacity" to determine how things will go:

> Infrastructure space possesses disposition just as does the ball at the top of an incline. Few would look at a highway interchange, an electrical grid, or a suburb and perceive agency or activity in its static arrangement. Spaces and urban organizations are usually treated, not as actors, but as collections of objects or volumes. Activity might be assigned only to the moving cars, the electrical

current, or the suburb's inhabitants. Yet the ball does not have to roll down the incline to have the capacity to do so, and physical objects in spatial arrangements, however static, also possess an agency that resides in relative position. Disposition is immanent, not in the moving parts, but in the relationships between the components.[36]

The idea of the ordering disposition of nuclear infrastructures is central to the most canonical works of nuclear apocalypse literature, from Mordecai Roshwald's infrastructural melodrama *Level 7* (1959), whose apocalyptic unfolding emerges from the spatial arrangement of its underground fallout shelter community; to the ghostly nuclear reactor that organizes Riddley's journey through postapocalyptic England in Russell Hoban's *Riddley Walker* (1980); to the nuclear blueprint in Walter M. Miller's *A Canticle for Leibowitz* (1959) that determines the course of historical progress over thousands of years to produce a second nuclear apocalypse. These texts capture something of what it means for apocalypse to be infrastructured, narrativizing the paradoxes of a society whose most expensive infrastructures, far from being dispositioned to perpetuate the common good, are designed to produce no outcome other than human extinction.

Nuclear Apocalypse from Below: Hot Spotter Aesthetics

In their depictions of a universal nuclear apocalypse in the future, however, novels like Roshwald's, Hoban's, and Miller's cannot capture the gradated levels of harm that nuclear infrastructures produce in the present. The nuclear mundane is the slow violence of the atomic age; like all slow violence, it distributes its damage unevenly.[37] Poor people, people of color, Indigenous people, queer people, and women receive the least benefit from the nuclear complex and are most exposed to its harm: the most toxic nuclear technology sites are located on Indigenous land and in proximity to poor communities and communities of color; predominantly Black cities are established as nuclear bait to protect the white suburbs, with the result that by 1984, an estimated 88 percent of the African American population would have been wiped out in the first minutes of a full-scale atomic conflict; safety standards regulating exposure to radiation are established based on the male body when women exposed to the same sources are 37.5 percent more likely to develop cancer; homosexuals are purged from the government at twice the rate of communists as the security of the nuclear complex is perceived to be threatened by their vulnerability to blackmail.[38] As the activist Jan in Toni Cade Bambara's *The Salt Eaters* (1980) argues to a friend who semijokingly wants to keep the struggle focused on "good ole-fashioned" racism, "They're connected. Whose community do you think they ship radioactive waste through, or dig up waste burial grounds near? Who do you think they hire for the dangerous dirty work at those plants? What parts of the world do they test-blast in? And all them illegal uranium mines dug up on Navajo turf—the crops dying, the sheep dying, the horses, water, cancer, Ruby, cancer. And the plant on the Harlem River. . . . Hell, it's an emergency situation, has been for years. All those thrown-together plants they built in the forties and fifties are falling apart now. War is not the threat. It's all the 'peacetime' construction that's wiping us out."[39]

This damage is occluded by conceptualizations of nuclear apocalypse that can only imagine it as universal, even when that universality is being invoked to antinuclear ends; as Peter Coviello notes, "one of the primary discursive effects of something like 'nuclear criticism' . . . is the radical leveling of all markers of difference—most notably class, race, and nationality—in response to a threat constantly invoked as 'universal'" such that "talking about nuclear weapons became a way to avoid talking about other, rather pressing inequalities."[40] Indeed, this critique might be extended in that speaking of nuclear danger as universal biopolitically enables the state violence that it also conceals. Taken as a national or species-level threat, nuclear annihilation justifies any action that might be taken in the name of its prevention. Such actions tend to sacrifice certain populations in the name of the survival of the whole; when the Nixon administration proposed dumping nuclear waste in Native reservations and redefining them as "national sacrifice zones," the sacrifice of Native lives and land was justified by invoking the nation as that which must be saved.[41] What Lisa Yoneyama has called "nuclear universalism" thus not only obscures the violence of the nuclear complex but also permits its flourishing.[42]

Infrastructures of Apocalypse therefore offers a nuclear criticism from below—a "below" that invokes both the etymology of infrastructure as that which is below structure and the "history from below" that narrates history from subaltern perspectives. In this, it works to counter the focus of the overlapping fields of Cold War, nuclear, and apocalypse studies on white Western thought and culture, fields that, as Andrew Hammond has argued, kept themselves remarkably isolated from the postcolonial theory that was reshaping the academy at the time of their emergence with the result that they came to share a "tendency to define 'Cold War' by the conditions where war was coldest."[43] By turning to nuclear criticism from below, this book contributes to the growing body of criticism that seeks, instead, the Cold War's hot spots.[44] In *Hot Spotter's Report: Military Fables of Toxic Waste* (2013), cultural geographer Shiloh Krupar activates the nuclear term *hot spot* as a critical heuristic. Radiation hot spots are locations where, thanks to environmental, social, and political factors, radioactive particles collect over time. For Krupar, hot spots "are areas where something remains unassimilated and nagging; they are reminders of the 'stickiness' of radiation and the impossibility of pure spaces, pure categories, or a pure self"; the practice of "hot spotting" is a diagnostic involving "the operations of identifying, making visible, and keeping open the possibility that more will be identified."[45] Krupar's focus is on military spectacle and the visual realm, and her hot spotting is a critical practice based in social science. Taking up her term to analyze literature in relation to the nuclear complex requires a slight reorientation, which I propose to call *hot spotter aesthetics*.

In this project, *hot spot* will refer to spaces and subject positions that are historically and structurally positioned to receive the most damage from the nuclear complex. Failing to adhere to the concentric "bull's-eye" diagrams of fallout that define the nuclear imaginary, hot spots appear in unexpected places and produce zones of intense vulnerability; hot spots might be literal, producing bodily exposure to radioactive damage, or metaphorical, in that indigeneity, for example, places persons in a position of extreme vulnerability to various forms of violence from the nuclear state. Hot spotter aesthetics emerge in hot spots both literal and metaphorical wherever subjects and collectives are most vulnerable to the violence of the nuclear complex. A hot spotter might be someone like Youngman Duran, a Hopi/Tewa Pueblo Indian deputy in Martin Cruz Smith's apocalyptic horror novel *Nightwing* (1977), whose innate skill in perceiving infrastructures lands him an army promotion in Vietnam, reading night photos of enemy installations to guide bombers. When he begins to perceive his own connection to the brown-skinned Vietnamese that he is bombing, Youngman starts diverting planes to bomb the ocean instead and is subsequently jailed. Upon his return home, his ability to sense both infrastructure and infrastructural violence enables him to perceive the ways in which the nuclear complex has become embedded into Hopi and Navajo land, rendering his heroic aversion of a vampire bat apocalypse deeply ambivalent in its juxtaposition with the slower apocalypse wrought by the demand for uranium and oil.[46] Requiring a critical perspective that can perceive the differentially distributed vulnerability of the hot spot, hot spotter aesthetics provide a subaltern imaginary for the nuclear age, foregrounding modes of imagination, knowledge production, and representation that are developed under conditions of imposed futurelessness.

Infrastructures of Apocalypse turns to a diverse range of locations to identify the expertise and aesthetic interventions that are produced in hot spots. Each chapter locates a hot spot where structural and historical violence intersect with the nuclear mundane: Orientalism comes to define how white Americans receive the threat to individual sovereignty posed by the legal infrastructures of the nuclear complex in chapter 1; legacies of slavery and logics of white supremacy intersect with civil defense in chapter 2; the weaponized nostalgia expressed by the Strategic Defense Initiative shapes the murderous nonresponse to the AIDS epidemic in chapter 3; and the history of settler colonialism and Indigenous genocide determines the placement of nuclear waste in chapter 4. Each chapter then turns to one or more artworks that have emerged from within these hot spots: Ayn Rand's *Atlas Shrugged* (1957); James Baldwin's *Tell Me How Long the Train's Been Gone* (1968) and Samuel R. Delany's *Dhalgren* (1975); Tony Kushner's *Angels in America* (1996); David Foster Wallace's *Infinite Jest* (1996) and Leslie Marmon Silko's *Almanac of the Dead* (1991).[47] Across the four chapters, hot spotter aesthetics emerge as both response and resistance to the apocalyptic foreclosures of the future imposed by the infrastructures of the nuclear mundane.

What kinds of aesthetics, then, emerge from within hot spots? Or to rephrase the question more broadly, what forms are appropriate to the task of liberation, when the world is structured to foreclose its possibility? In his analysis of Black nuclear poetics, Joshua Bennett has argued that "this is where one turns for critical instruments in the Anthropocene. To those who have already survived against all odds; those who have already seen the end of the world, and have managed to build new ones in its wake."[48] Inhabiting the apocalyptic position that Bennett describes, the texts in this study take up the foreclosed futures imposed upon them and intervene with a particular mode of apocalypticism that I will argue is central to their liberatory projects. To understand this intervention, however, it is first important to specify what *apocalypse* means in this project.

Throughout this book, I put into articulated opposition two different apocalyptic modes. The first is the teleological Genesis-to-Revelation temporality that has structured both Christian and secularized time in the West. Feminist theologian Catherine Keller captures this temporality beautifully: history organized through its relation to the events foretold in Revelation, she writes, produced "the temporality of creation-fall-cross-church-eschaton. Its linearity conducted the multiple spatiotemporalities of the earth into a single forward-moving momentum. In the next millennium this surged powerfully forward in the secularized translations of progress, with its vastly uneven distribution of rewards. Modern optimism horizontalized the heavenward eschatology, while modern pessimism cast the perduring shadow of apocalypse."[49] Time becomes linear in relation to its foretold ending; as Kath Weston notes, "if Apocalypse had a fifth rider, it would be Foreshadowing."[50] This trajectoral apocalyptic mode is the object of Frank Kermode's analysis in his influential study *The Sense of an Ending* (1968), which linked the end-directed macrostructure of apocalyptic history with the end-directed microstructure of the novel. In both apocalyptic imaginaries and the novel, Kermode suggested, the end is what allows the unity of the whole to be grasped as such, making its meaning available to the viewer (here we find the overlapping meanings of the word *apocalypse*: ending, but also revelation). Standing as we do in the middle of time, we imagine a past and a future that are consonant with each other, forming a meaningful whole that charges our own position with meaning.[51] In Kermode's famous example, we experience time in relation to its end as the charged interval between the *tick* and *tock* of a clock; if the clock runs *tick tick tick,* then we are reduced to mere succession. As emplotters of narrative time, novelists "have to defeat the tendency of the interval between *tick* and *tock* to empty itself; to maintain within that interval following *tick* a lively expectation of *tock,* and a sense that however remote *tock* may be, all that happens happens as if *tock* were certainly following. All such plotting presupposes and requires that an end will bestow upon the whole duration and meaning."[52] The art of the novel is, for Kermode, the art of creating consonance between beginnings and endings that will create humanly meaningful time in the same way as does eschatologically structured history.

It is important to note that while we think of apocalypse as in some way threatening the future, the apocalyptic mode that Kermode theorizes fully depends on an imagined future that provides the outer limit of time such that we can see time whole. Such a relationship to the future tends to produce conservative effects in the present in two primary ways. In the first, the future is something that exists out there in front of us as something desirable, something that should be protected from the apocalypse that threatens to destroy it. Any Hollywood movie that harvests its dramatic tension from the imminent destruction of the world by asteroid, alien, or virus serves as an example of this kind of futurity; it also appears in negative form in apocalyptic works, such as Nevil Shute's *On the Beach* (1957) and Cormac McCarthy's *The Road* (2006), that mourn the passing of that potential future by depicting elegiacally the final days of a dying world. In texts such as these, a determination to save the future works simultaneously to invest the present with a vulnerability that is essentially conservative; when McCarthy's protagonists have a quasi-mystical encounter with a can of Coke, it makes readers clutch their Coke cans a little tighter, newly aware of the possibility of their loss. A conservationist attitude toward an imagined yet valued future also organizes much of progressive politics, in both activism and theory; as Robin Wiegman wrote of "Feminism's Apocalyptic Futures" in 2000, movements that rely on an affective attachment to what we are progressing toward often find themselves experiencing the "hyperbolic anxiety that the future may now be unattainable because the present fails to bring the past to utopic completion."[53] In such cases, the drive to "save" a future in which one has invested one's dreams becomes a limit on the kinds of presents that feel acceptable, unfailed, with the result that only the past's futures become worth fighting for.

The second apocalyptic relationship to an imagined future sees a chosen community surviving beyond the end of Man or civilization in a New Heaven/New Earth scenario in which whatever the present sees as bad has passed away and whatever the present sees as good is able to flourish. This can be defined variously: as a fantasy of absolute patriarchy in novels like Robert Heinlein's *Farnham's Freehold* (1964), where the nuclear destruction of society creates the necessity of pastoral father-dominated communes; as the creation of a world in which Evangelical Christians are uniquely equipped to survive, as in Tim LaHaye and Jerry B. Jenkins's Left Behind series (1996–2004); but equally in texts that earnestly try to think beyond the human of humanism, as in Christopher Nolan's *Interstellar* (2014), where, after planetary starvation and a near-death-by-his-own-mansplaining experience, the protagonist is redeemed by becoming the "alien" for which he has been searching. Such postapocalyptic fantasies also tend toward conservative ends; in Claire Colebrook's trenchant critique of posthumanist theory and literature, "this seeming revolution of overturning man for the sake of the life that man has denied is—far from being man's other—the very hallmark of the end of man. Man has always existed as a being who ends himself: as soon as the human is given some natural or limited definition, man discovers that his real, creative, futural being lies in some not-yet realized becoming that will always save him from a past that he can denounce as both misguided and as at an end."[54] Cartesian Man is dead; long live Deleuzian Man!

In contrast to the apocalypse that depends on an imagined future to give the present coherence or inspiration, I trace in this study an alternative form of apocalypse that I see practiced by Black, queer, ethnic, female, and Indigenous writers in their engagements with the nuclear complex: apocalypse as *radical futurelessness,* as a *formal afuturity* that transfigures the present. Apocalypse is not, here, a historical rupture after which things continue differently than they did before, either better or worse; indeed, this pattern of crisis and new beginning has been central to the colonial project in America where, as Darieck Scott observes, "the rhetoric of new Edens, new slates, New Worlds has long constructed the historical as a narrative abruptly ended and then begun anew."[55] I therefore diverge from Kermode's canonical account of apocalyptic narratives, which states that by imagining the End, "we project ourselves—a small, humble elect, perhaps—past the End, so as to see the structure whole, a thing we cannot do from our spot of time in the middle," as well as from more recent theories of apocalypse after 1945 that argue for a general sense of postapocalypticism that defines the period, as in James Berger's definitive *After the End*.[56] Apocalypse is not, in this account, an opportunity to access the future anterior, the "will have been" that makes sense of the present according to how it will appear from an imagined future, the imagined future apocalypse that, as Rebekah Sheldon has argued, protects "against the possibility of a harmed future . . . through the fantasy of a fully formed future already present in the present."[57] Rather, I focus on minoritarian texts that depict a present that is oriented toward futurelessness and transformed by this orientation.[58]

The importance of a futureless present for hot spot writers lies in the politics of time itself. Apocalypse is often thought of as the end of time, but the exact quality of the time that is being ended is rarely questioned or defined. For subaltern writers, however, the chronopolitics of white Western society has serious material consequences, and the writers in this project all have a very clear idea of the temporalities into which they are intervening with their apocalyptic foreclosures. These temporalities have been theorized in the field that we might call critical temporality studies, a transdisciplinary research focus across the humanities and social sciences that finds its sharpest expressions in Black, queer, Indigenous, ethnic, and postcolonial studies. Such scholarship analyses how power and legitimacy are activated through different temporal frameworks, whereby time becomes, in Johannes Fabian's influential argument, "a carrier of significance, a form through which we define the content of relations between the Self and the Other . . . [and] give form to relations of power and inequality."[59] In *Against Race*, Paul Gilroy describes the Enlightenment origins of what Fabian calls the "denial of coevalness" to racialized others, showing how Kant and Hegel theorized modernity as "mediated by 'race' as both period and region"; while white Europeans were the proper subjects of a teleological history ever moving in the direction of progress, Africans were fundamentally outside of history and thus excluded from participation in social life, understood as "not only prehistoric but prepolitical also."[60] This temporal exclusion from the political space of the present was easily transferred to other minoritized subjects, as Valerie Rohy has demonstrated with regard to queerness in *Anachronism and Its Others* and Mark Rifkin has analyzed in the Indigenous context in *Beyond Settler Time*. By the twentieth century, the concepts of race, sexuality, and imperial position had become temporally fixed to produce an understanding of the racialized, Indigenous, and/or queer subject both as excluded from an active or political role in history and as occupying a different point in the historical timeline altogether, from the "sterility imagined as deathly regression" ascribed to queerness against the futural demands of what Lee Edelman has termed "reproductive futurism" to the trope of the "Vanishing Indian" that "constitutes one of the principal means of effacing Indigenous sovereignties."[61]

Hot spot writers thus enter the nuclear age already marked by a particular kind of imagined futurelessness imposed upon them by the racist, homophobic, and colonial chronopolitics of settler capitalism. The world as it is understood within the framework of the nuclear complex is one where atomic science is the natural result of white mastery over nature, fitting easily into existing teleological frameworks of modernization, progress, and predestination.[62] And as these teleological frameworks enter the nuclear age, they necessarily bring their abjected others with them. In practice, this divides both the practices and the imaginaries of the nuclear complex down existing social lines. Educated white men benefit from increased opportunities for work, while the white suburban family is the only imagined survivor of a future atomic war and thus the only community for whom fallout shelters are designed, making their survival in fact more likely.[63] Black, queer, and Indigenous Americans, meanwhile, remain futureless in the dominant imaginary, which then follows its own logic to render access to a flourishing future ever more diminished in practice: what's the point in investing in the inner city, mid-century governments reasoned, when either atom bombs or its minoritized residents will ensure its future destruction?[64] The disposition of nuclear infrastructures has, in other words, been structured by the politically potent denial of coevalness and continues to structure the world according to its logics.

Taken in this context, apocalypse as radical afuturity becomes visible as a targeted intervention into the social temporalities that structure and perpetuate the infrastructural violence of the nuclear complex. If the dominant culture pairs white heterosettler futurity with minority futurelessness along a determinately teleological timeline, then cutting out the future from this timeline becomes a way of disrupting the temporal structures that organize social domination. Such a disruption holds the potential to alter the dispositions of infrastructures themselves, as it does in John A. Williams's radical historical/nuclear novel *Captain Blackman* (1972). After constructing a counterhistory of American nation building that centers Black soldiers, unsettling the hegemonic historiography that recognizes only whiteness as capable of making history, Williams ends the novel in the speculative mode, imagining an alternative history of the nuclear age in which white-passing African Americans have infiltrated the nuclear infrastructures of the military and redispositioned them to destroy white supremacy instead of upholding it. In Captain Blackman's analysis, militarization has rendered the white nation "*more vulnerable now than at any other time in history, man, since all aspects of its society were gathered at the toe-jam-smelling feet of its military monuments.*"[65] Given such centralization, it doesn't take much to recruit light-skinned African Americans and "*set them in NORAD, the Skylab probes, SAC, the Pentagon; to the tracking stations at Kano, Tananarive, Santa Cruz, Canton Island, Kauai, Woomera, Houston, Kennedy; to Grand Forks, Denver, Cheyenne, Omaha, to the ice stations. And sit there looking white, but* be *black as a mothafucker.*"[66] After an internationalist pan-African alliance takes over the nuclear complex in one fell swoop, forcing its infrastructures to produce a story of Black liberation, Williams declines to describe the future that his apocalyptic ending might produce. Like the rest of the subaltern texts with which this book engages, *Captain Blackman* does not offer a political program that would fix the future into a better shape. Instead, the apocalyptic ending serves an Adornian function within the scope of negative dialectics: to negate the imagined future of white nuclearity that would legitimize the repeating cycles of the white production and exploitation of Black injury that structures the rest of the novel. Williams, along with Baldwin, Delany, Kushner, Silko, and Ozeki, raises the possibility that changing the structure of history by destroying hegemonic futurity might yet change the world.[67]

Apocalypse and Transfiguration:
Toward a Narratology of Futurelessness

It should be clear by now that time, emplotment, and imagined trajectories structure the world in a concrete sense.[68] Literary analysis is therefore an appropriate critical practice to bring to bear on a world that thinks about and structures itself in profoundly literary ways. But how do we think about literary texts themselves as not only representing a narratively constructed world and experimenting with alternative emplotments in a kind of textual laboratory but also as reemplotting the world in a way that has real phenomenological impacts on readers? Taking up a mostly forgotten term from narratologist Paul Ricoeur, *transfiguration,* this book proposes a new narrative theory by which to analyze the interaction of worldly and textual emplotments and, in particular, how emplotments without futurity can alter our lived experience of the world.

Ricoeur's three-volume *Time and Narrative* (1984–88) establishes emplotment as the link between the phenomenological experience of time and narrative representations of reality. Ricoeur "[sees] in the plots we invent the privileged means by which we re-configure our confused, unformed, and at the limit mute temporal experience."[69] He begins phenomenologically, with a reading of the twelfth book of Augustine's *Confessions,* where Augustine attempts to solve the problem of where, exactly, the past and future reside. For Augustine, the human experience of time simultaneously requires that the past and future be real, because we experience them as real and time consists nowhere but in our experience, and acknowledges that the past and future have no proper location. Augustine thus develops the model of the threefold present, a lived experience of present time that includes the act of remembering and the act of predicting. The nouns of *past* and *future* become adjectival, such that "what is in question here is an entirely different present, one that has also become a plural adjective (*praesentia*), in line with *praeterita* and *futura,* and one capable of admitting an internal multiplicity."[70] Past and future are located within the present of the soul, Augustine writes: "It might be correct to say that there are three times, a present of past things, a present of present things, and a present of future things. Some such different times do exist in the mind, but nowhere else that I can see."[71] Ricoeur characterizes the threefold present, "an extended and dialectical present," as the lived experience of time, in which the horizons of the past and future act upon the present as we experience it despite having only a virtual presence.[72] When we think about futurelessness, then, we can think about it as something that significantly alters our experience in the present: the third fold of our threefold experience of the present, futurity, has disappeared.

Ricoeur then turns to the question of how fictional emplotments act in relation to the world. The world, he insists, is already temporally figured ("prefigured") inasmuch as *time becomes human to the extent that it is articulated through a narrative mode, and narrative attains its full meaning when it becomes a condition of temporal existence.*"[73] Textual emplotment, what Ricoeur will call *mimesis*$_2$, takes up the existing emplotment of time in human experience (*mimesis*$_1$) and configures it through mediation between the real world and the reader (with the reception of the text by the reader performing the final operation, or *mimesis*$_3$). In the simplest possible terms, the world for us is composed temporally (mimesis$_1$). Literature configures the already emplotted world through its own emplotments and formal structures (mimesis$_2$). In the act of reading, the world of the text opens into the world of the reader, acting upon it through the juxtaposition of the world's original configuration and the text's refiguration of it (mimesis$_3$). This action of the text upon the world is what Ricoeur calls *transfiguration,* whose action lies in "the plots that configure and transfigure the practical field."[74]

All narrative texts thus have the potential to be transfigurative for Ricoeur, although Ricoeur does not seem particularly invested in the term; he uses it only a handful of times across the three volumes of *Time and Narrative* and does not acknowledge any difference between it and his most common synonyms, *configuration* and *reconfiguration* (although I concur with George H. Taylor's analysis that "transfiguration accounts for change and its deep possibilities to recast reality, while configuration and reconfiguration seem to project a more modest reworking").[75] In taking up the term here, I both adopt Ricoeur's sense of literary emplotment as something that can "transfigure the everyday" and seek to explore further the *trans* aspect of transfiguration that takes one figure and moves it "across" to some other semantic field where it will signify differently.[76]

Looking back to Erich Auerbach's classic essay "Figura" gives us a starting point to think from. Just as Ricoeur wants to keep *mimesis* (the act of representing) and *muthos* (the act of emplotting) as active verbs, so Auerbach seeks to restore to figuration the active sense of the classical *figura* as "something living and dynamic, incomplete and playful."[77] The figure for Auerbach should never be seen as fixed in meaning, because "the notion of the new manifestation, the changing aspect, of the permanent runs through the whole history of the word."[78] Auerbach traces the ways in which this fluid conception of *figura* became tangled up with emplotment, as through Christian models of biblical exegesis Western readers and writers were trained to see historical people and events as figures or types that will be fulfilled by the arrival of future people and events (antitypes). The meaning of the figure in this tradition is established by that which comes after it in time; the Law of Moses is fulfilled and superseded (in this hermeneutics) by the spiritual Law of Christ, while Christ himself is both the fulfilment of Moses and a new figure that will be fulfilled in the Second Coming. Figures gain their meaning from their position in an emplotted history, and the final arbiter of meaning can only be the Second Coming and the end of time. Thus, while our tradition of figural reading trains us to seek the postapocalyptic perspective from which all figures could authoritatively be interpreted, as Kermode describes in his theory of narrative consonance, Auerbach insists that from the mundane perspective, figures—including plots themselves—"have something provisional and incomplete about them," a meaning that can only be fixed from the perspective of eternity.[79] It is this provisional aspect of figuration within varyingly emplotted time frames that the trans-ness of transfiguration captures so beautifully: in different emplotments, figures will come to signify differently, moving across realms and orders of signification. And in the futureless emplotment that I am calling apocalypse, figuration in the present must remain provisional, for there is no future to serve as meaning's guarantor.

For hot spot writers, the provisional nature of figuration and meaning in the futureless present takes on a crucial political significance. Where oppressive chronopolitics seek to fix the potential meanings and emplotments of minoritized subjects, apocalypse as futurelessness restores a liberatory flexibility of both meaning and emplotment to the present. Situated in the heart of the nuclear complex's hot spots,

Bambara's *The Salt Eaters* exemplifies such an emancipatory transfiguration. The world that is being configured by the novel, as the excerpt quoted earlier in this introduction describes, is one that is structured by environmental as well as other kinds of racism; the Black community of Claybourne is situated next to a nuclear power plant, and unmarked trucks regularly carry radioactive waste through the center of the town; the town's medical clinic and educational centers have been built to counter unequal access to health care and schools; and the story is organized around the healing of Velma, an activist whose spirit has been fractured by the never-ending nature of the struggle for justice. Throughout the novel, Bambara juxtaposes the linear, teleological time of dominant temporalities with both deep, circular connections to African pasts and antifutural emanations of nuclear apocalypse. In the most intensely suicidal moment of her breakdown, for example, Velma longs to become an hourglass: "To be that sealed—sound, taste, air, nothing seeping in . . . to pour herself grain by grain into the top globe and sift silently down to a heap in the bottom one" (19). Identical and sequential, the time of the hourglass that Velma longs to lose herself into is the manifested temporality of what Walter Benjamin called the "homogenous, empty time" of the oppressive state.[80] Similarly, the nuclear complex is characterized in microcosm by the board game that Campbell, café worker and nuclear-issues writer, develops after hearing nuclear engineers from the power plant talking about their work.[81] "Disposal" captures the enervating routines required to stay one step ahead of unruly nuclear materials; each square represents a storage location, but each location necessitates another move merely to stay in the game: "'trench'—but one had to move within the next throw before the food chain was affected, 'storage plant'—but there was a card announcing build-up which obliged the player to move off the spot" (208). "Disposal" embodies the empty teleology of the nuclear complex, as pieces move around the board in a single direction that in the end leads them nowhere.

Both of these images and temporalities are exploded in the apocalyptic transfiguration of the world that takes place at the end of the novel.[82] Something that might be a storm also appears to be more: "A grumbling, growling boiling up as if from the core of the earthworks drew a groan from the crowd huddled together under the awning, in the doorway, as if to absorb the shock of it, of whatever cataclysmic event it might turn out to be, for it couldn't be simply a storm with such frightening thunder as was cracking the air as if the very world were splitting apart" (245). This splitting apart of the world, a transition of the world and grammar of the novel into the apocalyptic mode, produces a multiplicity of figurations and a constant switching between them: transfiguration. The final event is one yet multiple: it is an accident at the plant, an atom bomb dropping, the destruction of the earth by the gods, the energy released by Velma's healing, an environmental disaster; each of these figures of apocalypse is equally real to the text at the moment that it is being narrated. This multiplicity of figuration signifies in the text the arrival, through the arrival of an apocalyptic futurelessness, of "new possibilities in formation, a new configuration to move with" (293). The imminent end of the world suspends the teleological forward drive of the hourglass and the board game: "Rain. Delay. New possibilities in formation, a new configuration to move with" (293). The ending of the novel can seem jarring, switching genres into something like sci-fi as it incorporates radically new potentialities within the present; added to the inventory of ways that Velma could have died before this (at birth, in a fire) are now potential deaths in a resource war over burial grounds or by feral child attack (273–75). The apocalyptic scenario is not the "real" future of the novel, however, but rather the suspension of futural definitions of possibility to produce the "new possibilities in formation" that transfigure the experience of the present to include such outlandish potentials.[83]

The Salt Eaters is a profoundly disorienting novel, and the experience of reading it is certainly not one of apocalypse-as-revelation, where the ultimate Truth of the world becomes clear. It shares this quality with the rest of the texts on which Infrastructures of Apocalypse draws, texts that not only represent the transfiguration of reality but produce this experience in readers. Subjectively, these texts are sticky, like Krupar's radiation; they permeate the reader's consciousness and alter, at least for a while, the lived experience of the world, foregrounding how "we are transfigured—the narrative acts upon us—rather than our being simply active agents of refiguration."[84] Part of this transfigurative power stems from genre: they share a peculiar formal relation to the world as it is that falls under neither realism nor science or speculative fiction. They might be set in the near future, as in Atlas Shrugged, Infinite Jest, and Almanac of the Dead, or in a present where the rules of reality are slightly different (at times in *Tell Me How Long the Train's Been Gone* and more fully in *Dhalgren* and *Angels in America*), but they are not set in another world. Rather, they are set in a transfigured version of our world, which makes the boundary between the world projected by the text and the world of the reader more porous than in more overtly science fictional worlds. In the opening out of the text's world onto the reader's that Ricoeur describes as the transfiguration of the everyday, their foreclosure of the future makes the facticity of the real world seem somehow contingent, as if things might signify differently under the text's futureless emplotment.[85] By suspending the trajectory of the social and its objects, they restore a politically vital dimension of contingency to lived sensations of reality, a sense, as in Bambara's novel, of the *otherwiseness* immanent to the world as it is. Apocalypse emerges in these texts as a way of inhabiting a provisional life-structure in the present, a way of making the present always provisional.

Bambara and the other authors with whom this book will speak thus use apocalyptic emplotments to produce a shift from the politics of fulfilment to the politics of transfiguration, an opposition theorized by philosopher and social theorist Seyla Benhabib. According to Benhabib, "the politics of fulfillment envisages that the society of the future attains more adequately what present society has left unaccomplished. It is the culmination of the implicit logic of the present." Conversely, "the politics of transfiguration emphasizes the emergence of qualitatively new needs, social relations, and modes of association."[86] For most of *The Salt Eaters,* the activist characters are working to ameliorate the existing conditions of the social world, within the logics of the politics of fulfilment. The arrival of the apocalyptic horizon, however, produces in the novel the qualitatively new imaginaries that define the politics of transfiguration. While Benhabib does not engage with apocalypse directly, she does draw on Marx and the Frankfurt School thinkers in a way that suggests apocalypse as one mode of access to transfiguration: "The term 'transfiguration,'" she writes, "is intended to suggest that emancipation signifies a radical and qualitative break with some aspects of the present. In certain fundamental ways, the society of the future is viewed to be, not the culmination, but the radical negation of the present."[87] As a narrative form that negates both the future and the present's claim upon the future, apocalypse

facilitates the politics of transfiguration as, under its futural foreclosures, the present begins to imagine itself *otherwise*.

For Benhabib, the counterrealist tradition connected to the politics of transfiguration is that of utopia. Hot spotter apocalypticism,
however, has a very different relationship to histories of damage than
utopia does, one that forms an important part of both its apocalyptic
mode and its political project. Unlike utopian texts, which can only
imagine a better future if it is absolutely ruptured from the present
either in time (Edward Bellamy's century-long enchanted sleep in
Looking Backward [1888]) or in space (Thomas More's distant island in
Utopia [1516]), or dystopian texts, which see the future evolving un-
avoidably from the worst conditions of the present, hot spotter texts
use apocalypse to imagine a present that neither abandons the past
nor is determined by it. This is a particularly vital task for populations
whose pasts are defined by destruction and whose futures promise to
perpetuate that destruction—often, in America, by wiping the history
of destruction from the historical record (think of the resolute anti-
historicism that allows for the ongoing onslaught against Black communities by the police and justice systems today). As Christina Sharpe
writes of Black life in the afterlife of slavery, "in the wake, the past
that is not past reappears, always, to rupture the present."[88] Apocalypse
here is a specific form of historical consciousness: not the end of time
or the abandonment of history but a way to mourn and remember histories of damage without making those histories the determining feature of the now, to reckon with the realities of infrastructural violence
without acceding to its colonization of the future. Velma's healing in
The Salt Eaters requires that she gather to herself the long histories of
pain and resistance that accompany Blackness in America; we might
also think of the queer melancholia that defines camp for Elizabeth
Freeman, a figure that refuses to let drop the cheap, cracked, precious
objects of its history, or the backward glance of queerness toward histories of damage in Heather Love's *Feeling Backward*.[89]

Transfiguration is not a New Heaven and Earth, here, to walk upon
unencumbered by the past. Instead, it is a commitment to create a
world in which all those destroyed things—including, sooner or later,
ourselves—can be treasured. This transfigured time might be something close to the *jetztzeit* that Walter Benjamin describes in "Theses
on the Philosophy of History" as a time wrenched from the "empty, ho-

mogenous time" of the dominant class and replete with revolutionary potential. "Redeemed" mankind, according to Benjamin, will be that for whom the past has "become citable in all its moments"; the apocalyptic mode on which I draw here is less redemptive than Benjamin's historical materialism and less triumphal, often failing to be "man enough to blast open the continuum of history."[90] Nonetheless, the transfigured present holds itself, as does Benjamin's *jetztzeit* or time of the now, in constellation with the past, refusing the colonial desire for utopian new beginnings at the same time as it insists on radical social transformations that will honor the things we carry, the ancestors who sustain us and the damage we sustain.[91]

The transfiguration of the present under the sign of futurelessness also suggests an ethical reorientation to contemporary social theory's thinking about the future. Arjun Appadurai, drawing on the writings of Ernst Bloch, Michael Hardt and Antonio Negri, and David Harvey, has offered a powerful theorization of the importance of access to futurity and hope for subaltern subjects in the contemporary world. In *The Future as Cultural Fact,* Appadurai proposes two possible ethics of futurity: the ethics of possibility and the ethics of probability. The ethics of probability is the most structurally powerful and the least desirable; it is "those ways of thinking, feeling, and acting" that stem from a statistical or risk-management approach to the future and "is generally tied to the growth of a casino capitalism which profits from catastrophe and tends to bet on disaster" as well as "amoral forms of global capital, corrupt states, and privatized adventurism of every variety." Conversely, the ethics of possibility are defined as "those ways of thinking, feeling, and acting that increase the horizons of hope, that expand the field of the imagination, that produce greater equity in what I have called the capacity to aspire, and that widen the field of informed, creative, and critical citizenship"; it is "part and parcel of transnational civil society movements, progressive democratic organizations, and in general the politics of hope."[92] Against a probabilistic ethics that seeks to profit from the risk of damage, the ethics of possibility stands for an expanded sense of social potential, a commitment to improving the future through hope and aspiration.

Juxtaposing Appadurai's theoretical framework with that of Benhabib, however, reveals the similarities rather than the differences between the two sides of his binary opposition. The "progressive" vision of the ethics of possibility and the risk-analysis approach of the ethics of probability are both examples of a politics of fulfilment, a present that seeks to ameliorate itself by gradual change into an imaginable future. Bambara's novel makes the limits of such a politics clear, as Velma's capacity for emancipatory struggle is slowly stifled by remaining trapped within the imaginative limits of an oppressive world. The transfigurative apocalypse at the end of *The Salt Eaters* conjures a present that is oriented neither toward a probable future nor a possible one but rather toward a set of impossible futures. It suggests that subaltern justice in the nuclear age demands an ethics of impossibility that is oriented toward the abjected outside of our capacity to think the social future: a life lived to produce liberation that we consistently fail to imagine but work to bring about anyway. Bambara captures this sense of impossible action beautifully elsewhere when discussing Black women's activism: "I despair of our failure to wrest power from those who have it and abuse it; our reluctance to reclaim our old powers lying dormant with neglect; our hesitancy to create new powers in areas where it never before existed, and I'm euphoric because everything in our history, our spirit, our daily genius—suggests we do it."[93] The ethics of impossibility implies those ways of thinking, feeling, and acting that are not guided by what seems possible or probable in the collective vision of the future. It is designed, instead, to orient toward those whom the collective future tends to exclude: the Black, queer, Indigenous, disabled, and other subjects who are marked as futureless in the nuclear complex as elsewhere. Such an ethics will be pursued throughout *Infrastructures of Apocalypse,* as we turn to hot spot writers seeking to transfigure the capacities of the present through their engagement with their own impossible futures.

Overview

Chapter 1, "White Sovereignty and the Nuclear State," opens the book with a demonstration of how the most empowered subjects of the nuclear age experienced themselves as threatened by it and how they countered their own apocalyptic loss of privilege by denying futurity to others. The chapter argues that fundamental changes in the legal relationship between the individual, the market, and the nuclear state in the 1940s and 1950s created a crisis of democratic sovereignty that was understood primarily in racial terms. A wide variety of public and state discourse, fiction, and film shows that white Americans represented this crisis as a new form of Orientalism for the nuclear age, a reflexive yellow perilism whereby being subject to state-sanctioned nuclear terror was also a form of racial degeneration. Through a reading of Ayn Rand's treatment of race, self-determination, and nuclear weapons in her 1957 apocalypse novel *Atlas Shrugged,* I demonstrate the ways in which whiteness was constructed in the post-1945 period as a violently sovereign force that could prevent the white American population from being recoded as a racialized mass: incoherent, powerless, and endlessly vulnerable.

Chapter 1 establishes settler-colonial masculine whiteness as having a unique, if threatened, access to futurity that it protects by casting all others into an apocalyptic futurelessness. My subsequent chapters explore how this paradigm comes to shape the nuclear complex itself and, subsequently, how writers who have been disallowed futurity transform their imposed futurelessness into a political and aesthetic position, taking up the apocalyptic mode to deemplot the present from its position within the overdetermined narratives of infrastructural violence and create the possibility of new, more liberatory emplotments. Chapter 2, "Civil Defense and Black Apocalypse," turns from legal and bureaucratic infrastructures to environmental ones, examining the reconfiguration of urban environments according to the racialized logics of civil defense. This chapter charts the discursive and infrastructural imbrication of civil defense and white millennialism through the re-emergence in literature, politics, and the burgeoning field of American studies of the image of the City on a Hill. Through readings of mid-century speeches and maps, novels and urban environments, I show that white America's exceptionalist future, as encapsulated in the image of the City on a Hill, was based on the promise of Black annihilation, as the inner city became both predominantly African American and a target that would protect the surrounding suburbs from nuclear attack. In opposition to these racialized infrastructures, James Baldwin's *Tell Me How Long the Train's Been Gone* (1968) and Samuel Delany's *Dhalgren* (1975) develop narrative forms that dismantle the determinate relationship between race and the city. Rejecting the typological emplotment of history that structured both mid-century liberalism and African American civil rights movements, Baldwin and

Delany deploy an apocalyptic futurelessness to reject the politics of fulfillment and demand a politics of transfiguration that would produce qualitatively new ways of being.

Chapter 3, "Star Wars, AIDS, and Queer Endings," extends my investigation of competing apocalyptic temporalities into the 1980s. Here I draw on the overlapping discourses surrounding the Strategic Defense Initiative (Star Wars) and the AIDS epidemic to argue that the obsession with the 1950s in 1980s America was part of a larger political and ideological shift involving the emergence of what I call *retrocontainment*: a replacement of the failed spatial borders of the Cold War containment doctrine with the temporal boundaries of a nostalgic return to a past that had been ideologically reconstructed as safe. Retrocontainment came to define both the AIDS body and the infrastructures of state responses to the epidemic, as fears of failed bodily boundaries promoted (non)responses that were oriented more toward a forcible recloseting of gay culture in an imagined return to a heteronormative 1950s than toward saving lives. This oppressive temporality is, I argue, both staged and critiqued in Tony Kushner's 1991–92 epic play *Angels in America* through its portrayal of Roy Cohn and Ethel Rosenberg, which, through formal techniques like simultaneous staging, makes retrocontainment only one of multiple temporalities in play at any given moment. Connecting my discussion of AIDS to Kushner's staging of the Cold War's ghosts, I historicize the emergence of queer temporality studies in the 1990s as a response to the apocalyptic experience of the AIDS epidemic. In the face of the singular timeline of retrocontainment, the multiplicity that defines queer temporalities becomes legible as a form of resistance to normative constructions of time that predicate the survival of the nation on queer extinction.

The final chapter, "Nuclear Waste, Native America, Narrative Form," returns to the first-order materiality of the nuclear complex: the millions of tons of radioactive waste that will continue to be dangerous to humans for billions of years. While most ecocriticism argues for a move from an apocalyptic mode to a realistic one when depicting environmental hazards, this chapter argues for the continuing importance of apocalypse to disrupt conservative realisms that maintain the status quo. Through a reading of Department of Energy documents that use both fictional description and probability modeling to produce a "realistic" account of the future Southwest that allows for the opening of a dangerous nuclear waste depository, I show how realism is used by the state to distribute risk unevenly onto Indigenous nations. I read David Foster Wallace's 1996 novel *Infinite Jest* as a critique of both nuclear colonialism and the form of realism that perpetuates it before turning to Leslie Marmon Silko's *Almanac of the Dead* (1991), a novel that uses apocalyptic form to transform nuclear waste into a prophecy of the end of the United States rather than a means for imagining its continuation. This revised emplotment of history transforms the present into an apocalyptic space where environmental catastrophe produces not only unevenly distributed damage but also revolutionary forms of social justice that insist on a truth that probability modeling cannot contain: that the future will be qualitatively different from the present, while the present, too, might yet be utterly different from the real that we think we know.

The book closes with a brief coda, "Nuclear Entanglements," that turns to the Fukushima Daiichi disaster to consider the nuclear problem at the planetary scale in the twenty-first century. Drawing on the history of nuclear power in the Atoms for Peace program and Ruth Ozeki's transoceanic novel *A Tale for the Time Being* (2013), I bring together the entangled fields of nuclear science and quantum physics to argue that the nuclear condition requires an ethical engagement with the world through the model of quantum superposition and entanglement, in which distant objects resonate with each other, cause and effect are unpredictable, and impossibilities flourish. The nuclear age in which the human species will now always live reveals us to be something other than we thought we were, unstable beings entangled with an unknowable planet. And if this revelation appears apocalyptic, then apocalypse is where we must reside, with futurelessness affording the chance to keep the present open to radical change just a little longer, suspended between the unbearable past and the impossible future, here, at the end of the world.

Why Apocalypse, Why Now?

These chapters, taken together, intervene in a central problem in contemporary environmental and social theory: how counterhegemonic work can continue when all avenues of possibility appear to be foreclosed. As late capitalism grinds inexorably on, as more and more lives are precarious, as the protections and promises of liberalism become increasingly hollow, as overt white supremacy seizes power, and as the irreversible environmental catastrophes of climate change, toxification, and the sixth mass extinction project an uncertain future for life itself, the affective function of hope and a belief in progress comes under increasing pressure. This is hard, as all of us know: it's *hard* to keep working when you don't know what you're working for; it's *hard* to keep working when you don't feel optimistic about your chances of generating change; it's *hard* to invest in action that doesn't fit into a narrative of amelioration, that doesn't promise that things will get better. Futurelessness is not a politics that feels empowered, agential, directional. Anna Lowenhaupt Tsing takes up this problem in *The Mushroom at the End of the World*: we think that we have grown out of progress narratives, left them in the last century where they belong, but at the same time, "progress felt great; there was always something better ahead. Progress gave us the 'progressive' political causes with which I grew up. I hardly know how to think about justice without progress."[94] Progress is how we know how to feel good, and progress requires futurity.

"It's hard for me to even say this: there might not be a collective happy ending."[95] I know what I'm asking. In *Conscripts of Modernity*, David Scott describes the crisis of postcolonial politics after Bandung when the horizon of utopian possibility that had defined earlier anticolonial movements seemed to contract into a "dead-end present," what Raymond Williams described in reference to modern tragedy as "the loss of hope; the slowly settling loss of any acceptable future."[96] This state of mind is both shared by the contemporary moment and intolerable to it, for all of the reasons described above. Scott diagnoses it, but his project is explicitly to find a way to get out of it. Mine is not. I'm asking us to stay there, to see what apocalyptic transfigurations of the world might be produced if we ceased to be oriented toward a futural horizon even if it doesn't feel good, even if it can't sustain the momentary punk euphoria of Edelman's "fuck everything" and for the most part is kind of depressing, even if it means by definition that we can never *get* anywhere.

Contemporary theory sees little of value in apocalypse. Addressing the question of how we live in precarious times, Donna Haraway asks, "How can we think in times of urgencies *without* the self-indulgent and self-fulfilling myths of apocalypse?"[97] Rebecca Solnit uses apocalypse as a synonym for "easy despair," while Timothy Morton argues that "the strongly held belief that the world is about to end 'unless we act now' is paradoxically one of the most powerful factors that inhibit a full engagement with our ecological coexistence here on Earth."[98] Kath Weston's note on the topic in *Animate Planet* establishes the conceptual outlines of the opposition between apocalypse and a serious/radical engagement with a precarious present that these thinkers share: "The perception that environmental changes are rendering life more precarious," she writes, "is not to be confused with an apocalyptic narrative, although the two may feed off one another. Meteor strikes, nuclear winters, and climate change–induced disasters all draw audiences to cinemas, especially in North America, but these stories focus on the end game, the time when human history stops, not the insecurities of a now. With their teleological bent, apocalyptic accounts are affectively quite distinctive."[99] Apocalypse, here and elsewhere, is the bad object (teleological, determinate, an overly aestheticized distraction) against which good thinking about present-day crisis defines itself.

But what if "the insecurities of [the] now" demand that we take apocalypse more seriously? Tsing defines precarity as "that here and now in which pasts may not lead to futures."[100] To be precarious, to be in crisis, is to exist in a condition of foreclosed futurity. The reaction formation to this is to double down on ideologies of survival, but this comes with its own problems; "in popular American fantasies, survival is all about saving oneself by fighting off others. The 'survival' featured in U.S. television shows or alien-planet stories is a synonym for conquest and expansion."[101] Even in less overtly Hobbesian fantasies, the logic of survival, as we noted with regard to the nuclear complex, is essentially biopolitical, such that survival as an ideological determining horizon makes the actual living-on of situated bodies less likely, especially if they are already precariously positioned. What if we were to think about life, and the social, and the here and now, in other ways? What if acknowledging our own foreclosed futurity led not to a commitment to survival at all costs but somewhere else?

The wager that this book makes is that radical apocalypticism, a commitment to struggle in a present that is oriented to futurelessness rather than to survival, an apocalypticism that interrupts teleologies rather than reproducing them, produces valuable forms of work, thought, solidarity, and care.[102] It traces the operations of such a struggle in hot spot writers in the hope that retrieving a counterhistory of apocalypse from below can help us reclaim a strategic apocalypticism as a weapon in the fight for liberation. In the face of a future whose impossibility seems to sediment with every new report on climate change, in a moment when the United States is committing itself to another $5 trillion nuclear buildup, where Blackness and Brownness are a license to be killed slowly by water or suddenly by cop, *Infrastructures of Apocalypse* offers a timely theorization of futurelessness not as an obliteration of possibility but as a place to stand, a place where we might yet construct a world in which to live.

1

White Sovereignty and the Nuclear State

> It is such a supreme folly to believe that nuclear weapons are deadly only if they're used. The fact that they exist at all, their presence in our lives, will wreak more havoc than we can begin to fathom. Nuclear weapons pervade our thinking. Control our behavior. Administer our societies. Inform our dreams. They bury themselves like meat hooks deep in the base of our brains. They are purveyors of madness. They are the ultimate colonizer. Whiter than any white man that ever lived. The very heart of whiteness.
>
> —Arundhati Roy, *The Cost of Living*

LET US BEGIN WHERE ALL INFRASTRUCTURE BEGINS: with bureaucracy. In the months following the end of World War II, the tangle of institutions that had taken shape under the name of the Manhattan Project were slowly formalized under civilian control. The Atomic Energy Act of 1946 created the Atomic Energy Commission (AEC) as a way of removing the new nuclear technologies from military governance and restoring them to the norms of democratic oversight. The disposition of these new legal and bureaucratic infrastructures, however, was toward secrecy, unaccountability, and radically expanded state power—a disposition that struck observers as closer to the totalitarianism of the United States' enemies than the free market democracy by which Cold

War America defined itself. Even the first chair of the AEC, David E. Lilienthal, warned of the totalitarian dispositions of the nuclear state. In 1948, Lilienthal published "Democracy and the Atom," alerting readers that "a principal danger to the people of this democracy is that atomic energy in our own hands can become a threat to our basic liberties." Writing against the more common fear that America would be existentially threatened by an atomically armed Soviet Union, Lilienthal noted pointedly that "it is not the plotting and design of evildoers, from without and within, of which I speak." Rather, the greatest danger lay in the new state practices of the nuclear age: "in our diligent efforts—the common goal of us all—to provide for this country the greatest possible security in a world in which the release of atomic energy may in some future day no longer be even a limited American monopoly, in our efforts to control and develop this majestic force for beneficial use, we must not unwittingly and carelessly adopt practices that are in reality authoritarian and dictatorial, that deny the essentials of our democratic faith and our democratic way of life."[1]

Lilienthal's jeremiad is exemplary of a widely shared concern across the political spectrum in the Cold War United States: that the legal and bureaucratic infrastructures put in place to maintain nuclear superiority would transform the United States into a totalitarian state. For Lilienthal and others, as Roland Végső writes, "the secret of the atom marks an internal limit of democracy: it is the force that can lead to the internal collapse of American democracy by turning it into a totalitarian system in the name of the security of democracy."[2] Even as more dramatic "end of America" narratives accrued around spectacular representations of Soviet invasions or nuclear war, a more mundane anxiety formed a consistent counterpoint: America in the atomic age would be defined by the fear that it was transforming into its own opposite as a result of the means of its defense.

What, though, is the opposite of America? What does transforming into the other look like in the specifically American context? A more recent extension of Lilienthal's 1948 argument gives us some indications, through a pattern appearing both at the beginning of the Cold War and after its end. Elaine Scarry's magisterial critique of the political economy of nuclear weapons in *Thermonuclear Monarchy: Choosing between Democracy and Doom* (2014) establishes the many ways in which the infrastructures of the nuclear state are fundamentally incompatible with the Constitution and with democratic sovereignty itself:

> Forms of government based on symmetry and distribution of power require weapons that entail symmetry and distribution of power. If an out-of-ratio weapon comes into being in the midst of a symmetrical form of government, one of the two must give way to accommodate the other. Either the out-of-ratio weapon must be renounced and dissolved, enabling the symmetrical government to survive; or the symmetrical form of government must be renounced and dissolved, replaced with an out-of-ratio government whose shape can accommodate the shape of the new out-of-ratio weapon. The second outcome has taken place in the United States following the invention of atomic weapons.[3]

The extreme weighting of sovereignty toward the president as a figure who controls the capacity to eliminate entire nations under his own counsel and in conditions of absolute secrecy produces, for Scarry, the political condition that she calls thermonuclear monarchy: a state that appears to be a liberal democracy but in fact shares the basic conditions of a monarchy due to the absolute power over life and death held by its head of state.

Scarry's description of the condition of thermonuclear monarchy, however, treats it not only as a shift in the ratio of political power but also as a shift in the nation's position in time. Thermonuclear monarchy is, for Scarry, an "archaic," "atavistic and infantilizing form of government"; "it carries us back to a territory that is not just anterior to democracy but anterior to social contract altogether."[4] Thermonuclear weapons are "savage and prelegal"; their use is "savage or atavistic."[5] Words like "savage" and "atavistic" ring bells, harkening back to the racial chronopolitics discussed in this book's introduction; Scarry performs here the denial of coevalness described by Johannes Fabian, positioning the prenuclear United States as the culmination of Enlightenment reason and the nuclear-age state as its racialized other, a step backward along an evolutionary timeline into a "territory . . . anterior to social contract" that starkly recalls Hegel's descriptions of Africa as outside the time and space of political being as well as more recent settler-colonial depictions of Native nations as prepolitical.[6]

Scarry's "savage," "atavistic" nuclear age brings into the foreground a theme that has remained mostly unrecognized in studies of the Cold War United States: that the fear of America transforming into its other under the internal pressures of nuclear security was not only an ideological anxiety but also a racial one. This chapter limns the contours of this fear of racial transformation, showing how the ideology of totalitarianism was itself racially coded as "Oriental" in a way that made becoming-totalitarian also becoming-Asian. While the sovereign subject of democracy was coded as white, the subject of totalitarianism— widely defined as "traditional Oriental despotism plus modern police technology"—was imagined in the United States through an Orientalist lens that coded Asian others as unindividuated, "savage," "atavistic."[7] As white Americans confronted the nuclear complex, they found themselves facing the loss of the individuated invulnerability to state violence that the state had guaranteed as a property of whiteness since its founding in settler-colonial genocide and slavery. As a result, whiteness developed a new relationship to the state that saw the apocalyptic threat of atomic weapons as inhering not in a future atomic war but in the everyday operations of the nuclear complex that threatened to remove the privileges of whiteness.

I take as my case study of this reflexive yellow perilism a text that has become a bible for a particular form of white sovereignty: Ayn Rand's 1957 novel *Atlas Shrugged.* One of the most successful and influential books ever published, *Atlas Shrugged* is both an exemplar of mid-century anxieties about race and sovereignty and, I will suggest, a significant actor in the renegotiation of those anxieties, laying the groundwork for the rhetoric of nuclear-state atavism that will come to function as common sense by the time of *Thermonuclear Monarchy*.[8] Rand's fervent defense of sovereign individualism draws on the aesthetics and ideology of yellow perilism to redefine changes in state power in the nuclear age as the creeping Orientalization of white America. By invoking this tradition, she also takes up the sense of apocalyptic threat to the white nation that lies at the heart of the yellow peril genre. While anti-individualist ideas, such as the monopolization of nuclear technology by the state, gained much of their rhetorical power by raising the specter of the atomic apocalypse that might attend their failure, Rand presents in *Atlas Shrugged* the apocalyptic consequences that would, in her view, follow from their success. Depicting American whiteness as simultaneously threatened and inevitably victorious,

Rand teaches her reader to sacrifice everything for its defense: society, the nation, the world.

Atlas Shrugged in the Nuclear Age

Ayn Rand is difficult to situate within the literary-historical matrix of the nuclear age. This is, at least in part, an effect of her own commitment to self-mythologizing. A staunch believer in her own rootlessness, she thought of herself and her philosophical system Objectivism as having sprung, in the words of her biographer, "Athena-like, fully formed from the brow of Zeus."[9] The only intellectual influence she acknowledged was Aristotle, and she recognized no heirs: not the libertarians who walked under her flag; not the anarchists or feminists who claimed her as inspiration; not even Ronald Reagan, for whose administration she was dubbed the "novelist laureate" by the *New York Times.*[10] Her aesthetics are equally resistant to a literary-historical reading, bringing together so many genres—philosophical treatise, novel, romance, science fiction, melodrama—that the end product comes to seem genuinely sui generis. Criticism tends to operate within the parameters laid out by Rand herself, debating whether the philosophy is coherent or how the multiple genres of her novels function, and these approaches have produced insightful critiques of Rand's work.[11] More recent work by Myka Tucker-Abramson and Andrew Hoberek has productively taken an economic approach to Rand's post–World War II work, analyzing the nature and function of capital and class in this arch-capitalist oeuvre.[12] What gets lost in these readings, however, are the ways in which Rand was both a product of and a player in some of the major cultural conflicts of the Cold War.

As a Russian immigrant whose family lost their haute-bourgeois status after the Bolshevik revolution, Rand was a fierce critic of communism long before anticommunism became the default position of American life. She despaired at the popularity of the communist and leftist positions that characterized intellectual trends in the 1930s and thought that the New Deal was the first step in America's collapse into collectivism. After World War II, she engaged actively in the flourishing anticommunist movement. Working as a script and scenario writer in Hollywood, she published several tracts describing how movies could combat collectivism and promote capitalism.[13] In 1947, she volunteered as a friendly witness in front of the House Un-American Activities Committee, which was engaged at the time in rooting out leftist/communist "subversives" from the film industry.[14] While never fully aligned with any of the existing range of anticommunist positions (she believed firmly that capitalism rather than abstract terms such as *freedom* or *democracy* was the moral system that stood opposed to collectivism), Rand was, in the years from 1945 to 1957 in which she was writing *Atlas Shrugged,* a dedicated Cold Warrior.[15]

Atlas Shrugged, then, emerges from a time in which Rand thought and wrote obsessively about the Cold War and its ideological battles, and it was understood by its author as a weapon in the fight against collectivism. The novel tells the story of John Galt, a superman who has initiated a strike of what Rand calls the "prime movers": high-powered industrial capitalists whose creative energy keeps the world running. As the collectivist world slowly disintegrates, Dagny Taggart, heiress to the Taggart Railway, must learn to reject her altruistic instincts to maintain the railway for the sake of the country and to join the strike instead, leaving the nation to collapse. As the corrupt, bureaucratic government takes full control of the economy and the prime movers retreat to the hidden capitalist utopia known as Atlantis, America degenerates apocalyptically into a third world country without law, electricity, or hope, clearing the way for the triumphant return of the heroic industrialists.

That the basic opposition of capitalist–collectivist operates within Cold War parameters is clear, but *Atlas Shrugged* in no way supports the state policies of the capitalist America in which it was written. In fact, the novel is deeply critical of the increasing bureaucracy, secrecy, and militarization of the American state, depicting a system that transforms itself into a collectivist nightmare without any external threat or enemy invasion. Rather than body snatchers or fifth columns, the decisive moment in America's apocalyptic transformation into its totalitarian other comes with the advent of nuclear technology, when the state finally reveals its death-driven lust for power and destroys its citizens' physical and mental freedom.

Attention to the implications of the atom for sovereignty is bricked into the foundations of *Atlas Shrugged.* In 1945, Rand was under contract to Hal Wallis, the producer of *Casablanca,* as a screenwriter. For six months of every year, Rand was on call to write treatments and screenplays for movies to be produced by Wallis. The rest of the time, she was free to work on her own projects. While Rand was never a particularly prolific screenwriter, this Persephone-esque working arrangement led to a fertile cross-pollination between her personal work and her paid projects.[16] One such transfer was her engagement with the atomic bomb. Rand started working on *Atlas Shrugged* on January 1, 1945. In late 1945, riding the contemporary wave of fascination with atomic scientists and their doings, Wallis suggested that Rand write a screenplay about the development of the atom bomb. Rand worked on the project, provisionally titled *Top Secret*, until March 1946, when MGM bought the script and buried it to prevent competition with their own Manhattan Project docudrama *The Beginning or the End*, which was released in 1947.[17]

Rand took the project seriously. She interviewed many of the key scientists at Los Alamos, including two sessions with J. Robert Oppenheimer. In a memo to Wallis on January 2, 1946, titled "An Analysis of the Proper Approach to a Picture on the Atomic Bomb," Rand, never one to underestimate her own importance or that of her projects, writes that "the responsibility of making such a picture is greater than that of knowing the secret of the atomic bomb. The atomic bomb is, after all, only a piece of inanimate matter that cannot set itself in use. Whether it's used and how it's used will depend on the *thinking* of men."[18] Rand asserts that writing about the bomb is even more significant than building the bomb, metonymically garnering to writing the apocalyptic force of nuclear technology. When *Top Secret* was quashed by MGM, she did not give up on the material that she had gathered. On June 11, 1946, Oppenheimer makes his first appearance in Rand's notes for *Atlas Shrugged*. He would end up playing a major role in the novel under the cover of the fictional Dr. Robert Stadler, the brilliant scientist co-opted by the state.

According to the script treatment preserved in Rand's journals, *Top Secret* presents the Manhattan Project in an extremely positive light, describing it as the objective correlative of a truly free capitalist society: "only free men in voluntary cooperation could have done it," says Oppenheimer.[19] This positive view of the atom and its implications for individual freedom was, however, short-lived. In *Atlas Shrugged*, the Manhattan Project reappears in allegorical form as Project X, a superweapon created by the State Science Institute from the theoretical work of Dr. Stadler that uses sound rays to destroy everything within a hundred-mile radius. This weapon plays a crucial role in the plot of the novel, as it is the detonation of Project X by a politician who wants to establish his own rule over a disintegrating America that delivers the final blow to the very idea of a United States by destroying the Taggart Bridge, the last remaining transport link connecting East to West over the Mississippi.

The demonstration of the weapon to assorted politicians, journalists, and military leaders recalls nuclear weapons tests such as the widely publicized Operation Cue in 1955, which involved building model suburban houses at various distances from ground zero, fitting them out with humanoid mannequins, and then dropping a bomb on them to see what happened. For the Project X test, the assorted viewers are placed in stands and given binoculars through which they observe the instantaneous destruction of a dilapidated farmhouse and a flock of goats. The details of the test, from the effects of the weapon to the building housing it that has "an air of silent malevolence, like a puffed, venomous mushroom" (754), are clearly atomic. In Rand's presentation of Project X, however, the function of the weapon is not its stated one, that of national defense against aggression from other states. While the collected dignitaries and spokespeople offer rousing speeches for radio broadcast about how the weapon will keep them safe, Stadler observes the crowd:

> They were sitting quietly now, they were listening, but their eyes had an ebbing look of twilight, a look of fear in the process of being accepted as permanent, the look of raw wounds being dimmed by the veil of infection. They knew, as he knew it, that they were the targets of the shapeless funnels protruding from the mushroom building's dome—and he wondered in what manner they were now extinguishing their minds and escaping that knowledge; he knew that the words they were eager to absorb and believe were the chains slipping in to hold them, like the goats, securely within the range of those funnels. (759)

Despite the platitudes offered by the assembled luminaries regarding the importance of Project X for the defense of the nation, we learn that this has never been the true function of the sound ray weapon: "Social systems are so precarious. But think of what stability could be achieved

by a few scientific installations at strategic key points. It would guarantee a state of permanent peace—don't you think so?" (760). This
technology, developed in secret, is presented as a defensive weapon
that operates solely as a deterrent but is in fact a set of bureaucratic,
legal, testing, and military infrastructures that are ultimately intended
to control Americans—an effect that, as Jackie Orr and others have
noted, was carefully constructed by state performances of nuclear terror in the real-world United States that sought to produce enough fear
in their audiences to maintain support for deterrence.[20]

What, then, can account for the shift in Rand's attitude toward the
atom bomb between her veneration of it as a symbol of individual freedom in *Top Secret* and her critique of it as a state-designed threat to
individual sovereignty in *Atlas Shrugged*? In many ways, Rand's shift in
thinking indexes a larger cultural shift in American perceptions of the
atom bomb that emerged in the years following World War II. The detonation of atomic bombs over Hiroshima and Nagasaki on August 6
and August 11, 1945, revealed to the world that the United States had
developed the capacity to split the atom, the technology to weaponize it, and the will to use it. Breathless accounts of the bombings presented the detonations as absolute historical ruptures, presaging the
world's transition into an atomic age. In the months that followed,
however, this historical rupture was revealed to have its own secret
histories as the bomb's infrastructural backstory was slowly released
to the public, with often equally breathless revelations as to the real
function of the massive military installations at Oak Ridge, Tennessee;
Richland, Washington; and Los Alamos, New Mexico.[21] As much of the
world settled into its post–World War II reality, Americans began to
come to terms with the fact that under the veil of wartime secrecy, the
legal and bureaucratic infrastructures of the United States had been
transformed, transforming in turn the lived reality of all Americans.

Within weeks of the revelation of the Manhattan Project's existence, fears began to surface that the development of the atomic bomb
would have serious implications for the relationship between citizen
and state. In a country whose founding document declared the right
to life of each citizen, life itself was now imperiled by government action. The bomb, a threat to life at greater magnitude than previously
conceived of outside imaginings of the Last Days, had been developed
by an elected government in secret and then used in the name of a

nation whose citizens not only had not voted for the bomb to be developed but had not been consulted or even informed. Dwight Macdonald, a left-wing cultural critic writing in September 1945, immediately connected the infrastructures of the bomb's production with its implications for political tradition: "there is something askew," he wrote, "with a society in which vast numbers of citizens can be organized to create a horror like The Bomb without even knowing they are doing it. What content, in such a case, can be assigned to notions like 'democracy' and 'government of, by and for the people?'"[22] In a 1946 *Collier's* article, Robert DeVore captured the mood of the moment when he wrote that "men are beginning to learn that the price of admission to the Golden Age of the Atom will be paid in freedom."[23] Dropped in the name of defending democracy, the bomb was almost immediately recoded by such writers as a threat to democracy itself.

The negative impact of the atomic bomb was not identified solely with its use but radiated out from the infrastructures of its production and the vision of a future in which an atomically armed government would have total control over all aspects of daily life. The passage of the Atomic Energy Act in 1946, which restricted atomic research to government-chosen private companies and automatically classified the results as top secret, was the first occasion in which, in peacetime, a new market had been established entirely under governmental control and under conditions of total secrecy, a move that was widely read at the time and in the following decades as inimical to the spirit of democracy. A legal review of the act written in 1953 described it as a mechanism by which "a whole new science and technology were imprisoned in the house of Government and walled about with secrecy."[24] The security conditions attached to the act were also the first indication that individuals would be under much greater scrutiny in the atomic age, as the act required that all AEC employees, including scientists working on AEC-funded research at other institutions, such as universities, pass a full FBI background check.[25] By 1950, the nuclear complex would fulfill Lilienthal's jeremiadic warnings with a set of state infrastructures that operated completely without democratic oversight. The CIA, established in 1947 by the National Security Act to act within the jurisdiction of the executive branch without congressional involvement, had gained the legal power in 1948 to undertake covert operations anywhere in the world, transforming it from an intelligence-gathering agency into a fully operational tool for covert warfare. In 1950, NSC-68, the policy paper that inaugurated the doctrine of containment and many other key protocols and practices of the Cold War, established that the full secrecy that had defined the Manhattan Project under wartime's suspension of democratic norms would now be the standard procedure of the nuclear state. The emergence of what Timothy Melley has called the "covert sphere," a set of institutions run by the state yet hidden from its citizens, "fundamentally—and perhaps permanently—transformed U.S. democracy" by replacing norms of informed consent of the ruled with new assumptions about the extent to which the state could operate in secrecy and without accountability.[26]

Even the writers of NSC-68 were not ignorant of the implications of their proposed infrastructural changes for traditional democratic sovereignty, and they acknowledged them in terms strikingly similar to those that Lilienthal had used several years earlier. In its attempt to grapple with the "moral, psychological, and political questions" involved in NSC-68's task, to undertake a "reexamination of this country's strategic plans and its objectives in peace and war . . . viewed in the light of the probable fission bomb capability and the possible thermonuclear bomb capability of the Soviet Union,"[27] NSC-68 finds itself caught in a paradox stemming from its premises: democracy is inherently stronger than totalitarianism because it promotes individual wellbeing (7–8), yet the communist state is strengthened because it has no internal disagreements. The United States is the greatest military power in the world, but the Soviet Union is better prepared for war because it can remain fully mobilized (not having to convince its citizens to bear the burden of constant militarization) (32). Even "the rights and privileges that free men enjoy . . . are but opportunities for the Kremlin to do its evil work" (34). As a consequence, the writers of NSC-68 are very aware that what strengthens the United States in the Cold War (as they see it) will be a structural shift to something that more closely resembles totalitarianism; like Lilienthal, they worry that "in pursuing these objectives, due care must be taken to avoid permanently impairing our economy and the fundamental values and institutions inherent in our way of life" (62). The belief that the new infrastructures of the nuclear state held the potential to turn America into its totalitarian other was thus not limited to Rand's antistatist position but was shared by commentators and political actors across the political spectrum.

This sense that the enemy is taking over the country from the inside is widely recognized as a defining feature of U.S. culture in the 1950s. Foundational accounts of the era, such as Alan Nadel's *Containment Culture* and Elaine Tyler May's *Homeward Bound,* describe both the increasing paranoia of the age and the strategies of containment, visible in foreign policy, domestic ideology, and cultural products, that developed to oppose it. In classic examples like *The Manchurian Candidate* (1962) and *Invasion of the Body Snatchers* (1956), American bodies become empty vessels for external enemies, taken over by Chinese–Soviet brainwashing or soulless alien parasites and threatening the American Way through their indistinguishability from the "real" Americans whom they have replaced.

In existing readings of such texts, however, ideology supplants race as a way to understand the permeable boundary between the external and internal enemy: the white body, even when taken over by a totalitarian force, remains white, with the Oriental body separate and elsewhere. Matthew Frye Jacobson and Caspar González, for example, deliver a detailed and biting critique of the Orientalism at work on every level in *The Manchurian Candidate,* from the content of the film to the conditions of its production, without noting that brainwashed American Raymond Shaw takes upon himself the definitive attributes of the "Oriental," becoming essentially, as the film's title suggests, Manchurian: inscrutable, passive, effeminate, robotic (100–129). David Seed's essay "The Yellow Peril in the Cold War" similarly describes the yellow peril as an external threat that might take control of white bodies but does not lead to racial degeneration; in Seed's account of *The Manchurian Candidate,* as in that of Jacobson and González, the yellow peril is embodied in the brainwashing villain Yen Lo rather than in Shaw himself. Timothy Melley captures the way in which "the vast security apparatus itself . . . tends to be seen as a source of irrationality, mystery, or supernatural agency," but he reads this threat to normcore America as feminization rather than as racialization.[28] The body that becomes taken over by a soul-destroying worm or Russo-Chinese communist remains for these critics a white body: this is the line that, in these accounts, cannot be crossed. Race is the final, impermeable barrier in the containment imaginary.

What *Atlas Shrugged* makes visible, however, is the extent to which becoming-totalitarian was racialized in this period as becoming-Oriental. Rand, as well as more fondly remembered mid-century authors like George Orwell and Arthur Koestler, defined totalitarianism through "the essential Orientalness of the Russian mentality"; as William Pietz argues, mainstream Western antitotalitarianists saw "communist Russia and totalitarian governments in general" as "nothing other than 'ancient oriental despotisms' plus modern police technology."[29] Jodi Kim also describes the transformation of Russia "from racially similar Westerners to the racially dissimilar 'oriental' Soviet Cold War enemies" as a key element of Cold War racecraft, emphasizing how older Orientalist tropes were transferred to the Soviet Union after World War II.[30] The anxiety in texts like *Atlas Shrugged* and *The Manchurian Candidate* about America's transformation into a totalitarian state should therefore be seen as participating in the much longer history of Western Orientalism and the genre of the yellow peril, but with a twist: while classic yellow perilism fears the invasion of the white nation by Asian bodies, the reflexive yellow perilism produced in the nuclear age fears the Orientalization of the white subject by the nuclear state. As communism was redefined by the West as totalitarianism and thus as Oriental despotism, the self living under totalitarian communism was, even if phenotypically white, fundamentally Oriental. Thus it is that the end product of the totalitarian nuclear state in *Atlas Shrugged* is not merely a disenfranchised populace but a racialized one: its political economy transformed into a Mao-esque "People's State" (906); its agriculture destroyed by a corrupt government subsidy of "the simple, wholesome foodstuff on which the peoples of the Orient have so nobly subsisted for centuries," soybeans (938); its rulers "moved forward [by] the vision of a fat, unhygienic rajah of India, with vacant eyes staring in indolent stupor out of stagnant layers of flesh, with nothing to do but run precious gems through his fingers and, once in a while, stick a knife into the body of a starved, toil-dazed, germ-eaten creature, as a claim to a few grains of the creature's rice" (872).

The history of the yellow peril genre provides a specific content to the racial form of nuclear Orientalism.[31] In the United States, yellow perilism both expressed and produced an affectively potent relationship to the Pacific Rim and to the Asian workers who migrated to America, as American legislatures repeatedly attempted to exclude Asian immigrants from white American life amid histrionically expressed fears of miscegenation, race degeneration, and Asian invasion.[32] Apocalypse was central to the genre, as fictions such as Jack London's "The Unparalleled Invasion" (1910) and Ignatius Donnelly's *Caesar's Column* (1889) projected a white Western world whose future was threatened by uncontrolled immigration, whether all at once or over the course of a century. During World War II, yellow peril discourse describing Japanese immigrants and Japanese Americans as an inherent threat to the future of the nation licensed the internment of more than 110,000 residents and citizens of Japanese origin despite the fact, acknowledged at the time, that there was no evidence of subterfuge or sabotage among the population.[33] Perceived as inalterably foreign, dangerous, and inassimilable, Asians, from the Chinese "coolies" of the 1860s to the Muslim "terrorists" of the present day, have long served in America as the racial other against which a particular model of highly individualized sovereign whiteness is defined; as Colleen Lye writes, Asiatic racial form is "a kind of difference that is marked by the lack of difference between individuals."[34] Against the Japanese, who must be interned as a population or not at all, stands the white subject who may plead his case as a sovereign individual.[35]

Inheriting this tradition, the basic algebra of the American racial ideology of anticommunism thus declared that freedom and individuality were equivalent to whiteness, while to be racialized as Oriental was equivalent to unfreedom and a reduction to being part of a deindividuated mass. To transform into a totalitarian society was, then, not only an ideological shift but also a racial one, and the threat to American democracy leveled by atomic infrastructures threatened whiteness as much as it did the more abstract concept of freedom.[36] At the Project X test, even the demonstration of "nuclear" technology makes its viewers less free, as they settle into obedience not only in terms of their behavior but in their minds, squashing free thought to continue to believe in the fallacy of democracy under the atomic regime. The scene becomes a vision straight out of the yellow peril–inspired anticommunist imagination: "a machine that had no center, no leader, no direction, a machine that had not been set in motion by Dr. Ferris or

Wesley Mouch, or any of the cowed creatures in the grandstands, or any of the creatures behind the scenes—an impersonal, unthinking, unembodied machine, of which none was the driver and all were the pawns, each to the degree of his evil" (748). And as they are deindividuated, the characters in the scene are Orientalized, drawing on a variety of tropes that were used to describe the Japanese during World War II: they are no longer human but animals, filled with "a plain, brute, animal fear of physical destruction" (765); they become a teeming mass of germs under the "veil of infection"; the machine itself is "a primitive structure unearthed in the heart of the jungle, devoted to some secret rites of savagery" (754).[37] Project X is a science fictional infrastructure of the nuclear state that works not as a ray to destroy bodies but rather as a ray to destroy freedom, individuality, and the privileges of whiteness: a race-ray, a technology that makes "savages" of people.

Antilife: Race, Rationality, and the Apocalypse of Goo

The concept of an Orientalized white population relies on a curiously fungible notion of race in which any body can become racialized at any moment. Such fungibility is possible because the axes along which race functions in *Atlas Shrugged* are drawn not upon lines of blood, phenotype, or national origin but rather along lines of rationality. In John Galt's speech, the sixty-page summation of the Objectivist philosophy allegorized by the rest of the novel, Galt runs the gamut of racist stereotypes in his description of the innate differences between rational and irrational approaches to the world:

> Let the caveman who does not choose to accept the axiom of identity, try to present his theory without using the concept of identity or any concept derived from it—let the anthropoid who does not choose to accept the existence of nouns, try to devise a language without nouns, adjectives or verbs—let the witchdoctor who does not choose to accept the validity of sensory perception, try to prove it without using the data he obtained by sensory perception—let the head-hunter who does not choose to accept the validity of logic, try to prove it without using logic—let the pigmy who proclaims that a skyscraper needs no foundation after

it reaches its fiftieth story, yank the base from under his building, not yours—let the cannibal who snarls that the freedom of man's mind was needed to *create* an industrial civilization, but is not needed to *maintain* it, be given an arrowhead and bearskin, not a university chair of economics. . . . A savage is a being who has not grasped that A is A and that reality is real.[38] (956–57)

Rand had criticized racism as both a form of collectivism and a limit to individual freedom, but her language here demonstrates the centrality of race to her conception of personhood.[39] Those capable of purely rational thought are men; those who are not are "on the way back to the sub-human" (963).[40] The apocalyptic scenario produced by this degeneration is not one of catastrophic violence, as it is for earlier yellow peril writers such as London and Donnelly, but a dissolution of reality itself in the face of irrationality: "it's as if the whole world were suddenly destroyed, but not by an explosion—an explosion is something hard and solid—but destroyed by . . . some horrible kind of softening . . . as if nothing were solid, nothing held any shape at all, and you could poke your finger through stone walls and the stone would give, like jelly, and mountains would slither, and buildings would switch their shapes like clouds—and that would be the end of the world, not fire and brimstone, but goo" (819, ellipses original).

As Judith Wilt has argued, "for Rand . . . the apocalypse of goo is the product of twentieth-century thought, Einsteinian, Heisenbergian, Freudian, deracinating, derationalizing thought dissolving the clean lines and stable constructs of nineteenth-century science, art, industry, and philosophy, which, in her view, restored man's Greek singleness (and singularity) after a long detour through 'religious' irrationality and otherworldliness."[41] Rand's writing-together of whiteness and rationality, however, suggests that the "apocalypse of goo" in which the world dissolves through irrationality also has a racial dimension. In "The Phenomenology of Whiteness," Sara Ahmed defines whiteness as "an orientation that puts certain things within reach. By objects, we would include not just physical objects, but also styles, capacities, aspirations, techniques, habits. Race becomes in this model, a question of what is within reach, what is available to perceive and to 'do' things with."[42] In Rand's theorization of race, whiteness is a worldly orientation that has sole access to both rationality and futurity. When the nuclear state threatens rationality, it shifts the position of whiteness within the network of objects in relation to which it defines itself, threatening the nature of whiteness itself. Race has an infrastructural dimension for Ahmed: because whiteness is an orientation toward objects, it defines where things are in relation to each other and how they are held together; it is an infrastructure that holds the world in a specific shape, such that "whiteness describes the very 'what' that coheres as a world."[43] Thus the apocalypse of goo: when whiteness is stripped of its access to "its" objects of rationality and futurity, the world that was cohered by it loses its shape as the infrastructure of whiteness that held things in fixed relation to each other begins to deliquesce.

Rand's depiction of whiteness, rationality, and futurity as mutually constitutive allows us to see the racial dynamics of whiteness at play in larger mid-century concerns about rationality and nuclear apocalypse. Many of Rand's peers were equally horrified by the turn to existentialism, pragmatism, and relativism that characterized intellectual life in Europe and the United States in the twentieth century. "Before the possibilities of physical atomization had become apparent," Catholic leader William J. Grace wrote in 1950, connecting the threat of irrational thought to the threat of nuclear technologies, "we had already undergone an accelerated process of intellectual atomization."[44] This philosophical debate was imbricated in the wider cultural and military conditions of the Cold War. The paradox that underlay the very idea of a Cold War, the condition of permanent crisis or the constant state of exception, struck many commentators as less a necessary response to the pressures of the age than as downright delusional. Cultural blockbusters such as Stanley Kubrick's *Dr. Strangelove* (1964) and Joseph Heller's *Catch-22* (1961) depict the insanity of a nuclearized world in which truth is inconstant, in which relativity is the condition of everything from particle physics to aesthetics and ethics. Rand's reassertion of Aristotle's premise that "A is A" as the foundation of her philosophy stands against what Frederick M. Dolan calls "Cold War metaphysics": "The Cold War preoccupation with whether American life is real or artificial," Dolan argues, "is powerful enough to cut across, or absorb, ideological differences. The right-wing articulation of simulation as fear of communism, and the left-wing articulation of simulation as consumer capitalism, are equally workable (or unworkable) attempts to think, judge, and protest the transition to a society of sheer artifice."[45] In fiction, popular texts such as J. D. Salinger's *The Catcher in the Rye* (1951) captured the enervating effects of life surrounded by "phonies," dramatizing life lived without access to "true" reality. The consequence of a society based on delusion was, for most commentators, seen as apocalypse via nuclear war. Journalist Fred J. Cook, criticizing the militarization of American society, argued that "the aims of the Warfare State . . . are aims that in the end, unless checked, must be ultimately suicidal"; sociologist Leander Boykin, confronting the paradox of a democratic state governed by totalitarian means, described the situation as a "fool's paradise" in which "we are stubbornly refusing to admit that anything is wrong with democracy in this era of big, dynastic, imperialistic, states. The question of maintaining peace, decency, and prosperity is now too immediate, too critical to continue such a course. The gravest immediate danger facing us is the possibility of being involved in another futile war."[46] For such critics, the phoniness of life lived without (white) rationality under conditions of permanent nuclear threat makes it impossible to guarantee futurity for either the individual or the nation.

For Rand, however, the violence that in these predictions lies farther down the road is already happening in the form of nuclear infrastructures. A society that brings the threat of nuclear violence into the everyday lives of its inhabitants in the name of safety damages the individual by forcing him to live irrationally. The ability to think independently and to act autonomously, without needing help from anybody else, is the basis on which Rand's "utopia of greed" will be built (694). In contrast to a Hobbesian view of life outside the social contract, however, in which the absence of interpersonal dependence leads to interpersonal violence red in tooth and claw, this kind of sovereign individualism is predicated on the use of force only for self-defense.[47] In John Galt's speech, Rand writes that "no man may *initiate* . . . the use of physical force against others" (940, emphasis original). Immediately following this, she extends the prohibition to preclude the threat of physical violence:

> Force and mind are opposites; morality ends where a gun begins. . . . To force a man to drop his own mind and to accept your will as a substitute, with a gun in place of a syllogism, with terror in place of proof, and death as the final argument—is to attempt

to exist in defiance of reality. Reality demands of man that he act
for his own rational interest; your gun demands of him that he
act against it. Reality threatens man with death if he does not act
on his rational judgment; you threaten him with death if he does.
You place him into a world where the price of his life is the surrender of all the virtues required by life—and death by a process
of gradual destruction is all that you and your system will achieve,
when death is made to be the ruling power, the winning argument in a society of men. (940–41)

Both violence and the threat of violence deprive man of his ability
rationally to choose according to his own self-interest. In Rand's theory of violence, there is no practical difference between action and
threat. Whether you shoot a man or force him to follow your dictates
at gunpoint, the end result is the same: "death by a process of gradual destruction."[48] The collapse of the distinction between war and
peace is usually associated with the use of nuclear weapons as a form
of threat in foreign policy, where "powers of terror are indistinguishable from powers of 'deterrence,' and technologies of war indissocia-
ble from practices of peace."[49] In *Atlas Shrugged,* however, it is on the
home front that the nuclear state exerts its force, both as a threat and
on the material plane: in the apocalyptic destruction of Rand's America, the damage to bodily, psychic, and national integrity that stems
from the nuclear state actually happens. Here the damage is cata-
strophically inflicted and the world of whiteness really does collapse.

The irrational man, the "savage," thus becomes for Rand the product of life in the nuclear age. To live under the contradictions involved
in Cold War metaphysics, man must sacrifice the motor behind his sovereign individuality, the power of rational thought, and thus degenerate into a racialized form: the caveman, the anthropoid, the witchdoc-
tor, the headhunter, the pigmy, the cannibal. Separating the content
of "race," defined as an orientation toward backwardness, irrationality, and vulnerability, from its embodied form, Rand radically expands
the size of the population who can be understood and represented in
those terms. By the end of *Atlas Shrugged,* the number of people who
are acknowledged as "white"—defined as rational and invulnerable—
can fit into a single Colorado hamlet.[50] The rest of America has become a "nation of sharecroppers" (84), where even Dagny's fantasy of a

science fiction railway line produced from the futuristic Rearden Metal has to pass through "the rotting shanties of half-starved settlements" (132). The real-world America's Orientalized populace, long subject to exclusion acts, labor and property restrictions, and internment orders, becomes in Rand's novel the entirety of the population, with their labor and property controlled by Directive 10-289, prohibiting changes of employment and migration and transferring ownership of all intellectual property to the state.[51]

At the same time as she critiques the operations of the nuclear state that produces this state of affairs, however, Rand depends—philosophically, aesthetically, and narratively—on these racialized others. Her mission is never to save those who have become disposable; rather, it is by depicting the degeneration of the American people into "yellow fools" marked by a "yellow complexion" that Rand can produce a new and improved white American (191, 774). The "apocalypse of goo" is terrifying to Dagny and disturbing to the reader. Pedagogically, however, the lesson that Dagny, and, by extension, the reader, must learn is not to resist the apocalypse or to attempt to save the world but to find the Orientalized world despicable and to participate in its destruction; the central story of the novel is not, in fact, the apocalyptic destruction of America but rather Dagny's journey from fiercely attempting to keep the world going to joining the strike. By recoding race in the terms of the right kind of thought, of rationality, Rand creates a world in which "correct" thinking can restore whiteness and its privileges: the power to think, to survive, to flourish, to be counted as human. Referring to the imperative to beat the "yellow fools," steel magnate Hank Rearden reassures Dagny that "there are still a few men in existence" (191). If the carrot that Rand offers her readers is that of an integrated philosophy that insists on the importance of the individual, then the stick is that rejection of this philosophy makes you not only wrong but also "subhuman."

Rand's solution to the paradoxes of Cold War culture reveals the centrality of race to an intellectual tradition that is more usually understood in the abstracted terms of metaphysics and logic: what Daniel Grausam names as the psychic drama of "unthinking the thinkability of the unthinkable" and Végső calls a "crisis of representation."[52] We thus see in *Atlas Shrugged* the beginnings of the racial metaphysics that we saw organizing Scarry's critique of nuclear weapons well into the twenty-first century; for Scarry, too, nuclear weapons are "unreachable by the human will" and constitute a call to "suspend thinking" and exist irrationally: "the structures of power in the nuclear age have corralled populations into a philosophically untenable proposition according to which we are in charge of our own self-preservation except where our actual preservation is at stake."[53] The conditions of vulnerability, uncertainty, and irrationality have long been outsourced in white imaginaries to the world's nonwhite populations. With the advent of the nuclear threat and the subsequent constitutional shifts in the nature of American democracy, white Americans found themselves for the first time expected to experience these conditions not just fleetingly but as the new norm. *Atlas Shrugged* registers the impact of this transition precisely as a loss of race privilege, demonstrating the immense power of the fear that one could lose one's whiteness through its presentation of the world-ending consequences of the Orientalization of the West. If the West loses through its own nuclear contradictions its access to rational reasoning, its "own precious racial superpower,"[54] then it will not require the gradual yellowing of miscegenation in order to be destroyed but will immediately degenerate, decay, and die.[55]

Atlas and the People's Globe: Vulnerable Whiteness in the Global Imaginary

The potential for sudden Orientalization was not, however, limited to intra-American conditions. In the years before World War II, as Colleen Lye, David Palumbo-Liu, and others have demonstrated, a transnational consciousness of the Pacific Rim region was central to America's understanding of itself, particularly on the West Coast (where *Atlas Shrugged* was conceptualized and begun). Whether the perceived threat lay in the influx of Asian workers into California, as in Lye's account, or the permeability of the Pacific border as the correlative of a belief that America's national destiny involved pushing forward "to form a bridge westward from the Old World, not just to the western coast of the North American continent, but from there to the trans-Pacific regions of Asia," as Palumbo-Liu writes, Asia formed a buttress—an unnervingly uncertain buttress, but a vital one—against which white identity could be formed and tested.[56]

After 1945, however, the global politics of the Cold War demanded that America reconceptualize its relationship to Asia. Even as Maoist China and North Korea were demonized, noncommunist Asia became vital to America's economic, military, and diplomatic needs; Asian countries provided export opportunities, military bases, and ideological bastions against the spread of communism. In *Cold War Orientalism: Asia in the Middlebrow Imagination, 1945–61,* Christina Klein demonstrates the enormous ideological shift that was required to produce the necessary "reworking of national self-definition" as America moved from its former isolationist position into one that embraced global power.[57] Klein describes the new consensus as a "global imaginary of integration."[58] Opposite to yet working in tandem with the "global imaginary of containment," integration doctrine, promoted as vital to American survival by the Eisenhower administration, imagined nuclear-age America as part of a global network whose bonds must be ever strengthened if the United States were to achieve victory in the Cold War.[59] While communist states had to be contained, noncommunist states needed to be integrated into the American globe through economic, cultural, and affective ties. At home, this required that culture start representing Asia not as the location of irreconcilable difference, as it had been imagined before and during World War II, but as a place that could be understood, befriended, and taught. Musicals, plays, and books like *The King and I* (1956), *Teahouse of the Autumn Moon* (1956), and *Fifth Chinese Daughter* (1950) "narrated the knitting of ties between the United States and noncommunist Asia, and were infused with a structure of feeling that privileged precisely the values of interdependence, sympathy, and hybridity. These narratives and structures of feeling, far from undermining the global assertion of U.S. power, often supported it."[60] If Americans could accept that Asians were "like them," then they would be more likely to support the costs and difficulties of America's neocolonial activities abroad.

In *Atlas Shrugged,* Rand recoils from this integrative global imaginary like a finger from a hot stove. In the near-future of the novel, every country in the world, except America, has been Orientalized into China-esque collectivist "People's States." There is no longer any such thing as international trade; "with the world turning into People's States, this is the only country left where men are not yet reduced to digging for roots in forests for their sustenance—so this is the only market left on earth" (380). Instead, foreign aid sustains a one-way flow of capital from America to the rest of the world; by the time of John Galt's speech, the "People's Globe" has run apocalyptically into bankruptcy: "All those damned People's States all over the earth have been existing only on the handouts which you squeezed for them out of this country. But you—you have no place left to sponge on or mooch from. No country on the face of the globe. This was the greatest and last. You've drained it. You've milked it dry. . . . What will you do, you and your People's Globe, after you've finished me? What are you hoping for? What do you see ahead—except plain, stark, animal starvation?" (906). When the rest of the world has become "savage," racialized—even the People's State of Europe has "slave camps" (507)—America only speeds up its own degeneration through continued contact with it.

Rand was not alone in her fervent isolationism. If middlebrow culture as a whole embraced integration, many Americans did not; while Eisenhower pushed foreign aid as "the best mechanism for integrating the decolonizing world . . . a means to stimulate struggling economies, open new markets, and increase the overall flow of goods and resources," the idea of sending American money abroad became "the most contentious foreign policy issue of his presidency."[61] If, as Klein argues, *The King and I* acts as a model of an imagined community that could span the Pacific, then *Atlas Shrugged* speaks for a public—and a Congress—that utterly rejected such a community; Congress "fought and cut every aid allocation that the president requested."[62]

Rand was not, however, motivated solely by isolationist sentiments but also draws out the hypocrisy and violence behind American aid. Toward the end of the novel, the cadre of businessmen and politicians that now forms the U.S. government schemes to take over the D'Anconia mines, located in Chile and owned by one of the three original prime mover strikers, international playboy Francisco D'Anconia. The group sets up the Interneighborly Amity and Development Corporation, a corporation with "an exclusive contract to operate, on a twenty-year 'managerial lease,' all the industrial properties of the People's States of the Southern Hemisphere" (796). Barbara Grizzuti Harrison declares Rand wrongheaded on this, arguing that "she implies that American economic intervention in the 'pestholes of Asia' and in the underdeveloped countries of Latin America is motivated by demented, savagely liberal altruists who wish wrongheadedly to lend a hand to the undeserving poor."[63] By the time that the Interneighborly Amity and Development Corporation is established in the novel, however, it is obvious that the rhetoric of friendship and aid is merely an unconvincing cover for rapacious value extraction. When James Taggart, Dagny's worthless brother and the nominal CEO of Taggart Trains, insists to his wife, Cheryl, that "this is not an old-fashioned grab for private profit. It's a deal with a mission—a worthy, public-spirited mission—to manage the nationalized properties of the various People's States of South America, to teach their workers our modern techniques of production, to help the underprivileged who've never had a chance" (800), his explanation is convincing neither to Cheryl nor to the reader whose response she models. Rand may view this neocolonial action as a crime against prime movers rather than the citizens and residents of South America, but she sees the language of aid and international development for what it is: a way of maintaining American power abroad under conditions of absolute nonreciprocity.[64]

The idea of the global acquired a new potency in the nuclear age, as some conception of world government seemed, for many observers, to be the only way to prevent future wars that, with the advent of atomic weapons, might imperil the survival of humanity.[65] With the establishing of more and more bureaucratic infrastructures for nuclear internationalism under Eisenhower's Atoms for Peace program in the early 1950s, forms of international governance were indeed central to what nuclearization meant in that decade. For Rand, however, it is the concept of nuclear-powered global integration that appears as an apocalyptic threat to sovereign whiteness. If whiteness and its corollary, sovereign individualism, are represented by the ability to exist only for one's own benefit (John Galt's slogan is the vow that "I will never live for the sake of another man, nor ask another man to live for mine" [675]), then to be tied economically to another country is a catastrophic extension of the kind of nonsovereignty that threatens to overturn this ability. As Galt declares, "once, you believed it was 'only a compromise': you conceded it was evil to live for yourself, but moral to live for the sake of your children. Then you conceded that it was selfish to live for your children, but moral to live for your community. Then you conceded that it was selfish to live for your community, but moral to live for your country. Now, you are letting this greatest of countries be devoured by any scum from any corner of the earth, while you concede that it is selfish to live for your country and that your moral duty is to live for the globe" (970).

The devastating impact of this globalizing consensus on sovereign whiteness is presented in miniature in the story of the Twentieth Century Motor Company, the little dioramic allegory of collapsed industrial modernity that appears in the center of the novel. Led astray by the dim-witted heirs of the company's industrialist founder, the workers at the factory decide to collectivize both the factory and the company. This leads to the economic, physical, and moral collapse of the community and leads Galt—who, we discover later, had been an engineer there—to declare his strike. The tramp who tells the story to Dagny expresses the horror of having to consider oneself connected to others on a global scale:

> this was the moral law that the professors and leaders and thinkers had wanted to establish all over the earth. If this is what it did in a single small town where we all knew one another, do you care to think what it would do on a world scale? Do you care to imagine what it would be like, if you had to live and to work, when you're tied to all the disasters and all the malingering of the globe? . . . To work—with no chance to rise, with your meals and your clothes and your home and your pleasure depending on any swindle, any famine, any pestilence anywhere on earth. To work—with no chance for an extra ration, till the Cambodians have been fed and the Patagonians have been sent through college. To work—on a blank check held by every creature born, by men whom you'll never see, whose needs you'll never know, whose ability or laziness or sloppiness or fraud you have no way to learn and no right to question—just to work and work and work—and leave it up to the Ivys and the Geralds of the world to decide whose stomach will consume the effort, the dreams and the days of your life. And this is the moral law to accept? (618–19)

Like the nuclear infrastructures that de-whiten the sovereign individual, to be enmeshed in a global network with the Cambodians and the Patagonians does more than impoverish Americans by funneling capital away from them. The global imaginary here makes the white American functionally equivalent to the racialized Cambodian—he is not more important than the Cambodian; he is not more free than the Cambodian; he is not more white than the Cambodian. The horror that attends globalization is a vulnerable whiteness that can imagine economic and affective integration with the globe only as the end of its own privilege, the end of the world. While a world government was presented in the early Cold War as the only way to prevent an apocalyptic world war, for Rand and her followers, it is globalization itself that leads to the collapse of (white) civilization.

It is for this reason that Rand calls so frequently upon the language of the frontier in describing the aims of the striking prime movers. As Colleen Lye demonstrates, the impact of the closing of the American frontier in the late nineteenth century was not limited to the new anxieties that emerged regarding the end of frontier life and the over-civilizing of the American subject.[66] Rather, it created a relationship to Asia in which expansion into China was the only way to continue going west—requiring more contact with Asians, with the potential for the degeneration of the white race that this implied—while leaving the United States without a white buffer zone in between itself and Asia. In writings of the period, Lye notes, "a theme consistently struck is that, despite the U.S. 'opening' of China, 'Chinese' is a metonym for the closing of unique American conditions of possibility. The rhetoric of expansion's end and consolidation's onset, shared by writers from Brooks Adams to Jack London, repeatedly articulates the sense of the end of the American frontier with the image of Asia and Asians' new proximity."[67] When the frontier is closed and China is close, white America loses access to its own futurity. In *Atlas Shrugged,* Rand thus shares a set of concerns with the yellow peril writers of half a century earlier. In the face of an integrated world that insists on East–West networks, Rand follows "the degenerative logic of East–West contact" and sees only a contagious racialization and the decline of the white race.[68] To reverse this process, it becomes necessary to reopen the frontier. Whiteness can only be quarantined and reestablished if the border between East and West can also be reestablished, if the frontier can be rolled back away from Asia.

This is precisely what happens in *Atlas Shrugged.* California and the West are marked as irrevocably Oriental, providing a consumer's market for "the simple, wholesome foodstuff on which the peoples of the Orient have so nobly subsisted for centuries," soybeans—the production of which, incidentally, is the final nail in the coffin of the more American Midwestern wheat industry (938). When Dagny tries to tell the government to prioritize saving industry over the maintenance of the Union, the industrial East Coast stands in contrast to a degenerately racialized West Coast: "give us leeway to save the Eastern states. That's all that's left of the country—and of the world. If you let us save that, we'll have a chance to rebuild the rest. If not, it's the end.... There's nothing left to save in the West. You can run agriculture for centuries by manual labor and oxcarts. But destroy the last of this country's industrial plants—and centuries of effort won't be able to rebuild it or to gather the economic strength to make a start" (870–71). Dr. Ferris's response indicates that a fall into Oriental despotism is precisely the goal of the nuclear state: "The importance of industry to a civilization has been grossly overemphasized," he states. "What is now known as the People's State of India has existed for centuries without any industrial development whatever" (871).

Despite Dagny's attempt to amputate the West Coast and save the Breadbasket, however, John Galt's goal is, perhaps counterintuitively, the same as Ferris's. In his statement to the nation, he makes it clear that he and the prime movers will not return until the nuclear Orientalization of the nation is complete:

> Act as a rational being and aim at becoming a rallying point for all those who are starved for a voice of integrity—act on your rational values, whether alone in the midst of your enemies, or with a few of your chosen friends, or as the founder of a modest community on the frontier of mankind's rebirth. When the looters' state collapses, deprived of the best of its slaves, when it falls to a level of impotent chaos, like the mystic-ridden nations of the Orient, and dissolves into starving robber gangs fighting to rob one another— when the advocates of the morality of sacrifice perish with their final ideal—then and on that day we will return. (982)

Throughout the novel, the Orientalized masses are opposed to prime movers who embody as well as re-create the frontier; Galt's house in Atlantis "had the primitive simplicity of a frontiersman's cabin" (708), while Francisco's "looked like a frontiersman's shanty thrown together to serve as a mere springboard for a long flight into the future" (710). By rewriting all except the East Coast of America as Oriental, Rand can roll back the frontier in both time and space, creating an eastern territory to which her prime movers can return at the end of the novel and perceive the country as "empty." As the prime movers watch, from their planes, the lights of New York going out, the image seems to render the city devoid of the residents it had only a second before: Dagny "knew that now, at this hour, their plane was carrying all that was left of New York City" (1065). Spreading across the country, this absence re-creates the nation as *terra nullius* in the same way that it was for Dagny's grandfather Nat Taggart, the railroad man (the man who masters infrastructure rather than being mastered by it) who sutured the nation together by train in the nineteenth century: "She looked ahead. The earth would be as empty as the space where their propeller was cutting an unobstructed path—as empty and as free. She knew what Nat Taggart had felt at his start and why now, for the first time, she was following him in full loyalty: the confident sense of facing a void and of knowing that one has a continent to build" (1065). Through this racial-psycho-geographic sleight of hand, the Orientalization of the American population that expands outward from California simultaneously vanishes them, following the settler-colonial practice of Asian racialization that, as Iyko Day argues, has always believed that "Asian bodies could be entirely excluded from the nation-state."[69] Whiteness, cocooned safely in its accouterments of money, technology, and rational thought, now has the security of an entire nation lying between itself and its nightmare opposite, the "savage," "subhuman," "contagious" Asia. Far from the "pestholes," the white subject can finally come into his own. "Do you see how much is open to us here, on an unobstructed earth? Do you see how much I am free to do, to experience, to achieve?" (708).

How Does It Feel to Be White?
Affective Isolationism

The American turn toward integration after World War II required a specific affective shift: a feeling of interdependence, of relationality, of sympathy. As Klein writes, "Eisenhower made sympathy—the ability to feel what another person feels, to share in his or her conditions and experiences—the defining feature of American globalism."[70] It is for this reason that the aesthetic genre of the sentimental narrative, in Klein's account, was central to renegotiating America's relationship with the East. Sentimental narratives, defined by the urge to forge empathic connections across worldly divides, were ideal arenas for the development of sympathetic bonds with an East that had more traditionally been rendered as inscrutable and unfeeling; a text like *The King and I,* for example, draws explicitly on the sentimental tradition as it translates *Uncle Tom's Cabin,* the text by which white Americans were trained to feel with enslaved people, into the world of the Siamese court.[71]

When Rand rejects integration, then, she does so not only at the level of content and symbol but also through the repudiation of specific affective structures and literary forms. If affective bonds and sentimental relations are what tie us, dangerously, to an East that might all too easily infect us with itself, then to be affectless and antirelational becomes a way of defending whiteness against the depredations of the Orient and the Orientalizing impact of nuclear infrastructures. In *Atlas Shrugged,* the "moral pedagogy" that Kathleen Woodward describes as central to the sentimental novel is turned on its head: rather than learning how to sympathize with the suffering other, Dagny's journey—with the reader traveling alongside her—is based on learning how *not* to care about the pain of the dying world.[72]

At the beginning of the novel, Dagny considers her duty to be the reduction of the suffering of the masses; she accepts her burden of responsibility "because they're a bunch of miserable children who struggle to remain alive, desperately and very badly, while I—I don't even notice the burden" (141). Even after the mid-novel interlude that she spends in Atlantis experiencing the heavenly reality of a life without affective ties to the world, Dagny cannot let the railroad (and consequently America) die. Only after realizing that the world in fact *wants* to die can she walk away with the "indifference" that Melissa Joan Hardie describes as the "ethical foundation of a laissez-faire narrative economy."[73] Her flash of insight simultaneously Orientalizes and dehumanizes the world: "This was the nature and the method of the rebellion against existence and of the undefined quest for an unnamed Nirvana. They did not want to live; they wanted [Galt] to die. The horror she felt was only a brief stab, like the wrench of a switching perspective: she grasped that the objects she had thought to be human were not. . . . He was in danger; there was no time and no room in her consciousness to waste emotion on the actions of the subhuman" (1044). That such an indifference is inherently violent is clear from the action that it enables in Dagny—her shooting, during the rescue of Galt from a government torture chamber, of a guard as he begs for his life: "'Wait! Wait! I haven't said yes or no!' he cried, cringing tighter against the door, as if immobility of mind and body were his best protection. . . . Calmly and impersonally, she, who would have hesitated to fire at an animal, pulled the trigger and fired straight at the heart of a man who had wanted to exist without the responsibility of consciousness" (1055). Constructing a system in which accepting a philosophy of indifference is the only evidence of a desire to live, Rand's moral pedagogy equates sympathy with an apocalyptic death drive and indifference with a passionate desire for survival.

This indifference—Atlas's shrug, as Hardie notes—is coded as white. There are two competing affect theories at work in *Atlas Shrugged*. The prime movers consider emotions to be rational "judgments of value," as Rand theorizes in her 1950 "Notes on Emotions."[74] The racialized masses, conversely, oppose "feeling" to rational judgment. "Whenever anyone accuses some person of being 'unfeeling,'" Dagny tells Cheryl, "he means that that person is just. He means that that person has no causeless emotions and will not grant him a feeling which he does not deserve. He means that 'to feel' is to go against reason, against moral values, against reality" (818). Denying reality, the mark of the "savage," is here tied to the concept of sympathy. Only the "rotter," Dagny argues, calls upon sympathy rather than justice, and "those who grant sympathy to guilt, grant none to innocence" (818). The access to a brutally Manichean objective reality that defines whiteness for Rand is denied by any call to sympathy or compassion; those who function through empathy are those "who leap like a savage out of the jungle of your feelings into the Fifth Avenue of our New York" (955). Sympathy, in Rand's account, calls for acceptance of the other *despite* the truth, while "proper" feeling only emerges from the truth itself.

The white superman thus becomes the figure without sympathetic ties, oriented only toward himself. Just as America, to survive, must cut its bonds with the globe, so Rand's Objectivist must disentangle himself from the networks of feeling that would lay unsustainable claims upon him. As in Palumbo-Liu's reading of Lonnie Kaneko's classic tale of life in an internment camp, "The Shoyu Kid" (1976), whiteness is the power "to affect without being affected": Kaneko's kids playing at becoming-American "are voyeurs who witness and define other bodies while thinking themselves dis-embodied, deracialized, and powerful, and this empowerment is not coincidentally linked to their 'de-orientalization.'"[75] John Galt, Rand's perfect man, typifies the myth of the nonrelational or self-made man; describing the three leaders of the strike, their teacher Hugh Akston names them as "Francisco, the richest heir in the world—Ragnar, the European aristocrat—and John, the self-made man, self-made in every sense, out of nowhere, penniless, parentless, tie-less" (725). The myth outweighs, of course, the reality: "Actually, he was the son of a gas-station mechanic at some forsaken crossroads in Ohio, and he had left home at the age of twelve to make his own way—but I've always thought of him as if he had come into the world like Minerva, the goddess of wisdom, who sprang forth from Jupiter's head, fully grown and fully armed" (725). Galt is the only American of the three, and the only one to be fully autopoietic; while Francisco is tied to the family company and Ragnar carries his aristocratic history, Galt springs Horatio Alger–like from nothing, from the void that Rand sees when she thinks of working-class America.

Impeccably rational, Galt is the one character in *Atlas Shrugged* who never loses control of his emotions. He has attained the goal that he describes as the most difficult one of the strike: "what we now feel for their world is that emotion which they preach as an ideal: indifference—the blank—the zero—the mark of death" (684). Other prime mover disciples, still students following Galt's path, are shown learning to repress the feelings that they can't help having: when Francisco expresses anger, "the sentence sounded involuntary, as if, trying to suppress the sound of emotion, he had uttered suppressed words" (388), and when Dagny loses her temper and shouts "I'm so sick of them," "her voice startled her: it was an involuntary cry" (307). The ideal emotions, represented by moments of feeling with Galt at the center, are those that are experienced somehow nonrelationally; they are shared without language, making them self-identical and whole. Feeling is acceptable here only if it can be experienced without putting people into relation with each other. Galt's nonrelational being exemplifies the dynamic that Melley describes emerging in opposition to state and corporate consensus culture in the 1940s and 1950s, in which the "antidote" to consensus-based anti-individualism is "a 'paranoid' suspicion of social connections—and a commitment to the idea that persons are atomistic units threatened by various forms of social communication and collective identity."[76] Faced with the encroachments upon selfhood by others, in this case the nuclear state, the white sovereign self must be purely nonrelational.

At the same time that Rand establishes whiteness as the opposite of the sentimental, however, the pedagogical power of the novel is drawn from the affective ties that it inculcates in its readers. The central relationship that emerges between text and reader is paradoxical: if the reader were, in fact, as advanced as John Galt, the reader would not need *Atlas Shrugged*. Brian Jackson describes the interminable sermonizing of the novel as a kind of *mise-en-abîme* in which "*Atlas Shrugged* is riddled with long-winded speeches by characters who seem to have read *Atlas Shrugged*" (4–5); in fact, the only character who is excluded from this narrative economy, who needs no education, is Galt himself. Because the narrative is focalized through Dagny, the reader is established alongside her as a learner, and Rand's correspondence demonstrates the power of the novel to give the experience of having learned something new: fans describe the educational power of the book to combine "all my stray thoughts into an orderly, workable pattern" and transition them from "a very confused person" to someone with "the answers."[77] In keeping with Rand's self-described genre of "romantic realism," which she defines in *The Romantic Manifesto* as a portrayal of life "as it could be and should be," in contrast to life as it is, Rand's hero is not like us.[78] This creates an alarming structural gap for the reader: a character such as John Galt is held up as an ideal to emulate, but perfect emulation is rendered impossible by his very ideality. However hard a reader might try to follow Galt in being fully autopoietic, she will never be free of that last, failing but indispensable relation to John Galt himself.

A narrative strategy that calls upon affective ties to break the ties of affect may seem paradoxical. But this strategy is exceptionally powerful both pedagogically and in terms of the racial dynamics that Rand is negotiating. If the sentimental text of the 1940s and 1950s is invested in sympathizing with the figure of the inscrutable Oriental, then Rand simultaneously draws upon and alters its techniques to redirect the relational urges of her readers toward identification with an inscrutable whiteness.[79] The middlebrow text, in Klein's account, assumes a reader secure in her own whiteness and able to risk the danger of imaginative integration with the East. Rand's implied reader, by contrast, is already at risk of losing the privileges of whiteness through her vulnerable position within the infrastructures of the nuclear state. The effort that is required of this reader is not to integrate with raced others but to double down on her investment in her own whiteness by identifying ever more strongly with Galt. That this identification is doomed to fail makes it only more pedagogically powerful; as Philip Fisher writes, in the face of unexpressed emotion, "the reader or spectator *volunteers* passion, stepping in to supply the missing fear, grief, shame, or anger. Volunteered passion is a stronger demand on the spectator and a more perfect aesthetic strategy for the eliciting of passion than sympathy, understood in the narrow sense of feeling alongside another's explicit emotional state, can ever be."[80] The ultimate bad boyfriend, Galt's emotional unavailability only stokes the flames of the reader's desire for identification; the whiteness that he represents is more treasured as a goal desperately to be striven toward than it would be as a quality securely possessed.

Whiteness thus becomes in *Atlas Shrugged* simultaneously an ideal (an autopoietic subjectivity immune to nuclear infrastructures) and the practice by which that goal might be attained (a perfect rationality). Never quite attainable, whiteness is transformed from a secure position to a threatened one even as its superiority—indeed, its unchallenged position as the only "human" race—is supported. In this, Rand's novel could be read as part of a longer cultural tradition that redefined whiteness as an ethnicity, no longer the master race but one competing set of cultural traditions among many.[81] *Atlas Shrugged*'s aggressive racism and overt degeneration anxiety might seem a holdover from earlier times, the time when Jack London could celebrate genocide with utopian aplomb in the pages of popular fiction. The massive and continued success of *Atlas Shrugged* demonstrates, however, the extent to which the apocalyptic imagination, turned toward racialized others, is still the best and last hope of a whiteness threatened by nuclear Orientalization: better dead than yellow, or more accurately, better that everyone on earth should die so that sovereign whiteness might be maintained.

One Nation under Capitalism; or, The Octopus

The yellow peril genre emerged into American literature, culture, and law when the greatest threat facing white sovereignty came from monopoly capitalism. Accounts of late nineteenth- and early twentieth-century yellow peril writings by Lye, Tchen and Yeats, and Edlie Wong all depict the ways in which images of the Asian laborer, working at lower wages and living in worse conditions than white workers, became imbricated with monopoly capital as both perceived cause and effect of the decline of working conditions for the white man; industrialism in its Gilded Age form threatened to Orientalize the United States with "forecasts of declining wages, mass unemployment, and political authoritarianism."[82] In reinscribing the yellow peril into the nuclear age, Rand's most lasting achievement, in the end, was to reroute the source of the Orientalizing threat from capitalism to the nuclear state. While in the early part of the twentieth century, yellow peril rhetoric was used to seek protection for white workers through state legislation, Rand redefined the government as the enemy of the white self. Threatening whiteness through the development of nuclear weapons and the rise of a secretive, bureaucratic technocracy, it was the state, in Rand's view, that most endangered the survival of white American subjectivity after 1945.

In turn-of-the-century America, the image of the octopus did double duty as a symbol for the grasping East and for the predations of monopoly capitalism. Frank Norris's 1901 novel *The Octopus: A Story of California* shows white farmers caught between the tentacles of the railroad monopoly and the Pacific Rim, while popular cartoons from 1873 to 1936 depict an octopus representing the railroad trust eating "congressional honor" and the yellow octopus of Asia encircling the globe.[83] In *Atlas Shrugged*, however, the railroad has been resurrected as a symbol of hope while "the octopus" is transformed into the torture device by which John Galt is tormented, fruitlessly, by the government. In her description of the machine, Rand contrasts the history of (white) civilization with the "savage" prehistoricity of the Orientalizing state:

[Galt's] naked body looked strangely out of place in this cellar. . . . The long lines of his body . . . looked like a statue of ancient Greece. . . . And as the meaning of a statue of ancient Greece— the statue of man as a god—clashed with the spirit of this century's halls, so his body clashed with a cellar devoted to prehistorical activities. The clash was the greater, because he seemed to belong with electric wires, with stainless steel, with precision instruments, with the levers of a control board. Perhaps—this was the thought most fiercely resisted and most deeply buried at the bottom of his watchers' sensations, the thought they knew only as a diffused hatred and an unfocused terror—perhaps it was the absence of such statues from the modern world that had transformed a generator into an octopus and brought a body such as his into its tentacles. (1049)

God versus octopus; rationality versus diffuse and unfocused affect; individual versus state—in this scenario, it is not the state that must protect white workers from an Orientalized/Orientalizing industrial capitalism but capitalism that must save sovereign whiteness from the Oriental octopus of the state. And this state is defined for Rand by its nuclear nature; the state functionaries torturing Galt do so in a scene lifted directly from the *Top Secret* script treatment, with the American state officials screaming "we order you to think!" (1050) stepping into the role of the totalitarian Nazis who try to force "Bohr" to develop the atom bomb on their behalf and Galt embodying "Bohr's" dismissal of their paradox: "How are you going to force a mind?"[84]

Turning back to the beginning of the Cold War, we find in *Atlas Shrugged* a potent connection between the birth of the nuclear state and a form of antistatist white identity politics that reinflected the relationship between whiteness and apocalypse for the nuclear age. While Rand's prenuclear novel *The Fountainhead* (1943) depicts the bureaucratic state as little more than an oppressive irritation for the heroic individual, nuclearization transforms the state into an apocalyptically racializing threat that must be resisted at any cost. As the nuclear state became the enemy of whiteness, whiteness once again became the sole currency with which to purchase access to futurity. And as *Atlas Shrugged,* with its genocidal imaginary, demonstrates, the futurity of whiteness in the nuclear age would be purchased at the

cost of the futurelessness of others; the white, straight, wealthy settlers that are produced as sole survivors at the end of the novel can
only fully experience their survival by watching the lights of the city
blink out beneath them. What goes on in those futureless spaces of
alterity, however, is nothing as simple as disappearance. It is to these
hot spots—cities, ghettoes, bodies, reservations—and the lives that are
lived within them, impossibly, beneath the apocalyptic shadow of nuclear whiteness that the rest of this book will now turn.

2

Civil Defense and
Black Apocalypse

What would John Winthrop have thought if the hill upon
which he was to build his city was honeycombed with
cells for omnipresent defeat? Why should he have left
Europe at all? It is difficult to construct a Heavenly City,
when the contractor's plans, of necessity,
allot a space for Hell.

—Charles Newman, "Reflections on Protection
[Fallout Shelters]"

STANDING "LIKE A GIANT," like a "long-awaited conqueror at whose feet
flowers would be strewn," the young John Grimes stares at the city of
New York.[1] Decades later, Leo Proudhammer, not an old man but a
man older than his years, with his heart dying in his body and Hiroshima fresh in his memory, looks out across San Francisco: "San Francisco unfurled beneath us, at our feet, like a many-colored scroll. . . .
I had conquered the city: but the city was stricken with the plague."[2]
How are we to read this scroll, this futureless city? Meanwhile, somewhere out of time, in a city called Bellona, a protagonist with no name
stands in the street and wonders if the scroll is a script for infrastructural violence, for the city itself to produce futurelessness. A Black man
rapes (maybe) a white girl; the white girl, curdled with lust and shame,
pushes (maybe) her brother down an elevator shaft: "it would be just
like the myth: her lust for George, death and destruction! Only—only

suppose it *was* an accident? . . . That's the thing I'm scared of most. . . . Because that means it's the city. That means it's the landscape: the bricks, and the girders, and the faulty wiring and the shot elevator machinery, all conspiring together to *make* these myths true."[3] Sharing a peculiarly dislocated relationship to space and time, the protagonists of James Baldwin's *Tell Me How Long the Train's Been Gone* (1968) and Samuel R. Delany's *Dhalgren* (1975) find themselves lost, wandering in memory and in cities that cannot be read, scrolled environments that operate under lawless grammars.

When Ralph Ellison wrote in "Going to the Territory" (1979) that for the enslaved in America, "geography was fate," he was referring to the relationship between location in the United States and modalities of freedom and enslavement: "[enslaved people] knew that to be sold down the Mississippi River meant that they would suffer a harsher form of slavery, and they knew that to escape across the Mason–Dixon line northward was to move in the direction of a greater freedom."[4] In his analysis of the relationship between geography and fate, however, Ellison, like Baldwin and Delany, was participating in a much older hermeneutic practice of reading the environment as emplotted in what is now, and for now, the United States.

Combining colonization with a typological hermeneutics, the 1492 encounter between Christopher Columbus and Hispaniola marked an epochal shift in how the environment would be conceptualized as a temporal object. Typological interpretation of the Bible is based on the premise that "the persons and events of the Old Testament [types] were prefigurations of the New Testament and its history of salvation [antitypes]"; it is a prophetic form of history that makes present or future events the inevitable correlative of prior events and that sees the fulfillment of biblical prophecy in the present as an eschatological sign.[5] While in the medieval tradition, undiscovered paradises were thought to be an encounter with the lost Eden of humanity's past, Columbus interpreted his experience in the New World typologically as the first contact with an eschatological future: "of the New Heaven and Earth which our Lord made, as St. John writes in the Apocalypse," Columbus wrote in 1500, "He made me the messenger thereof and showed me where to go."[6] Casting himself as the apocalyptic prophet of empire, Columbus bends time around into space: the end of the world will no longer be found in the future, *then,* but in the West, *there.* By the time the Puritan settlers landed in North America, the belief that the New World was an inherently millennial landscape where Christians must work to bring about the Second Coming was widely shared. Echoing Columbus, Cotton Mather declared in 1702 that the Pilgrims had been carried to America to "create a New Heaven, and a New Earth in, new Churches, and a new Common-wealth together."[7] The New World was an emplotted environment whose physical elements were also narrative elements, fulfillments of biblical prophecy that wrote the story of settler colonialism into the Christian apocalypse narrative.

Settler colonialism's emplotment of the New World environment produced an American apocalypticism divided on racial lines, whereby the millennial redemption of white European settlers would be achieved at the cost of the apocalyptic destruction of racialized others. North America would be stripped down and remade according to the eschatological logics of its colonizers, logics that assured settlers of their divine election within providential history and produced African slavery and Indigenous genocide as scripted acts in the end-times drama. If the Indians were, as they were for Mather, the antitypes of the "Seed of the Serpent," then it is prophetically ordained that the "Souldiers of Christ" annihilate them to bring about the millennium,[8] while African slavery brought more and more souls into the realm of Christian salvation, hastening the arrival of the millennium through universal salvation while also providing free labor to build the New Jerusalem.[9] Under the regime of colonial typology, time itself is racialized: for the Puritans and their heirs, white supremacy and its actions are mandated by divine providence or historical necessity, while racialized life functions as its other, never the subject of historical narrative but only ever fate's object en masse.

Cold War America was no less structured by the apocalyptic emplotment of space than the Puritan settlements had been centuries before. But while Columbus and the Puritans had seen the millennium as inherent in the New World's "wildernesses," in the nuclear age, it was the built environment that would signify providential redemption and annihilation distributed along the lines of race. This chapter traces the resurgence of a secular form of typology after World War II in which the history of America itself became the type for which Cold War America was required to become the antitype. On the home front of the Cold War, the extent to which America could remake itself as the fulfillment of its own prophetic history would determine its ability to defend itself against nuclear attack. Following the established pattern of New World typology, however, discourses of civil defense in both official and fictional texts cast Black annihilation as the price of white redemption. America's predominantly Black cities were consistently imagined as the inevitable targets of a future nuclear war, an imaginary that was supported by the West's long history of conceptualizing Blackness as backward, futureless, or unshielded by destiny.[10] This imaginary, in turn, produced enormous infrastructural changes in the built environment, as under the racialized aegis of dispersal the American landscape was restructured by suburbs, highways, and massive redistributions of resources that allowed white citizens to fulfill their millennial destinies as nuclear-age pioneers in the suburbs while African Americans remained in the apocalyptic cities as useful atomic targets.

At the same time that typology was reemerging as a powerful infrastructural force for white America, however, it had reached a different kind of crisis point in African American life. Perhaps ironically, given the long history of white eschatology being used to justify the extermination of people of color, the most consistent strategy used by Africans in America and then African Americans to counteract this historiographical disempowerment has been to reimagine the story of African slavery and its afterlives in apocalyptic terms. Apocalyptic typology has functioned in African American thought not only as a way of imagining deliverance in the future but also as a way of refashioning historical time into a narrative that includes a future for Blackness. After the Puritans read themselves typologically as the "New English Israel" to justify their colonial mission, the Exodus and Revelation stories became central to a new Black philosophy of history in which slavery and suffering in the present guaranteed a future redemption not after death, as white ministers insisted, but as a collective liberation from slavery: because God had freed the Israelites (the original prophetic types), it was only a matter of time until he freed the Israelites' contemporary antitypes, the Black slaves in America.[11] From slavery-era spirituals such as "Go Down, Moses" to Martin Luther King's visionary 1968 speech "I've Been to the Mountaintop," African Americans have interpreted their history of slavery and oppression as the typological fulfillment of the Exodus narrative, a reemplotment of history with the crucial political and narrative functions of making freedom imaginable and "viewing the folk as subjects on a historical stage rather than as objects in the white historian's perspective on Africa and America, where blacks often find themselves portrayed as bestial, passive, and unheroic."[12] In the face of an oppression that relies on the logic of Black ahistoricity, typology provides a potentially liberatory historiography.[13]

The liberatory nature of this alternative historiography relies on a prophetic emplotment: promise and its fulfillment. By the 1960s, however, the typological infrastructure of time that had sustained liberatory endeavors from the struggle for abolition to the civil rights movement seemed finally to have exhausted itself. Dr. King's vision from the mountaintop had failed to bring redemption, and it seemed more and more likely that the journey of the United States was not toward a future of racial integration and harmony but of ever-increasing segregation, the "sacking" of cities for the benefit of the suburbs, and a nuclear conflict that would, by the end of the Cold War, have killed at least 80 percent of African Americans in its first minutes.[14] As Katherine Bond Stockton observes, in the post–civil rights era, the pattern of Black history was no longer imagined as prophecy and fulfillment but rather as "promise and letdown."[15] The emplotment of typology, which guaranteed progress toward justice as the basic structure of historical time, had turned out to be "a sad tale that, if it were a novel, would be noted for its repetitive events and remarkably nonrising plot structure."[16] At the same time, African American life within the Cold War city, a newly racialized chronotope of Black futurelessness, gave a renewed urgency to the question of emplotment as the forms of redemptive historiography that had previously countered the white emplotment of Black annihilation failed. This chapter thus takes up a key question posed by David Scott in *The Conscripts of Modernity*: what do we do when the emplotment that we have been working toward freedom within fails? When deliverance fails to arrive again and again, when "the conditions that created these explosions in 1963 are still here; the conditions that created explosions in 1964 are still here?"[17] "What if the imagined futures that had given point and direction to the intervention in the present and the rehistoricization of the past suddenly evaporated as a possible horizon of hope and longing?"[18] When both Blackness and the urban environment are being constructed as futureless in the nuclear age, how might Black urban fiction imagine ways of living without a future, of hoping without redemption?

This chapter juxtaposes the white supremacy of Cold War liberalism and civil defense with two works of urban fiction by queer African American writers that interrogate the typological relationship between the environment, race, and emplotment as it is manifested in the infrastructures of the nuclear city. Both James Baldwin's *Tell Me How Long the Train's Been Gone* (1968) and Samuel R. Delany's *Dhalgren* (1975) take as a structural stipulation the premise of Black futurelessness that both subtends and is reproduced by the infrastructures of civil defense. Rather than reiterating stories of futurelessness as despair, however, they use the lack of a future as a way of transfiguring the present to invoke forms of liberation that are not dependent on typological emplotments of redemption. Inhabiting the everyday apocalypticism of the nuclear city, Baldwin and Delany follow its logics to their conclusion: not to destroy the world or to express despair but to imagine new ways of living in time. In their works, we find a transfigurative temporality where the present need not be determined by the past, where the stifling, stunted forms of race that have structured and continue to structure time and space in the New World might yet become a casualty of the nuclear complex.

Ground Zero at the City on a Hill: The Cold War Typology of Civil Defense

For the nuclear commentators and legislators in chapter 1, the arrival of nuclear weapons marked an absolute rupture between the preatomic past and the nuclear present. In a 1951 training film for the Federal Civil Defense Administration (FCDA), however, President Truman frames the nuclear threat not as a break with traditional warfare but rather as a revival of the familiar past of American settler colonialism: "if there should be a war today," Truman tells civil defense trainees, "our cities would be like the frontier settlements in the days of Indian warfare." Within this framework, "our civil defense program is a revival of the old American tradition of community defense," established "in the early days of our history" when "the pioneer settlements along our frontier were exposed to attack by Indian tribes." Just as "every member of those pioneer communities joined together to meet the common danger," so can present-day civil defense "meet this danger, just as our forefathers did." If the old stockades were secured against the Cherokee, Seminole, and Apache nations, then during the Cold War, the new Fortress America would need to be proofed against the weapons detonated at the Cherokee, Seminole, and Apache test shots. For Truman and the FCDA, the nuclear age was to be imagined as the fulfillment of an earlier America: a land of Pilgrims and pioneers tasked with a redemptive errand into the wilderness, a land embattled from without yet needing only to hold fast to its mission to secure its providentially guaranteed victory.[19]

President Truman's invocation of the Indian Wars as the original type of the Cold War translates earlier typological traditions into a fully secular realm; the type is no longer a consecrated biblical figure but rather a historical event from the mundane history of the nation. In so doing, Truman indexes a larger turn in American self-fashioning during the Cold War. After 1945, the new superpower entered a time of frenzied national autopoiesis in which secular typology took a leading role: the burgeoning field of American studies created America as the object of its own study and produced influential accounts of the nation's founding ideologies; sociologists drew on history to describe and prescribe the particularities of American national character; and in its most popular genre, Hollywood told and retold its fables of western expansion. Looking to its past to justify its present, the United States began to understand its relation to its own history in typological terms, interpreting its present actions as the inevitable consequences and fulfillments of previous events in the nation's history.

Classics of post-1945 American studies, such as Perry Miller's *Errand into the Wilderness* (1954) and Ernest Lee Tuveson's *Redeemer Nation* (1968), participated in this broader turn to the past as a way of justifying and naturalizing the Cold War present. They function as something like historiographic Magic Eye pictures, with their accounts of early America requiring only a slight perspective shift to come back into focus as arguments about the role of the United States as a Cold War global superpower. Tuveson's historical study of American millennialism, for example, while often highly critical of the violence brought about by a millennial-exceptionalist interpretation of America's place in the world, closes with an unexpected endorsement of the Marshall Plan as the fulfillment of America's millennial destiny. In a pattern that Truman would surely find intuitive, a national narrative of apocalypse produces a matching infrastructure, since "[American millennialism] certainly must have done much to make the Marshall Plan accepted with so little difficulty; in what other country would such a scheme, apparently so contrary to traditional ideas of national self-interest—and so expensive—have been undertaken?" This infrastructure will, then, according to Tuveson, perpetuate that narrative to its apocalyptic/redemptive conclusion: "the practical success of the Plan indicates, too, that millennialism was by no means wholly an idealistic dream: Christian principles, if really triumphant, would redeem the world."[20] As William V. Spanos writes, "like so many Americanists of his (Cold War) occasion, Tuveson in the end appropriates the millenarian narrative on behalf of exceptionalist America's 'epochal struggle' against Communist totalitarianism."[21] Cold War interventionism becomes, even in works critical of early America, the inevitable redemptive outcome of the nation's history.

Perhaps the best example of America's newly framed relationship to its own past is to be found in the resurrection and strategic repurposing in the early Cold War of an image that has operated as shorthand for America's role in the world ever since: that of the city on a hill. First used to describe the Puritan settlement in the New World by John Winthrop in 1630, the phrase "city on a hill" positioned the future colony in a position of global significance:

> Wee shall finde that the God of Israell is among us, when ten of us shall be able to resist a thousand of our enemies; when hee shall make us a prayse and glory that men shall say of succeeding plantations, "the Lord make it likely that of *New England*." For wee must consider that wee shall be as a citty upon a hill. The eies of all people are uppon us. Soe that if wee shall deale falsely with our God in this worke wee haue undertaken, and soe cause him to withdrawe his present help from us, wee shall be made a story and a by-word through the world.[22]

For Winthrop and the original settlers, city on a hill status meant influencing world affairs only inasmuch as the example of such moral superiority and its correlated material flourishing would inspire the rest of the world to remake itself in its image. Yet the idea that America was providentially fated to a more proactive role in remaking the world emerged relatively quickly, as "by the nineteenth century, this 'errand into the wilderness' had transformed into the teleology of 'Manifest

Destiny,' with the persistence of the underlying assumption that the work of building a Christian democracy gave white Americans a divine entitlement to their land."[23] The phrase "city on a hill," however, did not function as shorthand for this form of aggressive exceptionalism until the start of the Cold War.[24] It was not until 1949 that Perry Miller, a historian and public intellectual, used the phrase as the one quotation necessary to summon the nexus of ideas that Miller himself had been promoting for the previous decade: that Winthrop's sermon connected civic government to a messianic, interventionist national mission. After World War II, the phrase "city on a hill" itself came to stand not for an America held to a higher moral standard but for an America understood as what Tuveson had called a "redeemer nation," destined to intervene in—and guaranteed to be on the side of right in—international affairs.

That this transition was connected to the geopolitical situation of the Cold War can be seen in the language that Miller uses to describe the Puritans' mission in a speech given at Brown in 1952, later published in *Errand into the Wilderness*. Miller writes that

> Winthrop and his colleagues believed fully in the covenant. . . .
> They could see in the pattern of history that their errand was not
> a mere scouting expedition: it was an essential maneuver in the
> drama of Christendom. The Bay Company was not a battered
> remnant of suffering Separatists thrown up on a rocky shore; it
> was an organized task force of Christians, executing a flank attack
> on the corruptions of Christendom.[25]

The preface to *Errand in the Wilderness* contains an account of a young Miller sitting on the banks of the Congo River, thinking about Gibbon's *Decline and Fall of the Roman Empire*, watching American oil being unloaded in Africa, and being struck by the necessity of writing an intellectual history of the Puritans to account for America's current expansionist position in the world. This quite bizarre passage has been central to the transnational turn in American studies, as Amy Kaplan and others have analyzed Miller's autobiographical vignette as illustrative of the ways in which empire has been the invisible center of American representations of itself.[26] Perhaps because the passage describing the Bay Company is (marginally) less odd, it has not been accorded the same kind of importance. Yet Miller was in his own way a Cold Warrior, and his interpretation of Winthrop's situation collapses the roles of exemplar and redeemer nation to produce a new understanding of the national mission that would be central to America's understanding of itself throughout the Cold War and into the War on Terror.[27] When Miller describes the exemplary role of America here, it is in the language of World War II military maneuvers, with "task forces" and "flank attacks" replacing Winthrop's "prayse and glory." If Winthrop's city on a hill is to be an exemplar, then its exemplarity is to be understood in the active terms of military actions abroad supported by a militarized sensibility at home.

The phrase "city on a hill" thus comes to represent in Miller's work an elision between exemplar and redeemer nation that legitimates the ever-expanding military activity of the nuclear complex in the mid-century.[28] And far from being limited to the world of academia, this new ideological formation found a welcoming home in Cold War politics. When John F. Kennedy uses the phrase in a speech to the Big Brothers of America in 1961, the whole of American Cold War policy is held in the tension between his sentence and its dependent clause: "I feel we are a city on a hill and that one of our great responsibilities during these days is to make sure that we in this country set an example to the world not only of helping and assisting them to fulfill their own destiny, but also demonstrating what a free people can do."[29] The process by which exemplarity and interventionism become one and the same, previously embodied in the ideology of Manifest Destiny, is now crystallized in the Cold War formation of the city on a hill. Typologically connecting Cold War America to Winthrop's America through this formation, Kennedy both legitimates and requires a set of actions and attitudes in the present; acting within a narrowly construed patriotism on the home front and "assisting" foreign nations are not only morally correct but also prophetically foretold, such that decisions that might otherwise be seen as political and contentious are presented instead as the inevitable outcome of America's providential history.[30]

As Truman's speech to the FCDA suggests, the home front of the Cold War was very much a part of the mid-century reformation of the relationship between the United States and its own past, as the success of civil defense came to be seen as the extent to which America could become the antitype of its earlier pilgrim/pioneer type.[31] For mid-century politicians and military strategists, the ideal citizen/community that would be produced by civil defense was not a new phenomenon but rather the typological fulfillment of American history: the pilgrim, founding father, or pioneer was the type and the civil defense citizen was to be the antitype. For Leo Heogh, federal administrator of civil defense in 1958, a commitment to suburban home fallout shelters would be the path to fulfilling the prophecy of early America: "every home a fortress! That can well be our watchword as we strive to attain the freedom won so dearly by our pioneer forefathers."[32] A 1956 civil defense pamphlet illustrated by Li'l Abner creator Al Capp illustrates the temporal palimpsest conjured by Truman and Heogh, depicting the present-day character Mr. Civil Defense superimposed onto a scene of settlers in covered wagons defending themselves against Indian attack. Katherine Howard, deputy administrator of the FCDA during the 1950s, sidesteps the politically contentious issue of civil defense funding through a similar removal of historical agency from the present

Mr. Civil Defense narrates the Indian Wars. Panel in *Mr. Civil Defense Tells about Natural Disasters* (New York: Graphic Information Service, 1956).

into the past: for Howard, the decision of whether to protect homes from nuclear attack "was made for us generations ago by the Pilgrims, and the Minute Men, and the Western pioneers."[33] Heogh's and Howard's statements seem grammatically peculiar: how can Americans still be striving to attain freedoms that have already been won? As typological claims, however, they make perfect sense: the first victory (type) has already been secured, while its fulfillment in the present (antitype) must yet be striven for. Within this framework, the task of Americans and America is not to debate policy in the present but to fulfill the prophetic figure laid down by the original types by embodying them sufficiently, whether at the individual scale of the stockade-protecting pioneer or at the national scale of the exemplar-redeemer city on a hill.

The Cold War fulfillment of antebellum national prophecy was therefore simultaneously inevitable and vulnerable. Within the typological model, victory is inevitable if Americans and America can successfully resemble their types. Two obstacles, however, stood between the United States and its self-fulfillment. The first was the country's cities. By the time of Truman, Heogh, Capp, and Howard, the frontier where the pioneer/pilgrim subjectivities that would guarantee victory were formed had been closed for more than half a century. Until its closing in 1890, the frontier had been the space where the American spirit could go to challenge itself, to recover the qualities of manliness and self-sufficiency that it lost by being softened and modernized by city life in Europe or back East. In Frederick Turner's famous 1893 thesis, "the frontier is the line of most rapid and effective Americanization. The wilderness masters the colonist. . . . It strips off the garments of civilization and arrays him in the hunting shirt and the moccasin."[34] Influential strategists, including George Kennan, updated the frontier thesis for the nuclear age, worrying both privately and publicly that urban life had led to a decline in the American national character that might not be reversible despite the dire importance for civil defense of fulfilling a frontier subjectivity. If the United States' inevitable victory will be won through the superiority of its national character, then the moral failure of urban America, where the traditional values are "now generally [held] in contemptuous disregard," writes the city into its own irredeemable declension narrative: in the light of dawn, Kennan writes in 1950, the city's "dreams are disturbed, its pretense, its ugliness, its impermanence exposed, its failure documented, its verdict written."[35] In Kennan's view, judgment has already been passed on urban America, and while Cold War victory depends on America redeeming itself, its cities are irredeemably doomed. The inexorable nature of this characterological failure is matched only by the new reality of total war in the atomic age: that cities would be the first targets of a nuclear strike and that there would be no way to defend them.[36] Both the typological and the material aspects of civil defense are therefore foreclosed in the city: it can be redeemed neither as a stockade manned by pioneers nor with fallout shelters and evacuation plans.

The second obstacle to America's typological fulfillment appeared at both the national and international levels, as the racial crisis in America's cities evacuated the moral superiority upon which the claim of the United States to world leadership relied. Just as the phrase "city on a hill" was being rebooted as a shorthand for American exceptionalism, America's urban blight, segregated space, and highly visible institutional racism were, as historian Mary Dudziak has shown, a major problem for an America whose foreign policy rationale depended entirely on being a democratic exemplar, a land of freedom for all. As early as 1944, the Myrdal report had stated that "America, for its international prestige, power, and future security, needs to demonstrate to the world that American Negroes can be satisfactorily integrated into its democracy."[37] As the Cold War progressed, successive administrations sent amicus curiae briefs to the Supreme Court as it debated cases like *Shelley v. Kraemer, Brown v. Board of Education,* and *Cooper v. Aaron,* informing the court of the impact of their rulings on America's potential dominance in foreign relations: domestic race relations were now a military problem.[38] The "race problem" had become a Cold War concern because the city on a hill was, very visibly, segregated.

As Dudziak and others have argued, this aspect of Cold War politics had a partially progressive impact on domestic civil rights struggles as the Truman, Eisenhower, Kennedy, and Johnson administrations attempted to enact a racial liberalism that would live up to America's strategically necessary ideals. At the same time, however, the spatial redistribution of race known as suburbanization/ghettoization offered a far easier and less equitable infrastructural solution to both the country's race problem and civil defense's urban problem. In the nuclear age, suburbanization became not only a domestic concern but also a military issue, as strategists such as Bernard Brodie argued that the city was "a made-to-order target, and the degree of urbanization of a country furnishes a rough index of its relative vulnerability to the atomic bomb."[39] While initial suggestions that all cities be forcibly decentralized along horizontal lines were considered too expensive and probably unconstitutional, Brodie and others consistently enforced the relationship between suburban infrastructures and national security. Norbert Wiener suggested in 1950 that to "bolster the nation's civilian defenses," it would be necessary to "accelerate the current trend of many city dwellers toward the suburbs," and that this could be achieved through a system of roads that would resemble a wheel, with expressways leading out of the city center and circling the city to make commuting possible from any point in the metropolitan area; in 1956, the National Highways Defense Act fulfilled Wiener's vision with the largest public works project in history.[40] The highway infrastructure that would enable suburbanization was an explicit project of Cold Warfare, funded in part by the Department of Defense and described by its planners as designed "to disperse our factories, our stores, our people; in short, to create a revolution in living habits."[41] With the need for dispersal very much in mind, the federal government committed to encouraging this revolution by offering a variety of subsidies, including tax breaks for subdivision builders and homebuyers and mortgage guarantees for suburban housing—the vast majority of which, owing to racial covenanting and redlining practices, were available only to white Americans.[42]

As an additional benefit, life on what Kenneth T. Jackson has labeled the "crabgrass frontier" also promised to restore to twentieth-century white Americans the bracing contact with the wilderness and separation from the city that had been lost with the closing of the frontier and that was so necessary for the creation of the Cold War–winning citizen of civil defense. While the suburb by itself might offer too comfortable a life to bring out the inner pioneer in its residents, it took only the addition of an imagined nuclear attack to re-create the suburb as exactly the environment where the civil defense pioneer would come into being. In Pat Frank's 1959 best seller *Alas, Babylon,* for example, World War III is all it takes to transform the softened suburbanites into avatars of the Old West, as with the destruction of all cities and governments, they learn to hunt, fish, kill racialized bandits, and inhabit stereotypical gender roles. Suburbanization thus fulfilled the requirements of civil defense in two ways: first, by convincing the crucial voting bloc of white suburbia that they could survive a nuclear war in their bunker-like homes, and second, by creating the typological pilgrim/pioneer subjects that were necessary for civil defense to succeed.

The correlate of suburbanization was, of course, ghettoization, but this too served a counterintuitively positive function for civil defense. The history of ghettoization demonstrates the immense power of race as a virtual infrastructure that determines the disposition of more material infrastructures as well as the power of those infrastructures to privilege some outcomes over others, materially impacting the kinds of emplotments that those spaces can foster.[43] In the twentieth century, racial theories of the "one-drop rule" from the biological realm were translated into legal and bureaucratic real estate practices in ways that would significantly reshape the built environment. The redlining policies of the Federal Housing Administration codified into bureaucratic practice in the 1930s, 1940s, and 1950s an absolutely segregated approach to space: a new kind of one-drop rule, where "the presence of a single, non-white family on any block was sufficient to mark that entire block black."[44] In yet another iteration of the imbrication of race, place, and time, the recoding of a block as Black also rewrote the space into a decline, recalling Paul Gilroy's description of the concept of race as having the power "to both determine history and explain its selective unfolding."[45] Black families moving onto a block, the FHA argued, meant that the value of properties in the neighborhood would decline; this was indeed true, because without the protection and funds of the FHA, it was next to impossible to maintain urban property. As Jane Jacobs wrote in 1966, "credit blacklisting maps, like slum-clearance maps, are accurate prophecies because they are self-fulfilling prophecies."[46] Through the temporal logics of raced space that undergirded white flight, urban space was redefined as both Black and futureless.[47]

After 1945, the disposability of the city became strategically and materially necessary for both civil defense and the arms race. On a strategic level, completely to disperse the nation's cities into a network of decentralized suburbs would actually make white suburbia less safe; as Dean MacCannell has shown in his analysis of the domestic impacts of deterrence, "American cities can be transformed into effective defense weapons to the degree that they are vulnerable to atomic attack. In other words, the defense role of the city is not just to receive the hit, it is to absorb the hit so that damage minimally spills over to surrounding 'survival areas.'"[48] On an infrastructural level, recasting the city as disposable allowed administrations throughout the Cold War to funnel resources that would have gone to urban communities into the nuclear complex. In addition to subsidizing the building of suburbs, cities were impacted by the negative infrastructures of the nuclear age: the massive disinvestments in civilian (and especially urban) life that were the consequence of hyperinvestment in the nuclear complex.[49] In 1976, Southern Christian Leadership Conference member Reverend James Orange protested the causal connection between the arms race and domestic poverty: "we are now turning out one nuclear bomb in the U.S. every eight hours," he said during the Continental Walk for Disarmament, "while every hour eight families die of starvation." Negative infrastructures like high unemployment and poor housing were, according to disarmament organizer Frank Brown, "bombs that are dropped [on] our communities every day," but they directly funded the weapons that promised to protect the white suburbs.[50] In both strategic and material terms, then, white America felt safe not only despite the nuclear threat to the nation's cities but because of it.[51]

Finally, the annihilation of the Black city also served a function somewhere between strategic and imaginative: to provide an imaginary yet impactful solution to the racial crisis that was challenging America's strategically vital moral exemplarity. As Toni Morrison and others have argued, the language surrounding ending the "race problem" in the middle of the twentieth century tends to slide into ending "race" and, essentially, imagining the end of Blackness.[52] This was a central tenet of the liberal consensus during the Cold War; in Nikhil Pal Singh's argument, "one of the cruelest ironies of new liberal approaches to race was that its powerful new impetus towards social reform could not differentiate itself from the longer-standing wish that 'Negroes' themselves would simply disappear."[53] As the city on a hill sought to defend its exemplary status, it was American cities themselves that became the locus for imagining redemptive annihilations of Blackness that would underwrite the white future of the United States.

In civil defense novels like *Alas, Babylon* and Philip Wylie's *Tomorrow!* (1954), it takes a nuclear attack on America to solve America's race problem. In *Alas, Babylon,* the protagonist is a white man who has just lost a local election because he wants to desegregate schools. After the attack, Randy Bragg observes that "the economics of disaster placed a penalty upon prejudice. The laws of hunger and survival could not be evaded, and honored no color line. . . . There were two drinking fountains in Marines Park, one marked 'White Only,' the other 'Colored Only.' Since neither worked, the signs were meaningless."[54] However, as Jacqueline Foertsch points out, the society that the survivors manage to re-create in Fort Bragg—so ideal that when federal troops come to save them, the residents choose to stay—does not abolish racial inequality but rather restores a kind of idealized plantation community, in which the white family lives in the big house while their Black neighbors—never too busy to help—use their ancestral knowledge of planting and fishing to keep the whites alive.[55] The original sin of slavery thrusts a stick between the spokes of America's typological wheel: how can the present be both a reenactment of the past and exemplary if the past itself contains the origin of today's racial unrest? Rewriting the past even as it typologically reenacts it allows Frank to redeem the white present; slavery is rendered morally neutral and perhaps even desirable to all involved, so that the contemporary suburban pioneer can have his Black servant-slaves and his moral exemplarity, too.

Written by a civil defense consultant to the government, Wylie's novel, which is dedicated to the FCDA, is more startling because it relies more explicitly on the annihilation of Blackness. *Tomorrow!* is an oft-referenced text in discussions of race in atomic fiction because its language, describing the scene after the attack in the voice of baddie Kit Sloane, is so shocking: "[the immigrants'] area had not been annihilated, just set on fire here and there. . . . So they were on the move, on the way out of town. . . . Not many Nigs. He even thought, racing past a bleeding family, there was a reason for the dearth of shines in the stampeded mobs: Niggertown was right on Ground Zero."[56] The novel's spatial logics mirror those of the Hypothetical Test Exercises that were conducted in several major cities during the 1950s, in which entire municipal governments as well as emergency services and utility providers spent up to three days working through how the city would respond to a nuclear attack scenario written for them by the FCDA. In these and similar civil defense exercises, the detailed, ethnographically inspired depictions of the urban scene that had defined earlier representations of the city were replaced by the more infrastructurally focused practice of "vulnerability mapping," which combined panoptic cartographic representations of urban space with actuarial reports of the damage at Hiroshima to produce virtual accounts of the effect of nuclear weapons on American cities.[57]

That vulnerability was concentrated in urban centers meant that what Matthew Farish has called the "spatial hierarchy of risk" was simultaneously a racial hierarchy, as Black urban space comes to occupy a position of greater vulnerability than white suburbia.[58] In Philadelphia, for example, the vision of the city's nuclear destruction that was produced by the widely publicized Hypothetical Test Exercise in 1951 became racialized over the subsequent years, as white occupants moved away from the forecast Ground Zero in West Philadelphia to safer suburbs, such as Levittown (where Black residents were prevented from living first by racial covenants and then by white riots), such that the community under threat of nuclear destruction that had been 71.9 percent white in 1951 would become 72 percent African American by the end of the Cold War. In 1985, the imagined bombing itself would become a self-fulfilling prophecy when the Philadelphia Police Department used helicopters to firebomb the residence of the Black liberation organization MOVE. The bombing, three blocks from the 1951 Ground Zero of the Hypothetical Test Exercise, killed eleven people, of whom five were children, and burned down sixty residences. All of the citizens killed or affected by the bombing were African American.[59] The Hypothetical Test Exercise–style map that was published with *Tomorrow!* condenses this history into a synchronic image, as the path of the missile sails over the "Private Estates" on Green River's outskirts to demolish the "Negro District" and "Slums."

The city was the inevitable target of any future war with the Soviets; it also became, through a striking metonymy, itself a threat that fused Blackness with nuclear weapons. During the urban uprisings of the 1960s, Black sociologist Kenneth Clark wrote in *New York Times Magazine* that "the dark ghettos now represent a nuclear stockpile which can annihilate the very foundations of America," while "threat assessments" that had been developed by defense analysts to deal with nuclear attacks by enemy combatants were deployed against "blight" in Los Angeles and Washington, D.C., in the 1960s and 1970s.[60] Later in Wylie's novel, middle-aged straight white family man Ted Conner looks

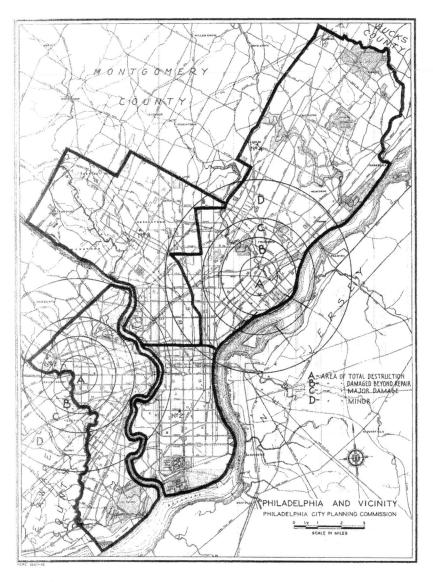

Hypothetical Test Exercise map showing the potential impact of atom bombs dropped on Philadelphia. In "General Outline: Civil Defense Plan for the City and County of Philadelphia," City of Philadelphia, Department of Records, City Archives, Box A5311 (1951). Reprinted with permission of the Philadelphia Department of Records.

out over the vista from his still-standing suburban home to where the new, decentralized city is being built. Through him, we learn that "by this time, unhit cities were considered 'obsolete.' Those that had been bombed provided people with a surge of exhilaration, for the bombing had proved an ultimate blessing by furnishing a brand-new chance to build a world brand-new—and infinitely better."[61] In a move that encapsulates the trope that Martha Bartter has called "nuclear holocaust as urban renewal," the annihilation of the city is the "secret salvation" of the nation.[62] For Wylie, as for Frank, the atomic destruction of the racialized city is America's second chance, producing not horror or grief but rather the exhilaration of Rand's characters at the end of *Atlas Shrugged,* the thrill of a pioneer subjectivity expressed in the chance to "build a world brand-new" now that the twinned threats of Blackness and nuclear annihilation have been neutralized with a single missile. For both Wylie and Frank, nuclear war offers the kind of racial do-over that mid-century liberalism so desperately wanted, a chance, in the words of a white character in an unfinished short story by Black writer Eugene Gordon, to "build an America we should've built from the outset."[63] Solving the race problem by destroying the possibility of racial strife while protecting the white pioneer suburbanite, civil defense thus ensures America's moral character and consequent Cold War victory. In the typological logic of civil defense, the price of a white *Tomorrow!* is the consignment of Blackness to yesterday.

Baldwin in the Promised Land

A Black, queer writer in Cold War America and an antinuclear activist, James Baldwin wrote a career-spanning tale of two cities across two novels, *Go Tell It on the Mountain* and *Tell Me How Long the Train's Been Gone,* that are set firmly in the context of the Cold War overdetermination of the city as a place where race, infrastructured space, apocalyptic narrative forms, and national identity are braided together. In 1953's *Go Tell It on the Mountain,* Baldwin describes the almost uncannily powerful affective force that irrupts when John Grimes feels himself aligned with the city as symbol of national belonging and its correlative, futurity. Approaching a concrete materialization of Winthrop's city on a hill, as "the slope stretched upward, and above it the brilliant sky, and beyond it, cloudy, and far away, he saw the skyline of New York," the affective charge of the moment comes from somewhere outside of John and overtakes him: "he did not know why, but there arose in him an exultation and a sense of power" as he declares that "he would live in this shining city which his ancestors had seen with longing from far away. For it was his; the inhabitants of the city had told him it was his; he had but to run down, crying, and they would take him to their hearts and show him wonders his eyes had never seen."[64] The irony of this description, of course, is that slavery and its legacies constitute the distance between John's ancestors and the "shining city," producing in them—in John's apostrophe, at least—a longing that matches John's own even as he assumes that the same distance will not apply to him. The fact that John returns home to find that his brother Roy has been stabbed in a fight with "some of those white folks *you* like so much" captures the limited access that Black bodies still have to the city on a hill.[65] In both constructing this irony and depicting John's blindness to it, Baldwin underscores the power of the image itself to structure the desire for national belonging even in those who are excluded by racism from the potential benefits of the nation.

In Baldwin's 1968 novel *Tell Me How Long the Train's Been Gone*, however, the same confrontation with the city is rewritten as an acknowledgment of the failure of John's vision: not the failure of his own dream to be realized but the failure of the city to deliver on its promise. In *Tell Me*, the protagonist, Leo Proudhammer, a successful actor now in middle age, thinks back across his life as he recovers from a heart attack in a San Francisco hospital. Like the young John Grimes, the young Leo dreams of success, this time in more specific terms: he wants to be a movie star. Having succeeded against all odds in this most American of occupations, Leo survives his heart attack and leaves the hospital. Standing with his lover Christopher, a younger man involved with revolutionary Black Power groups, Leo looks out across San Francisco and realizes that "there was a sense in which it certainly could be said that my endeavor had been for nothing. Indeed, I had conquered the city: but the city was stricken with the plague" (478). Christopher elaborates the nature of the plague a few lines later, connecting the contemporary urban crisis to a longer settler-colonial relationship between race, place, and extermination: "them laws they keep passing, shit, they just like the treaties they signed with them Indians. Nothing but lies. They never even *meant* to keep those treaties, baby, they wanted the land and they got it and now they mean to keep it, even if they have to put every black motherfucker in this country behind barbed wire, or shoot him down like a dog" (479). John's conquering dream in *Go Tell It* is revealed to have been for nothing: what would national belonging look like in a country founded on and infrastructured to produce constitutive exclusions and genocide? Nobody ever fights to get *into* a plague town.

The disappointment in the American ideal that comes across so clearly in comparing these two scenes of a Black citizen facing the city on a hill is central to Baldwin's later work. In his earlier writing, Baldwin's prophetic voice was tied to a belief in the emplotment of promise and fulfillment; as Hortense Spillers writes of *The Fire Next Time*, Baldwin "kept the eye fixed on the symptoms of movement toward the fulfillment of promise," while his conception of a "prophetic dimension would be borne out in the democratic promise as the route to the achievement of 'our country.'"[66] But Baldwin begins to sound distinctly apocalyptic after the mid-1960s. He continues to foretell disaster for America, but he no longer seems able to bear the conviction that things will improve, that justice, however elusive, will one day arrive as the inevitable fulfillment of a past suffering that has already paid the price of the ticket. In *No Name in the Street,* published in 1972 but written in part concurrently with *Tell Me,* Baldwin looks back on what he elsewhere calls "that betrayed and co-opted insurrection that American folklore has trivialized into 'the civil rights movement.'"[67] Whereas in *The Fire Next Time,* he had, in the tradition of the jeremiad, threatened America with destruction if it did not atone for its past and change its behavior in the present, here Baldwin, in an apocalyptic rather than a prophetic mode, sees destruction as inevitable. In "the American crisis, which is part of a global, historical crisis," Baldwin writes in the book's epilogue, "an old world is dying, and a new one, kicking in the belly of its mother, time, announces that it is ready to be born. This birth will not be easy, and many of us are doomed to discover that we are exceedingly clumsy midwives."[68] No longer able to exhort the "relatively conscious whites" and the "relatively conscious blacks" to "end the racial nightmare, and achieve our country, and change the history of the world," Baldwin now presents America and Americans as caught up in the inevitable end of the world as we know it, which, like any birth, will be more or less bloody depending on the skill of the midwife, but which can in no way be stopped.[69]

This shift toward the apocalyptic has not been much beloved of Baldwin's critics, being considered both an aesthetic and a political failure. What Cora Kaplan and Bill Schwartz describe as "a consensus . . . that his literary career represented a diminishment of sensibility, in which the early achievements (A) were followed by literary decline (B)," was matched by Baldwin's growing (in the eyes of others, never in his own) political irrelevance: in the years of Black Power, he was the wrong kind of Black; in the years of gay liberation, he was the wrong kind of queer.[70] Irving Howe's 1968 review of *Tell Me*, titled "James Baldwin: At Home in Apocalypse," typifies this view, stating that "Baldwin is now a writer systematically deceiving himself through rhetorical inflation and hysteria, whipping himself into postures of militancy and declarations of racial metaphysics which—for him, in this book—seem utterly inauthentic."[71] Describing Baldwin both as inauthentically Black and, through the term "hysteria," as a stereotype of homosexuality best described as inauthentically female, Howe sees little literary merit in *Tell Me* and even less political power. He also criticizes *Tell Me* for repeating tropes found in earlier Baldwin novels, a critique repeated in several other reviews, which argued that the book "rambles like a milk train over the same run that Baldwin covered in *Another Country,* creaks over the same hard ground, sounds the same blast about the Negro's condition, rattles the same rationale for homosexuality"; in this view, *Tell Me* is "nothing but a reshuffling of the same old cards on the same old games."[72] For these critics, the appeal of Baldwin's earlier work comes both from the power of his prophetic voice and from its novelty. Apocalyptic Baldwin, cursing the same old racism and the same old inequalities with ever-decreasing levels of optimism, has no such appeal.[73]

A welcome correction to this canonical hierarchy of Baldwin's work has arisen in the last twenty years, both within Baldwin scholarship and in the rise of Black queer studies, for whom Baldwin is a central figure.[74] Drawing on the epistemologies of nuclear physics, Michelle Wright, for example, has argued for a "quantum Baldwin" who, rather than being flattened into linearity and self-contradiction, should be permitted the full "multidimensionality of his Blackness."[75] In this reading, however, it is a different temporal analysis that I wish to undertake: that of the relationship between disappointment and repetition in Baldwin's work. The critiques of *Tell Me* as repetitive imply that Baldwin has lost his vim, his edge; he repeats scenes and characters because he cannot come up with anything new. This makes him, as well as his fiction, a failure and a disappointment. What I would like to suggest in place of this reading is that *Tell Me* is precisely about failure and disappointment: not the novelist's, however, but the nation's. As George Shulman asks in his excoriating defense of late Baldwin:

> did Baldwin betray himself by performing a script not his own, or did he change his script to register changing political judgment? Might he have been disillusioned and radicalized by the assassinations of Malcolm X, King, and Black Panther leaders, by the failure of the civil rights movement in the North, by invasive spying on political opposition, by the violence linking the Vietnam War to the repression of black and student radicalism, and by the ascendancy of white backlash, an emerging Republican majority, and the election of Nixon twice? How *does* one digest the bloody, hysterical termination of the second American Reconstruction by a repressive regime invoking "law and order"?[76]

Tell Me How Long the Train's Been Gone is, I argue, Baldwin's most sustained fictional attempt to reckon with the disappointment of a second reconstruction that failed almost as bloodily as the first. In his turn to a nonprophetic apocalypticism, Baldwin addresses the failure both of the American promise to be fulfilled and of the day of racial equality to arrive. But he also explores the limits of this emplotment of promise and fulfillment. What if, he asks, this was always a too-limited and limiting form of hoping?

What Baldwin depicts in his intertextual tale of two cities is the failure of the typological narrative form that had structured African American resistance to a white-authored script of Black ahistoricity for centuries. David Leeming and Lynn Orilla Scott both describe *Tell Me* and *Go Tell It* as a kind of diptych: they are Baldwin's two most autobiographical novels, their titles and epigraphs serving as a kind of call and response across fifteen years, and, of course, the latter returning to the city scene of the former. Through the multiple connections between *Go Tell It* and *Tell Me,* Baldwin creates a microcosm of history that is defined not by promise and fulfillment but by prophecy and its failure.[77] This, perhaps even more than his orthogonal relationship to identity politics, marked Baldwin out from his contemporaries; as the lukewarm reception of Baldwin's brand of apocalypticism by his critics suggests, there remained a vital affective force to the older, typological form of apocalyptic prophecy in the mid-twentieth century. From Martin Luther King's promise at the Mason Temple in Memphis the night before his assassination that "I may not get there with you, but . . . we as a people will get to the promised land" to Eldridge Cleaver's ecstatic claiming of the image of the New Jerusalem on earth at the end of *Soul on Ice,* the typological interpretation of history was still an immensely powerful social force.[78]

Why, then, does Baldwin represent only the failure of this practice in *Tell Me How Long the Train's Been Gone?* One answer, and I think it a correct one, is a loss of faith. Typology, unlike a chronology that understands the present and future as developing sequentially from the past, requires a significant amount of faith that one's own position is related to the past in precisely the way that one thinks it is. When Frederick Douglass wants to critique white America's sense of providential destiny, for instance, he accuses them of incorrect typological interpretation. In "The Meaning of July Fourth to the Negro," Douglass defines Independence Day as "to you, as what the Passover was to the emancipated people of God" that "carries your minds back to the day, and to the act of your great deliverance" before establishing that it is in fact the Black slave, not the white American, who is the antitype for God's chosen people: "I can today take up the plaintive lament of a peeled and woe-smitten people! 'By the rivers of Babylon, there we sat down. Yea! we wept when we remembered Zion.'"[79] By asserting that white America has misread typological history, that it is an antitype not of the enslaved Jews but of the enslaving Pharaoh or the tyrannical British, Douglass redefines America's faith in itself as bad faith. By the time that Baldwin is writing, if typology guaranteed deliverance, then the repeated deferral of deliverance's arrival might well come to look like a failure to correctly interpret one's position in a typological schema. In an essay composed shortly before his death, Baldwin writes that "my diaspora continues, the end is not in sight, and I certainly cannot depend on the morality of this panic-stricken consumer society to bring me out of—Egypt."[80] Not only has typology failed to bring deliverance but it has become almost unspeakable, as the stuttering punctuation before "Egypt" suggests.

Baldwin's treatment of deliverance in *Tell Me*, however, suggests that his staging of typological failure might work not only to reflect a lack of faith or to mourn the failure of the typological liberation narrative but also to critique the infrastructuring form of typology itself. In a scene that takes place, in the chronology of the plot, shortly before the heart attack that opens the book, Leo is waiting to speak at a civil rights rally in New York. On stage is a young girl singing a gospel song: "*Deliverance will come,* she sang, *I know it will come, He said it will come. And again, Deliverance will come. He said it will come. I know it will come.* I watched her face as she sang, a plain, black, stocky girl, who was, nevertheless, very beautiful. Deliverance will come" (110, emphasis original). The paratactic repetition here suggests a temporality both unbearably stretched out and claustrophobic, both the steadfastness of faith and the impossibility of maintaining that faith when deliverance is so long deferred: "Deliverance will come. Would it? We on the platform certainly had no patent on deliverance—it was only because deliverance had *not* come that we sat there in all our uneasy rage and splendor. Deliverance will come, it had not come for my mother and father, it had not come for Caleb, it had not come for me, it had not come for Christopher, it had not come for this nameless little girl, and it had not come for all these thousands who were listening to her song" (110–11). The dream endlessly deferred and the longing for deliverance are powerful tropes that Baldwin is hardly the first to invoke. What makes Baldwin's treatment of them unusual, however, is that his account reckons not only with the cost of deferral but also with the cost of deliverance.

For every form of deliverance that Leo tries to imagine, there are constitutive exclusions. Looking at Christopher, standing in here for the new generation of armed Black revolutionaries, Leo sees possible victory against the failures of his own generation. But, he asks, "was Christopher's manner of deliverance worth the voices it would silence?" (111). The silencing of other voices is not limited to acts of physical violence. Of the "other luminaries" on the platform with him Leo says, "In many ways, perhaps in nearly all ways, they disapproved of me, and I knew it; and they knew that in many ways I disapproved of them" (109). The differences between them "were reducible to one:

I was an artist" (109). Well. One difference it may be, but *Tell Me* was
written in the wake of homophobic attacks on Baldwin from "other
luminaries" in the movement, and Leo's doth-protest-too-much insistence that "we were responsible, commonly, for something greater
than our differences" suggests that "artist" stands in here for a nonnor-
mative lifestyle more generally, including the sexual and transnational
deviations from the norm that made Baldwin a target from many different angles.[81] Leo is left to wonder what deliverance means if there
is no room in it for him: "and yet—yet—was it not possible that the
mighty gentlemen, my honorable and invaluable confreres, by being
unable to imagine such a journey as my own, were leaving something
of the utmost importance out of their aspirations?" (110). The journey that these men, rendered positively stolid by Baldwin's swing into
the Dickensian language of "mighty gentlemen" and "honorable confreres," cannot imagine is one that does not model itself on inclusion
in the national polity. For what these men are fighting for—and what
Leo tells us his younger self used to want, recalling John Grimes's passionate urge for national belonging—is for everyone to be "at home in
the world" (109). Deliverance means the end of estrangement: the end
of the endless days of wandering in the desert after the escape from
slavery, the crossing of the river Jordan into, as the old song "Wayfar-
ing Stranger" testifies, a form of freedom that is also death, homoge-
neity, stasis, home.[82]

What Leo cannot accept, however, is that in the New Jerusalem
across the Jordan, or as the result of the inclusion of Black citizens in
American national belonging, there will be no more room for wandering. It is precisely his homelessness that has given him, a poor, queer,
Black boy in a country that values whiteness, straightness, and wealth,
a voice: "I had never been at home in the world and had become incapable of imagining that I ever would be. I did not want others to en-
dure my estrangement, that was why I was on the platform; yet was it
not, at the least, paradoxical that it was only my estrangement which
had placed me there? And I could not flatten out this paradox, I could
not hammer it into any useful shape" (109). Deliverance, as a word, is
central to the Exodus story that provides the bedrock for American
typological practice. The tension in this scene between the desire to
arrive and the desire to keep wandering is also the tension between
the desire to fulfill the typological promise and the desire to resist such

closure. For Baldwin, the cost of typology's fulfillment is those it would exclude: the voices silenced by violence and those silenced by a normative drive for belonging.

Baldwin's critique of typological hermeneutics is not, however, limited to the civil rights movement but rather extends to the shared emplotment of African American liberation rhetoric and the language of American universalism. If Black typology looked to the Bible to find a promise in the past whose fulfillment in the present would mean freedom for all, then Cold War liberalism, as Dudziak demonstrates, found the same promise in the Declaration of Independence and the U.S. Constitution. In 1965, Robert F. Kennedy, with whom Baldwin and other civil rights activists had met unproductively in 1963, braided the story of American universalism and that of the civil rights movement into a familiar typological image when he told the National Council of Christians and Jews that "America is still in the middle of its journey. When millions of people suffer the injustice of discrimination and poverty, we know that we are only half way to our goal—only half way to the city upon the hill."[83] When faced with the "race problem," typology allowed for the narrative of an exceptional America that is only ever one step away—ending slavery, ending Jim Crow, ending segregation—from perfecting democracy. This typological narrative was, in fact, the shared ground upon which Black and white Americans could stand to talk about race. As many scholars have noted, the theory of American universalism, which sees the founding promises of America as a land of liberty for all as a valid theory that only fails to be practiced correctly, has been a vital rhetorical resource for African American writers and activists.[84] From Frederick Douglass's insistence on the value of the liberty mandated in the Constitution to Martin Luther King's characterization of the Declaration of Independence as a "promissory note" that had yet to be cashed for the nation's Black citizens, universalism insists on the fact of a superior form of American statehood to which all citizens should have equal access.[85]

While the younger Baldwin did appeal to the brand of exceptionalism shared by Black activists and white liberals, *Tell Me* evidences a different kind of fulfillment narrative. Here the inevitable fulfillment of America is not in racial harmony but in nuclear destruction. Debating leaving America during his convalescence, Leo thinks that his countrymen "would not change, they could not. . . . The very word caused their eyes to unfocus, their lips to loosen or to tighten, and sent them scurrying to their various bomb-shelters" (331). The nuclear infrastructures of civil defense function for Baldwin as the end point of white supremacy, suggesting that America has been so rigidly oppressive from its very beginning that its fulfillment would be fatal: "the metamorphosis of the framework into which we had been born would almost certainly be so violent as to blow Christopher, and me, and all of us, away" (331). In raising the nuclear specter, Baldwin presents it as thoroughly involved with American racism; when hearing of the bombing of Hiroshima later in the novel (although earlier in its chronology), Leo "kept thinking, *They didn't drop it on the Germans. The Germans are white. They dropped it on the Japanese. They dropped it on the yellow-bellied Japs*" (364, emphasis original).[86] Baldwin had spoken of this connection as early as 1961 in his role as a member of the advisory group of the antinuclear group SANE, telling a *Washington Post* journalist the day before a speech on SANE's behalf that "it is just as difficult for the white American to think of peace as it is of no color."[87] Nuclearization is a racial issue for Baldwin as well as other African American commentators, appearing as the fulfillment of a long history of militarized racial terror.

Black responses to the atom bomb have long noted that the "atom belongs to white folks," both as its possible beneficiaries and as the culmination of the technological/scientific progress narrative of Enlightened whiteness.[88] For Barbara Omolade, for instance, writing in 1984, "a direct historical line of military terrorism can be drawn from the guns used during the slave trade against Africans and American Indians to the building of nuclear arsenals by the world's current superpowers."[89] Bringing together the nuclear-apocalyptic history of American racism in his description of Hiroshima with the fulfillment narrative undergirding both exceptionalism and the civil rights movement, Baldwin indicates that the only possible fulfillment of America's real story is the destruction of the world, with its nonwhite populations the first to be sacrificed. Writing in advance of the presidential elections of 1980, Baldwin says of Reagan's blatant racism and hawkish nuclear policies that "no black person can afford to forget that the history of this country is genocidal, from where the buffalo once roamed to where our ancestors were slaughtered (from New Orleans to New York, from Birmingham to Boston) and to the Caribbean to Hiroshima and Nagasaki to Saigon. Oh, yes, let freedom ring."⁹⁰ In *Tell Me,* Baldwin ironizes the typological hopes of a civil rights movement that would stand against this slaughter while inhabiting the same exceptionalist system of belief that allowed for it to happen: "perhaps God would join us later, when He was convinced that we were on the winning side. Then, heaven would pass a civil-rights bill and all of the angels would be equal and all of God's children have shoes" (331–32).

American exceptionalism has long been grounded upon nonwhite futurelessness, as Baldwin's list of righteous massacres suggests. Baldwin rejects the typological narrative form of history because he knows that, in a country that has used the same form of history to justify racist atrocities, there is no future in it for Blackness. Taking up the liberal image of the city on a hill, he connects it to other cities: Hiroshima, Saigon, New York, San Francisco. The history of American racism is suffused into the physical and affective infrastructured space of the American city in *Tell Me*: as the graffiti on the walls that "were full of information which I could scarcely read" (28); as "the town's emotional economy" that Leo disrupts by his presence in an all-white café (166); as "that invisible frontier which divides American towns, white from black" (185). In this city, Leo's father plays out the role assigned to him: he struggles to pay rent, to save his children from his own fate; in both, he fails. Elsewhere, he might have succeeded; but "this was America, America, America, and those people out there, my countrymen, had been tearing me limb from limb, like dogs, for centuries" (253). The liberal appeal through the image of the city on a hill to American history as guarantor of immanent racial equality is countered by Baldwin through other combinations of race and place: the real America, founded not in democracy but in slavery; the segregated city of civil defense; the atomic target of Hiroshima, outlined in yellow. From this perspective, turning to the fulfillment of a promise as the keystone of Black liberatory desire is deeply problematic, not only because of its potential failure but also because of the possibility of its success. Shulman writes of Baldwin that "depicting a nation founded in slavery, whose ideals have been practiced only in viciously exclusionary ways, he denies that progress is the telos of American history."⁹¹ In Baldwin's later writings, however, the fear is rather that progress is precisely the telos of American history. The question is whether there is room, at all, for Blackness in the American ideal that might lie at that telos. In rewriting the city on a hill as an atomic target, infrastructured to reproduce racist oppression, Baldwin suggests that Black annihilation is, in fact, what success might look like within the true American narrative.

Dhalgren: When the Case of Blackness Is Dismissed

In a speech given at the Harlem Museum in 1978, Samuel Delany echoes Baldwin's description of the violence contained within segregated urban space. As a Black child attending a mostly white school in a white neighborhood, the young Delany of the 1950s sees 110th Street as "an absolute social barrier" separating the white world from the Black one. And, as in Baldwin's argument that "the metamorphosis of the [racial] framework into which we had been born would almost certainly be so violent as to blow . . . [all] of us away," Delany describes the breaking of that barrier in terms akin to the explosive energy release of splitting the atom: each journey to school "was a journey of near ballistic violence."[92] These imaginative resonances between Baldwin, usually considered a writer of nonfictional essays and realist fiction, and Delany, one of America's greatest writers of science and speculative fiction, might be unexpected for anyone other than Delany himself, who writes in the same speech of reading "James Baldwin's early essays that were to be first collected in *Notes of a Native Son,* and I thought they were as wonderful as . . . well, as science fiction" (28, ellipses original). For Delany, realist fiction by Richard Wright and Chester Himes seemed to say "that, in any realistic terms, precisely what made [the condition of the Black man in America] so awful also made it unchangeable" (28). Conversely, Baldwin and Delany are aligned in Delany's speech as writers of science fiction, the counterrealist genre whose vital function is to ask *what if,* to conceptualize the world as radically otherwise from its present reality.

To read *Tell Me How Long the Train's Been Gone* as a work of speculative fiction would be to ask a different set of questions than we might bring to it as a realist novel: not *what,* but *what if*? What if the Cold War vision of the futureless Black city came to pass? What would happen to American cities, and to the racialized logics that underlie American ontologies, if the infrastructural role of Blackness *were* annihilated—if, in Fred Moten's powerful formulation, "the case of blackness [were] dismissed?"[93] It is precisely this question, I argue, that Delany takes up in his 1975 epic novel *Dhalgren,* this question that makes this strange yet very much of-this-world novel a work of speculative fiction.[94]

The novel takes place in Bellona, the ultimate failed city located somewhere in the American heartland whose geographies and temporalities shift continually in some kind of ongoing catastrophe stemming from uncertain causes: postapocalyptic, or mid-apocalyptic, or caught up in what W. Gilbert Adair calls a "semi-apocalypse."[95] That *Dhalgren* is a response to both mid-century urban crisis and the relationship between race and the national narrative has been well documented. In a 2001 interview for *Sci Fi Weekly,* Delany described the "deserted, burned-out, inner-city shells, just ruins and wrecks" that functioned as "the basic images that I used to create *Dhalgren* from."[96] Bellona's strangeness, however, runs deeper than the mere destruction of physical infrastructure. Time and place are unmoored here. The nameless protagonist, who comes to be known as Kid, seems to enter Bellona at the beginning of the novel and leave it at the end, but the last line of the novel loops back around to the first, with a stutter ("I have come to" / "to wound the autumnal city" [801, 1]), and Kid writes poetry in a notebook that he finds soon after his arrival that already contains the writing of someone who seems, to the reader, to be Kid himself. This instability is matched by the shifting landscape of the city; as Bellona resident and leather daddy Tak Loufer tells Kid, "the whole city shifts, turns, rearranges itself. All the time. And rearranges us . . ." (36, ellipses original). Reader and protagonist alike are disoriented by the unstable infrastructures of the city and the novel, lost, unable to find our bearings.

For Delany as for Baldwin, however, both spatial and temporal surety are deeply suspect for Blackness in nuclear-age America. White supremacy has produced the segregated American city, fixed in space, as well as the apocalyptic narrative of urban Blackness, fixed in time. The Richardses, a white middle-class family who refuse to accept that anything has changed in Bellona, appear in *Dhalgren* as an example of what comes to pass when fixed stories play out in fixed infrastructures. A sexual encounter between the Black proletarian George Harrison and the fragile white teenager June Richards results in the death of June's brother Bobby when he falls, or is possibly pushed, down an elevator shaft after threatening to tell their parents about the poster of a naked George (copies of which are being circulated all over town by the reverend of the Black church, Amy Taylor) that June has been obsessively hiding in her bedroom. Kid's response indicates the horror of encountering a racial myth captured and recapitulated by urban infrastructures, as the novel's affect shifts closer to horror than to science fiction:

> "I mean, I don't *know* what Mr Richards would do if he found out his sunshine girl was running around the streets like a bitch in heat, lusting to be brutalized by some hulking, sadistic, buck nigger. . . . It would be just like the myth: her lust for George, death and destruction! Only—only suppose it *was* an accident?" He took another breath. "*That's* what frightens me. Suppose it was, like she said, *just* an accident. She didn't see at all. Bobby just backed into the wrong shaft door. That's what terrifies me. That's the thing I'm scared of most." "Why?" Lanya asked. "Because . . ." He breathed, felt her head shift on his shoulder, her hand rock with his on his chest; "Because that means it's the city. That means it's the landscape: the bricks, and the girders, and the faulty wiring and the shot elevator machinery, all conspiring together to *make* these myths true. And that's crazy." (249)

Crazy, maybe, but not that crazy. In the essay "Of Sex, Objects, Signs, Systems, Sales, SF, and Other Things," Delany lays out his theory of the semiotics of space. He takes from Lacan the idea that geographic space is an expression of the human psyche.[97] Lacan writes, describing the view from his window of "Baltimore in the early morning," that "exactly all that I could see, except for some trees in the distance, was the result of thoughts, actively thinking thoughts where the function played by the subjects was not completely obvious."[98] Delany takes from this an understanding of the infrastructured urban landscape as a code or a language, not simply a static expression of human intention but with a grammar of its own that in turn affects the kinds of thoughts, affects, and intentions that can arise within it: "as we walk down any street, we read (or sometimes misread), consciously or unconsciously, this code. What it says affects us. It is the real world influencing (among many other things) our emotions and general psychology."[99] As in the elevator scene, where faulty wiring in an abandoned building "conspires" toward rendering the mythical association between female and Black

sexuality and "death and destruction" "true," the city itself can produce changes that while leading seemingly inexorably toward an expression of an ingrained idea cannot be reduced to a specific source of
that idea: "these signs, semes, or codons affect one another in purely
autonomous ways that change their meanings so that those meanings
cannot be traced back to any intention on the part of the initial human
actors: soot in the air (one seme) defaces a new building (another seme)
creating a new seme—a grimy building—with a new meaning for the
city itself."[100] Building a new block of affordable housing in the middle
of a slum, while supposedly meant to better life for its inhabitants, will
put it in grammatical contact with its surroundings—none of them designed, as Delany argues elsewhere, to sustain communities—as well
as with the larger bureaucratic and social systems that work together
to create a ghetto.[101] Grimy buildings and collapsing infrastructures
seem like an expression of one myth—people of color live in slums
because of a cultural pathology—when in fact they are the material
expression of a racist collective unconscious.[102]

    For Delany, then, as for Baldwin, and as the cityscapes developed
under civil defense attest, race is an infrastructural force. In the United
States, race and racism determine what gets built where, how bodies
can move in space, and what narratives can play out in the streets that
race has built. The Richardses' elevator is what Emily Apter has called
a "raced worldscape," in which race functions quite differently from
its usual bodily sense and instead becomes part of the constructed
world.[103] As Mark Chia-Yon Jerng observes, "race is often used to provide the background, the social context, for truly understanding the
terms of one's identity (race matters because it is an overdetermined social, legal, and economic category). In *Dhalgren,* though, Delany resists
this projection and importation of a background by insistently placing
racial markers in a foreground that gets related to the differential elements that constitute the world of the SF text."[104] But whereas Jerng
argues that race gets placed in the foreground of the text as a purely
cognitive procedure or "protocol of racial reading," I suggest that racialization not only makes the scene coherent but also builds the world
of the text in a more literal sense, as race becomes not one of many
contingent features of the landscape but the landscape itself. If one
of Delany's goals in writing science fiction was "to write about worlds
where being black mattered in different ways than it matters now,"

then *Dhalgren* concretizes that goal at the level of landscape: Blackness matters here as matter, as the material form of urban infrastructure.[105] When we encounter the labile urban landscape of Bellona, then, where the streets shift, rearrange, and crumble, we should see it not only as the aftermath of an uncertain catastrophe or as an uncannily active participant in making racial myths come true but also as an ongoing refiguring of race and racialization. This refiguring is a consequence of an apocalyptic assault on Blackness that recalls the civil defense imaginary: the originary crisis that has left Bellona smoldering is unclear, but the connecting thread that ties all of the possibilities together is the motif of Black annihilation. Most of the novel's characters place the origin of this attenuated apocalypse at a riot in Jackson, the city's Black ghetto, the cause of which is variously proposed as the shooting by a white sniper of Black activist Paul Fenster (who bears similarities to Martin Luther King Jr.), a house collapsing, and a plane crashing into the neighborhood. None of these events were unimaginable in the mid-twentieth century; indeed, some of them were regular occurrences as slum conditions left people living in collapsing buildings all over the country and Black leaders were assassinated. Even the plane crash theory is only one semiotic jump away from the fact that the only aerial bombings ever to take place on the American mainland have been launched by the U.S. government against its own Black citizens.[106] If the history of race and racialization has become a part of the infrastructural landscape of Bellona, as the elevator scene suggests, then Bellona before the origin point of the crisis would have been the material expression of race as it has historically been constructed in America, with its white neighborhoods and Black ghettos. But we see this Bellona only in the Richards household, clinging to older racial forms even as those forms wreak havoc. In the rest of Bellona, we see only the aftermath of the destruction of the Black urban space of Jackson that is, as the real-life analogues of these possible causes suggest, also the destruction of Blackness itself: the ultimate goal, as Baldwin argues, of a white national narrative that requires to maintain itself such things as segregation into slums where building codes are not enforced but restrictive covenants are, the assassination of Black leaders, and the bombing of Black neighborhoods.

To say that to destroy the buildings of Jackson is to destroy Blackness is not to say that it removes all of the Black bodies from the city.

We hear that Bellona has become a blacker city since the beginning of the crisis; even a speculative city is not immune from white flight, and as Fenster tells Tak, "Bellona was . . . what? Maybe thirty per cent black? Now, even though you've lost so many people, bet it's closer to sixty. From my estimate, at any rate" (282, ellipses original). But Blackness is uncannily absent from the city that we see. It is absent even when we encounter Reverend Amy's Black church, even when Kid visits George Harrison's more or less Black-only nightspot, and even though, as Sandra Y. Govan writes, "race as an issue is unavoidable and unmistakable in *Dhalgren.* Three-fourths of the scorpions are black. Bellona is still, after the holocaust, bifurcated by race. There are fewer goods and supplies in the city's black sections than in its white neighborhoods, and there are snipers who shoot blacks from the tops of deserted buildings and arsonists who burn black neighborhoods."[107] But behind this presence is an absence; as Kid thinks to himself, "between what Nightmare had said earlier and what Reverend Taylor had just said, he found himself wondering, granted the handful he'd seen, just where all the black people in Bellona *were*" (192, emphasis original). Hearing from Joaquim, an old white seller of the *Bellona Times,* about an exceptionally deprived area of Jackson called Lower Cumberland Park, Kid recalls being there the night before: "'Oh,' Kid said. 'Where I was last night. It says here something about nobody living there any more.' Faust hefted the bundle on his hip. 'Then all I know is that I leave a God-damn lot of papers in front of a God-damn lot of doors, and they ain't there the next day when I come back'" (491–92). The disappearance of Blackness is not, here, a genocide; rather, it seems to separate the physical existence of dark-skinned bodies from a raced concept called "Black." In this way, the Black neighborhood can be both empty and overcrowded. The destruction of Jackson has destroyed not Black people but Blackness as the organizing principle that holds America together, Blackness as "absolutely indispensable to normative order, normative form."[108]

For Baldwin, as for Fred Moten, Blackness serves as both an infrastructural and an epistemological support to normative whiteness: "the black man," Baldwin writes in *Notes of a Native Son,* "has functioned in the white man's world as a fixed star, as an immovable pillar: and as he moves out of his place, heaven and earth are shaken to their foundations."[109] But Bellona is a city whose racial astronomy has ceased to order the world below, where two moons rise one day, where one day the sun rises far too closely to the earth and sets far too quickly; its stars are moving unpredictably now. Whatever the devastating event in Jackson was, its main consequence has been to remove the pillar of Blackness from the novel's world, with a consequent unmooring of the organizational matrices of time and space. The most striking formal feature of *Dhalgren* is its use of multiple narrative temporalities, not only because it is difficult for a reader to establish the sequence of events underlying the narrative but also because different characters experience time in different ways: Kid experiences one day passing where Lanya experiences five. Spatially, the novel's most sustained "alternate reality" conceit is that the city continually rearranges itself; the sun comes up from one direction one morning, another the next. The novel's characters themselves trace the origin of Bellona's spatio-temporal unmooring to a disruption of racial infrastructures, situating it in the events of the Jackson riot. In a conversation with Joaquim, Kid learns about the riot for the first time as an explanation of why no one knows exactly what time it is in Bellona. Looking at the church steeple, Kid asks, "What happened to the . . . hands?" (70, ellipses original), to which Joaquim replies, "The niggers. The first night, I guess it was. . . . They went wild. . . . This guy told me there was a picture of them climbing up on the church. And breaking off the clock hands" (70–71). That this exchange takes place in a chapter called "The Ruins of Morning" underscores the connection between the physical destruction of Jackson (which Kid sees for the first time in this chapter) and the becoming-uncertain of time. So does the fact that Joaquim tells Kid to find the newspaper from that day; since we already know that the *Bellona Times* has been issued with entirely random dates on the cover since the beginning of the crisis (26), for a copy depicting the riot to be locatable, it must have been printed with the correct date, making it the last one of the old temporal order and positioning the riot as the tipping point from an ordered chronology to a fully unpredictable one. Now Bellona has many times, many cities, and, somewhere at the start of it all, the culmination of a national narrative that has constellated Blackness with a certain landscape and both with annihilation.

The apocalyptic destruction of Bellona, beginning with Jackson, thus refigures both the association of the Black inner city with nuclear destruction that was a prominent feature of Cold War discourse and the much longer history of race, place, and Black futurelessness.

If Wylie's depiction of the atomic destruction of "Niggertown" works to shore up a suburban-yet-exceptional American whiteness, then Delany relates the nuclear to the undoing of such epistemological categories. When the giant sun appears in the sky over Bellona, Kid's first reaction is to remember a time in New York when he experienced what he thought was an atomic explosion: "sirens woke him—he remembered no scheduled test. A jet snarled somewhere on the sky . . . Then the window filled with blinding yellow light. The fireball! he thought, beyond the pain in his terrified body. The light's here now. The shock and the sound will arrive in four seconds, five seconds and I will be dead . . ." (419, ellipses original). In *Dhalgren*, this memory is passed over fairly quickly. But in Delany's autobiographical work *The Motion of Light in Water*, the same scene is repeated verbatim. Here it is followed by a description of the same kind of epistemological uncertainty that runs through *Dhalgren*: simultaneously watching a speech by the Cuban ambassador to the United Nations (UN) during the Cuban Missile Crisis on CBS and listening to it on Riverside Radio, Delany has the jarring experience of two different, overlaid realities. On CBS, the speech cuts to commentary after a pause; on the radio, the ambassador keeps speaking and ends his speech to minutes of rapturous applause. Delany describes this moment as "terrifying" and connects both stories to a form of temporal confusion: "I'm not sure which of the above two incidents, the false bomb scare, or the U.N. General Assembly session, came first. I don't know whether both, one, or neither came just before (or just after) the incident below."[110] In this constellation of the nuclear and the city, official discourse, and its construction of reality, is undone because it goes too far; the effect of this is to unmoor reality itself, to render cause and effect uncertain. The catastrophe that has hit Jackson is not a nuclear strike; the possibility is raised and dismissed by Kid, who tells Mary Richards that "there was nothing about a bomb in the papers" (225), although given the media blackout surrounding Bellona, this evidence is not as conclusive as it might be. But through the metonymic logics that rule this novel in which cause and effect are no longer the primary mode of relation, the city itself has become nuclear. Described repeatedly as "saprophytic," it has become fungal, mushroom-like or mushroom cloud–like, and taken into itself the qualities that Delany ascribes to the nuclear in *The Motion of Light in Water*: it makes reality uncertain and confuses temporal order.

This nuclear city thus dramatizes not the imaginative remediations of civil defense discourse whereby nuclear apocalypse upholds the infrastructures and epistemological security of racial segregation but rather the fear that made those remediations necessary: that any form of civil defense would produce a radical "reconfiguration of the racial geography" of the United States[111]—not, this time, the reconfigurations of dispersal that upheld racial epistemologies but a racial mixing that would explosively break through the environmental color line described by Delany in "The Necessity of Tomorrows." The specter of disintegrating racial boundaries haunts the civil defense imaginary. In a memorandum commissioned to establish the kinds of sociological problems that the newly established FCDA might be expected to face, two hired consultants quail at the prospect of the desegregation wrought by civil defense: "it is awesome," they write, "to reflect on what would happen in one of those cities [New York, Detroit, Chicago] if colored people and white people were forced into close association in shelters, in homes, and even evacuation reception centers."[112] At an FCDA conference for women in 1954, America's own paragon of domesticity, Betty Crocker (Marjorie Husted), encouraged housewives to prepare to host community evacuees while simultaneously evoking the specter of "racial . . . invasions" from the cities as a result of the FCDA's own evacuation plans.[113] Even as the nuclear infrastructures of civil defense were themselves structured by logics of racial segregation, they always carried with them the threat of racial inmixing.

In *Dhalgren,* Bellona's racial geography and the epistemology of difference that it had upheld have collapsed as the city has become nuclear; speaking back to Truman's vision of civil defense as a stockade to keep out "Indians," Kid's own ethnicity, half Native American, stages the inevitable failure of segregation's dream. The Indian is already inside the city; he was here all along.[114] Taking up civil defense's nightmares of racial mixing and its redemptive phantasies of the annihilation of racial others, Delany, like Baldwin, pushes them to their limit and imagines what it would mean if they were to be fulfilled. Whereas Baldwin's nuclear city undercuts the liberal progress narrative by revealing the Black annihilation that lies at its end, Delany's novel takes place after that end. Tying Blackness to a doomed place and time, he suggests, is the cake; actually destroying that place and time would be eating it too, if you need Blackness to be secured to secure your own centrality and futurity. But Delany also finds in the destruction of this form of Blackness—Blackness defined as the bad neighborhood, idiot child, forbidden lover, atavistic past of whiteness, "the thing against which all other subjects take their bearing"—an escape from the same kind of determinism that Baldwin tried to move away from: the grammar that writes race, place, and time into a sentence heard too many times before.[115]

The futureless nuclear city of Bellona becomes, if not unreadable, then constructed through a different and uncertain grammar. Toward the end of the novel, Kid reports that

> today I cut down the block where I'd heard the scorpions had their nest. "What kind of street do they live on?" In the grammar of another city, that sentence would hold the implication: What kind of street are they more or less constrained by society to live on, given their semi-outlaw status, their egregious manner and outfit, and the economics of their asocial position? In Bellona, however, the same words imply a complex freedom, a choice from hovel to mansion-complex because every hovel and every mansion sustains through that choice some remnant of our ineffable catastrophe: In any house here movement from room to room is a journey from a place where twin moons have cast double shadows of the window sills upon the floors to a place where once, because the sun had grown so immense, no shadow was cast at all. We speak another language here. (754)

The inexplicable event rising from beyond edge of the real changes the nature of space, which becomes a place where the impossible has happened: next to the seme of the window is the seme of the two moons, creating new permutations in the "American grammar book" of race that makes experience make overdetermined kinds of sense.[116] If George Harrison is the Black rapist in Bellona, he is also the second moon that bears his name, the anything that can happen in this unmiraculous city: not the formation of a new racial myth but an assertion that even George can be something impossible, something beyond what we are capable of imagining. The choices that are made within this nuclearized geography are not all as fatal and determined as the death of Bobby in the elevator shaft, because the underlying grammar of race that insists on that myth is no longer the only language in which the city can speak.

I have framed my discussion of Delany as a speculation because that is, ultimately, the only mode of analysis one can bring to bear on *Dhalgren*, and it is this as much as the giant sun or hologram light shields that defines the novel as a work of speculative fiction.[117] Like Kid, we are consistently estranged from what we see and what we think we know; we lose our bearings, we get lost, we lose time and lose track of time. Kid's amnesia and namelessness, his uncertainty about his actions or the reality of what he sees, and his loss of days at a time call to mind nothing more than the fugue state to which Moten refers at the end of "The Case of Blackness," the essay from which I have taken my speculative impetus: what would happen if the case of Blackness *were* dismissed? In his essay, Moten expands on Fanon to ask a question that echoes uncannily the impossible city of Bellona with its cast of "semi-outlaws": "how do we think the possibility and the law of outlawed, impossible things?"[118] In answering this question, Moten describes the deconstructive movement of Blackness across the ontological frames that whiteness imposes on it as "fugitive movement," "stolen life," a being that is both against the law and against the very possibility of Law.[119] Moten's most extreme case study of fugitivity is the "fugue states" of certain inhabitants of Fanon's colonial Algeria, "those imagining things whose political commitment makes them subject to being committed . . . those things whose constant escape of their own rehabilitation as men seems to be written into their nature": "in such contrapuntal fields or fugue states," he writes, "one finds (it possible to extend) their stealing, their stealing away, their lives that remain, fugitively, even when the case of blackness is dismissed."[120] When Delany solidifies Blackness into the infrastructured landscape of the nuclear city and then subjects that landscape to an uncertain but racially motivated disaster, the "ineffable catastrophe" that results for the city transforms the whole world of the novel as well as the reader's experience of it into such a fugue state: Kid's amnesia and spans of lost time are fugue states at the smallest scale, but the same conditions define both the city of Bellona and the reader's own narrative experience. Taking up the central image of the failure of Blackness to be redeemed through American universalism, the blighted nuclear city,

Delany's speculative fiction imagines through the logics that created it and shows us the world that might exist on the other side of the veil, where, caught up in an apocalypse that refuses to resolve itself, Bellona is living not on borrowed but on stolen time.

Harlem Is Nowhere

The fantasy of redemption is a powerful one on both sides of the color line, combining the promise of forgiveness with the canceling out of past mistakes. Time will be redeemed, in theological historiography, when all of its typological prophecies and promises have been fulfilled; history, like a well-balanced checkbook, must have no loose ends. In literature, the redemption of time is what we call plot. The murder that starts the detective story must be solved at its close; the gun on the wall in the first act must go off in the third. It is this notion of promise and fulfillment that Peter Brooks reads in secular terms as central to plot and that Frank Kermode understands to be the full-scale importing of an apocalyptic plot structure into the novel form.[121] Plot as typological fulfillment, Kermode argues in 1968, gives meaning to an experience of time described as the tension between beats of the clock, the *tick* and the *tock,* where novelists

> have to defeat the tendency of the interval between *tick* and *tock* to empty itself; to maintain within that interval following *tick* a lively expectation of *tock,* and a sense that however remote *tock* may be, all that happens happens as if *tock* were certainly follow-ing. All such plotting presupposes and requires that an end will bestow upon the whole duration and meaning . . . the interval must be purged of simple chronicity, of the emptiness of *tock-tick,* humanly uninteresting successiveness.[122]

Delany wrote "bits and pieces" of *Dhalgren* sitting in Kermode's old of-fice at Wesleyan, and he summons Kermode's ghost toward the end of the novel: "people," Kid writes in his journal, "probably do hear watches go tic-tok. But I'm sure my childhood clock went tic-tic-tic-tic-tic-tic-tic . . . Why do I recall this in a city without time?" (720, el-lipses original).[123] For Kermode, plot requires *kairos*: the replacement of the "mere successiveness" of *chronos* with a significance achieved by the consonance of beginning and end. It is this narrative temporality that structures Cold War civil defense, where the imagined typological ending must be consonant with America's beginnings. But not only is Delany's "tic" not followed by a "tock"; "tock" is not even a possibility here. The concept of an end that gives meaning to the duration, "a concord of imaginatively recorded past and imaginatively predicted future," is structurally negated by the continuous present of the "tic," which has no "tock" against which to define itself.[124] Delany's "tic" is *Dhalgren*'s stutter: the narrative has no origin and no future, its last line and its first both forms of the "tic," bending time into a continuous present not "charged with meaning from its relation to the end" but meaningful because it resonates uncertainly across itself, because people live in it.

Both Baldwin and Delany interrogate the apocalyptic model of plot that requires a *kairotic* journey between any beginning and its predestined end, an end that combines closure and complete revelation, which so profoundly structured Black vulnerability in the nuclear age. In *The Devil Finds Work*, Baldwin distinguishes between story and plot: "a story," he writes, "is impelled by the necessity to reveal: the aim of the story is revelation, which means that a story can have nothing—at least not deliberately—to hide. This also means that a story resolves nothing. The resolution of a story must occur in us, with what we make of the questions with which the story leaves us. A plot, on the other hand, must come to a resolution, prove a point: a plot must answer all the questions which it pretends to pose."[125] Delany makes a similar connection between story, plot, and revelation, writing that "it has been known as long as narratives have been recognized for what they are that stories are made more coherent, vivid, exciting, and energetic by resonances leap-frogging from one section over another to relate to yet another." He goes on to ask, "What else is 'plot' other than something at the end of the tale relating clearly and strongly to something at the beginning? And if 'plot' is 'dead,' it is only because in most people's minds the only relations they will respond to have become far too limited, formalized, and restricted to a ridiculously narrow repertoire of revelatory actions."[126] While Delany and Baldwin differ slightly in the way that they frame the issue, both differentiate between a form of narrative that too easily provides resolution (what Baldwin calls plot and Delany calls dead plot) and one that does not resolve itself so readily, that relies on the reaction of an unpredictable reader, one whose endings are not consonant with its beginnings or whose resonances do not resolve the plot in the form of narrative closure.

The danger of typological plot is its essential conservatism: to pin one's hopes of redemption on the fulfillment of an earlier promise means that the future can only appear within the terms set by the past, a past defined in America by slavery and genocide. Nuclear infrastructural thinking within the nuclear complex has long been structured by typological assumptions, which insist that because nuclear technology has been invented, the only possible outcome of the nuclear age is ever-increasing nuclearization.[127] In their aesthetic reconceptualizations of nuclear infrastructural thought, Baldwin and Delany offer an alternative temporality centered on something like resonance: a narrative structure that registers the presence of the past in the present without making history the determining feature of the now.

Both writers inhabit the paradoxical position described so powerfully by Saidiya Hartman in *Lose Your Mother: A Journey along the Atlantic Slave Route,* whereby the urgency of remembering and acknowledging the past of the African diaspora is matched only by the impossibility of such a task in a country built on the suppression of Black, white, and Native histories. The amnesiac, Indigenous Kid feels, terribly, his lack of a history, of a name ("his missing name was a sudden ache and, suddenly, he wanted it, wanted it" [327]); when Delany writes in his autobiography that "history . . . is what most of us do *not* remember, what most of us *cannot* speak of," it resonates both with Kid's namelessness and across time to a later, mournful line of Baldwin's: "later, in the midnight hour, the missing identity aches. One can neither assess nor overcome the storm of the middle passage. One is mysteriously shipwrecked forever, in the Great New World. The slave is in another condition, as are his heirs: *I told Jesus it would be all right if He changed my name. If He changed my name.*"[128] The condition of the slave is to be ripped from one's origin, and "the only sure inheritance passed from one generation to the next was this loss"; how, then, could the heirs of the enslaved rely on a form of emplotment that required the consonance of origins and endings?[129] To believe that you can dispense with history is a luxury of whiteness, as Delany makes clear in his damning depiction of the steely middle-class security fantasies of Mrs. Richards, and as Baldwin insists throughout his career. But when history is *already* absent, absolutely lost, the presence of that absence must be registered as the lost origin of any plot: the impossible algebra of a Genesis-to-Revelation emplotment when the genesis of your story is lost at sea. Delany replaces Kermode's *tick-tock* with the ongoing resonance of the *tic-tic-tic,* and Baldwin, too, takes up what would in a Kermodian apocalyptic model be placed in the future to provide coherence and brings it insistently into the present. The effect of bringing the apocalyptic future into the present is transfigurative. In *The Black Atlantic,* Paul Gilroy takes up Seyla Benhabib's concepts of the politics of fulfillment and the politics of transfiguration to analyze two distinct strains in Black liberation rhetoric. The politics of fulfillment is based on the typological model; it rests on "the notion that a future society will be able to realise the social and political promise that present society has left unaccomplished."[130] As I have argued, late Baldwin critiques the limits of such a politics: that demanding the fulfillment of an old promise limits you to the terms in which that promise was made, terms that will never be redemptive for African Americans in the United States. In its place, Baldwin offers us something like Gilroy's politics of transfiguration. Such a politics "emphasises the emergence of qualitatively new desires, social relations, and modes of association within the racial community of interpretation and resistance and between that group and its erstwhile oppressors"; it seeks not the ideal version of existing social conditions but a new one.[131] While Gilroy defines the politics of transfiguration as essentially a future-oriented mode, emerging from a "revolutionary or eschatological apocalypse," however, Baldwin's novel, positioned within the futurelessness of the Black nuclear city, forecloses the futurity on which a postapocalyptic vision of an equitable future relies.[132]

In *Tell Me,* apocalypse functions not to evoke the better world that will come after the last days but a different way of living that does not rely on their arrival. The final pages of the novel, beginning with the city on a hill image repeated from *Go Tell It,* create a repetitive temporality that produces transfiguration without futurity, as Leo asks himself a Judgment Day question: "where will you be, when that first trumpet sounds?" (476–77). Christopher takes Leo to an underground nightclub where the trumpet sounds again, not in a rhetorical-question future but in the present: "And the dancers seemed, nearly, in the flickering, violent light, with their beads flashing, their long hair flying, their robes . . . and with the music assaulting them like the last,

last trumpet, to be dancing in their graveclothes, raised from the dead" (481–82). In contrast to the underground of the fallout shelter, where whites "scurry" to avoid changes in the racial order, this underground space full of "very, very young" people, "black and white," who "dared to embrace each other in the sight of all the world" and are "oblivious to the presence of the cops" (480), signifies a transformation in Leo's present, in this world. Leo describes the dance as a "rite," a ritual act, built on repetition (481). And in the final line of the novel, Baldwin balances the futural apocalypticism of the world that is soon to be overturned with a repetition that writes us back to the beginning, when Leo had his heart attack onstage: "and then I did a new play, and so I found myself, presently, standing in the wings again, waiting for my cue" (484).

In contrast to the futural imaginary of civil defense that defines "nuclear apocalypse as urban renewal," then, Baldwin's apocalypse thus insists on transfiguration not in the utopian future but in the resolutely non-utopian, repetitive, maybe even boring or aesthetically disappointing present. Transfiguration for Baldwin, as for Delany, lies not in the spectacular destruction and re-creation of urban infrastructures but in the radical shifts in perspective that would allow them to be redispositioned, to signify differently. Leo indicates what it might mean to live "presently" when he recognizes that the city on a hill is a plague town: "Not in my lifetime would this plague end, and, now, all that I most treasured, wine, talk, laughter, love, the embrace of a friend, the light in the eyes of a lover . . . would have to be stolen, each day lived as though it were my last, for my own mortality was not more certain than the storm that was rising to engulf us all" (478). The "as though" changes the present, giving it something of Kermode's *kairotic* immanence, but the futureless narrative form declines to fulfill the function that connects *kairos* to typological fulfillment. In Kermode's definition, "the notion of fulfillment is essential; the *kairos* transforms the past, validates Old Testament types and prophecies, establishes concord with origins as well as ends."[133] But Leo is resolutely cut off from his origins; his father—uniquely non-American among Baldwin's father characters—has come from Barbados and has failed to bring anything of his past that might provide such a concord. Ends are equally impossible within the narrative; while John Grimes in *Go Tell It* undergoes a personal crisis and resolution on the threshing room floor of his church that serves as the dramatic climax of the book, Leo Proudhammer has no such climax, nor does Baldwin hint that one is just around the corner. Indeed, the language of sexual tension and release that hovers behind the language of narrative tension and climax is troubled throughout the novel, as Leo repeatedly experiences situations where "I was sexually excited, too, but in an eerie way; it was a tension which contained no possibility of release" (291–92). The apocalyptic tide that Leo sees approaching is resolutely of this world rather than a future one and must be experienced in the mode in which he finds himself at the novel's end: "presently."

To acknowledge the severity of the catastrophe, the foundational quality of the absent origin of Black history, is not, for Baldwin or Delany, to lapse into a world of postapocalyptic anomie without political possibility.[134] Rather, it allows for the present to become the primary space of meaning as the future becomes unmoored from the past in an affective time frame in which we have always been, and will have always been, disappointed. This paradox has been at the heart of the relationship between Blackness, citizenship, and time in America and was acute in the 1950s and 1960s as Black liberation politics attempted to maintain hope in the face of ongoing disappointment. The temporality in which hope gives way to disappointment is, however, one that the history of race in the Americas renders unstable. As Malcolm X asked in 1964, "how can you thank a man for giving you what's already yours? How then can you thank him for giving you only part of what's already yours? You haven't even made progress, if what's being given to you, you should have had already. That's not progress."[135] The horizon of hope that David Scott's decolonial fighters see as so necessary to political struggle has always already failed in X's analysis; history is irredeemable, and so it would be necessary to position disappointment not in the future or the present, as something to be avoided, but structurally, as constitutive of African American relationships to the state. When Baldwin and Delany resist the logic of redemptive emplotment, they do so not only because such emplotments have tended to work out badly for Black bodies in America but because the story-without-origin of Blackness hollows out the temporalities upon which a redemptive emplotment relies.

What, then, of Baldwin's and Delany's deterministic cities? Both authors represent and deconstruct the great American myths of the city: the city on a hill, the Black inner city, the city as nuclear infrastructure.

In so doing, they combine an analysis of the nuclear city with a reckoning with the long history of how race, environment, and time have been braided together in the Western world, showing both the extreme power of this constellation to determine lives and infrastructures and the instability of any ideological system that is so thoroughly founded upon that which it claims to despise. Taking up the futurelessness imposed on Blackness by the nuclear complex and using it to negate the typological history of the Pilgrims, civil defense, and the African American Exodus narrative, these two novels reanimate a spectral counterhistory of the American errand that, failing to support the city on a hill justification for American interventionism, was not written into the history of the United States produced by Cold War American studies. In 1622, Robert Cushman argued against the Exodus analogy so beloved of early settlers traveling to America by rejecting the interpretation of colonial settlement as typological fulfillment. "Neither is there any land or possession now," he wrote, "like unto the possession which the Jews had in Canaan. . . . Now there is no land of that Sanctimony, no land so appropriated; none typical [that is, none that can serve as a type for Christians]: much less any that can be said to be given of God to any nation as was Canaan, which they and their seed must dwell in." In language strikingly similar to Delany's unreal Bellona and Baldwin's repeated motifs of the exile and the wanderer, Cushman argued that "now we are in all places strangers and Pilgrims, travelers and sojourners, most properly, having no dwelling but in this earthen Tabernacle; our dwelling is but a wandering, and our abiding but as a fleeting, and in a word our home is nowhere."[136] In *Tell Me* and *Dhalgren*, Delany and Baldwin show what a narrative might look like that negated the apocalyptic writing-together of time, space, and race that has characterized America from the start and that infrastructured its cities in new ways in the nuclear age: a present consonant with neither beginning nor ending but resonant with both, formed by and resistant to apocalypse, that must reckon with both disappointment and difference. Against a white American surety, they posit a contingent or speculative Black reality that unsettles the determinants of narrative and geography. For even as, in Ellison's words, "geography was fate," "Harlem" has always been the place that America might otherwise, speculatively following Cushman, Baldwin, and Delany, have been: outside of geography and free from fate—"*nowhere*."[137]

3

Star Wars, AIDS, and Queer Endings

Life is a window of vulnerability. It seems
a shame to close it.

—Donna Haraway, "The Biopolitics
of Postmodern Bodies"

IT SOUNDS LIKE THE BEGINNING of a joke: Roy Cohn and Ethel Rosenberg walk into a bar. Except that they don't. No, Roy has Ethel executed, sends her to the electric chair on June 19, 1953, by illegally influencing the judge at her trial for espionage. Ethel comes back in 1986, walking into Cohn's house at 244 East Eighty-Seventh Street, New York City, as he writhes on the floor, unable to control any longer the AIDS-related abdominal pain that he has been suppressing in his previous conversation. As Roy insults her, Ethel telephones an ambulance; as he lies dying, she taunts him with the specter of disbarment; in the moment of his death, she prays for him. In every staging of Tony Kushner's massive and now canonical play *Angels in America* (1991–92), these two emblematic figures of the Cold War face off from within a history that binds them together—a history, Ethel claims, that is about to "crack wide open."[1]

Ethel's historiographic statement places *Angels in America* firmly within a millennial setting. Apocalyptic sentiments abound in the play, surpassing distinctions of character, ontological status, race, gender, sexuality, disability, class identity, serostatus, or age: Harper Pitt, the miserable Valium-addicted wife of closeted Supreme Court clerk Joe, sees "systems dying, old fixed orders spiraling apart" (16); Joe imagines a world where "overnight everything you owe anything to, justice, or love, had really gone away" (72); his mother, Hannah, matriarch of their Mormon family, describes the times as "late in the day . . . for saints and everyone. That's all. That's all" (83). Ethel, ghost of McCarthyite eras past, apostrophizes the title of the first volume of the play when she tells Roy that "millennium approaches" (112); it approaches, we learn from Prior Walter, recently diagnosed with AIDS, like a nuclear warhead from above: "I feel like something terrifying is on its way, you know, like a missile from outer space, and it's plummeting down towards the earth, and I'm ground zero" (98). Finally, in the last, staggeringly effective moment of the first part of the two-part play, "a sound, like a plummeting meteor, tears down from very, very far above the earth. . . . We hear a terrifying CRASH as something immense strikes earth; the whole building shudders and a part of the bedroom ceiling, lots of plaster and lathe and wiring, crashes to the floor. And then in a shower of unearthly white light, spreading great opalescent gray-silver wings, the Angel descends into the room and floats above the bed" (118).

Prior Walter, touched by the "wine-dark kiss of the angel of death" (20), is the play's official "Prophet. Seer. Revelator" (88). The angel that crashes through his bedroom ceiling, named the "Continental Principality of America" (3), tells him that to prevent the oncoming dissolution of the world, humanity must "be still. Toil no more."[2] The intense feeling of impending doom that climaxes at the end of *Millennium Approaches* transitions into a more durational mode in *Perestroika*, as new alliances are formed, new possibilities are envisioned, and Prior rejects the Angel's terminal exhortation in favor of the blessing that he demands having wrestled her and won: "*More Life*" (146, italics and capitalization original). For Ethel and Roy, however, things aren't so simple. Ethel announces a new temporality that she also embodies; her appearance on the stage is evidence that history, understood as the unidirectional forward movement of time, is coming apart at the seams. She is the speaker of the play's most apocalyptic line, ventriloquizing the playwright in a way that suggests her centrality to the play's thematic concerns. Roy, too, is a central figure in the play, standing in for the worst aspects of Cold War politics and closeted homosexuality and serving as a connecting figure between the two. But neither Ethel nor Roy can enter into the future projected at the end of the play. While every other character is accounted for in the final scenes of *Perestroika,* Ethel disappears when Roy dies, having prompted Louis, a lapsed Jew and Prior's ex-lover, to recite the Kaddish over Roy's body.

This chapter takes as its starting point a very simple question: what are Roy Cohn and Ethel Rosenberg doing in *Angels in America*? This, as simple questions do, metastasizes into some larger ones. What does it mean to have an emblem of the 1950s show up in 1986? What does it do to a work of historical fiction to have one real historical personage prompting a fictional character to pray over the body of another real historical figure? And what does this tell us about history and apocalypse, about safety and risk, about how we wish to encounter the past and how the past in turn responds to us?

These questions touch on many broader debates. This chapter thus ranges widely, taking in the peculiar spatiotemporal politics of Reagan's pet military infrastructure project the Strategic Defense Initiative, the rhetorical construction of AIDS in the 1980s, the ontological status of historical characters in fiction, and contemporary theories of queer temporality. It locates in Reagan's America the emergence of a new form of public time: an insistent backward connection between the 1980s and the 1950s that allows neoconservative America to imagine itself as safe through a retroactive temporality that relocates the present to a prior era when conditions are imagined as having been more favorable. I call this temporal regime *retrocontainment,* bringing into the realm of time the spatial policy of containment that, as Alan Nadel has argued, defined the late 1940s and 1950s.[3] Beyond the realms of nostalgia and kitsch, the circle skirts and Elvis hairdos that appeared on screens and streets in the late 1970s and 1980s were also imbricated in Reagan's hawkish nuclear policies and the official nonresponse to the AIDS epidemic as the ruling powers tried to wish away the Soviet nuclear arsenal and the newly visible gay community. As a form of public time, retrocontainment had catastrophic effects, legitimating a massive increase in military spending, on one hand, and the brutal ignoring of the AIDS crisis, on the other. *Angels in America,* in creating a space where different temporalities, including retrocontainment, millennialism, prophecy, and radical futurelessness, coexist and challenge each other, stages both the prophylactic efforts of retrocontainment and its necessary rupture. The bonds of history can tighten, hurting you but drawing you toward that which you need to know; they can also just hurt you. This chapter is about the ties that bind, and the times that break them.

Back to the Past in 1980s America

Ethel and Roy are by no means the only figures linking the America of the 1980s to that of the 1950s. The cultural and political rhetoric of the Reagan era was built on the possibility of returning to an idealized version of 1950s America, one in which mother stayed home (but did not homosexualize her sons through over-mothering them), father went to work each day and came home ready to discipline the children, and little Tommy and Sally played outside without supervision and were as ready to obey their parents as they were to duck and cover on command.[4] As Michael Dwyer writes, "by 1985 American culture was deeply engaged in a fantasy of return to the more peaceful and prosperous fifties, a fantasy that was circulated and recirculated in American culture throughout the Reagan Era."[5] In the March 1986 issue of *Esquire,* TV critic Tom Shales described the eighties as the "Re Decade," in which America looked back to the fifties in order to "replay, recycle, retrieve, reprocess, and rerun."[6] Films such as *Diner* (1982), *The Outsiders* (1983), *Footloose* (1984), *Blue Velvet* (1986), *Stand by Me* (1986), and, paradigmatically, *Back to the Future* (1985) reflected a complex and hypercathected relationship between the two eras that served a number of purposes in Reagan's America.

These purposes are generally understood to be consonant with the rise to power of neoconservatism, even tautologically so. Neoconservatism refers almost exclusively back to the fifties, not as a ten-year span of time but as what Mary Caputi calls "a richly defined American metaphor," an overdetermined referent that brings with it an almost endless supply of connotations regarding security, prosperity, conformity, and the suburbanized American Dream.[7] It is impossible to imagine neoconservatism without the fifties; in calling for a return to family values rather than to, say, the gold standard, Reaganite neoconservatism established a connection to the earlier decade that came to define right-wing values as those of the metaphorized fifties—a rededication to the nuclear family and consumer culture, in this example—

rather than those of a metaphorized nineteenth century involving limits to financial speculation and slaughtering one's own pigs.[8] For Reagan and his ideological fellow travelers, an appeal to an idealized fifties worked to associate neoconservatism with a time remembered as the last haven of innocence before the social upheavals of the 1960s and 1970s. And it worked well—by the presidential election in 1984, Reagan's advisor Richard Darman was able to tell his campaign team to push the idea that "an attack on Reagan is tantamount to an attack on America's idealized image of itself—where a vote against Reagan is in some subliminal sense, a vote against mythic America."[9] Reagan, already himself a functioning metonym for the 1950s thanks to his B movie days, was able to fuse himself, the fifties, and the ideal form of America together so effectively that in the 1984 election, he walked away with the electoral college votes of forty-nine out of fifty states.[10]

That a nostalgic relationship with the 1950s is key to Reaganite neoconservatism has been well documented; so, too, has the fact that the "fifties" posited by eighties nostalgia was almost entirely fictional. Dwyer notes that "for the fifties to be considered 'a simpler time,' the emergence of feminism and civil rights movements, concerns over juvenile delinquency and global nuclear war, furor over the obscenity of the Beats or Elvis Presley, and sundry other cultural shocks from the Red Scare to Kinsey Reports must all be elided or forgotten," while Stephanie Coontz's *The Way We Never Were* describes the image of the traditional family associated with the fifties as "an ahistorical amalgam of structures, values, and behaviors that never coexisted in the same time and place."[11] This combination of repressed historical complexity and ahistorical bricolage is central to Fredric Jameson's theory of the eighties' relationship to the past in "Postmodernism; or, The Cultural Logic of Late Capitalism." In this essay, first published in *New Left Review* in 1984, Jameson described his contemporary moment as simultaneously obsessed with images of the past and incapable of any meaningful relationship to history. The fifties serve as Jameson's paradigmatic example; he describes them as America's "privileged lost object of desire" and claims that nostalgia for that time reflects "a new and original historical situation in which we are condemned to seek History by way of our own pop images and simulacra of that history, which itself remains forever out of reach."[12] Our own representations of history come to stand in for any real historical referent, marking the end of "our lived possibility of experiencing history in some active way."[13]

Jameson's theory has not gone unchallenged; his evocation of nostalgia as a unified and contentless affect, in particular, has been countered by more nuanced accounts of the role of nostalgia in psychic and political life.[14] My quibble with Jameson, however, comes less from his assumption that there is only one way in which the eighties encountered the fifties and more from the fact that he does not account for why the fifties in particular were able to fill the role of "lost object of desire" at that historical moment. If the past has become a simulacrum, fabulously textual, then there would be no inherent logic privileging the fifties as object of fascination; it was not, before the establishment of fifties nostalgia as a primary discourse, a necessary or even an obvious object. It took an enormous amount of cultural and political work to construct a fictional, idealized "fifties" to which the eighties could then refer back; the image of the fifties created by the eighties thus tells us more about the Reagan era than it does about the 1950s themselves.

Mary Caputi's account of the positive benefits of the fifties as constructed nostalgia-object describes fantasies of a singular American identity, a simple and righteous national purpose, an evil Soviet empire against which to define itself, a postwar economic boom, and a generally Edenic condition in which "an innocent state of moral rectitude is believed to have gone hand in hand with a lavish material generosity."[15] At the same time, as Alan Nadel has shown, the suturing of the 1980s to an idealized 1950s "reinvigorated a Cold War sensibility that bridged the Vietnam era," eliding the catastrophic (to neoconservatives) rise of social justice movements in the 1960s and 1970s as well as the national disgraces of Vietnam and Watergate through a willed act of historical amnesia.[16] Taken together, these fantasies indicate a desire in the eighties for a return to the ideology of containment, the paradigmatic late forties/fifties conceptual apparatus that construed America and Americans as singular, coherent, and protected.

There is something so elegant about this formulation that it almost seems a shame to question it. It seems logical that the fracturing of an imagined singular American identity in the rise of civil rights movements, the disastrous experience of the Vietnam War, and the impact of increasing globalization on American industry would lead to a desire to return to the good old days of strong borders, both personal and national. And this is, in many respects, true; Susan Jeffords, for example, convincingly depicts an eighties in which Reagan "reestablished the boundaries of the presidency," and the "hard bodies" that permeated Hollywood at the time "reestablished the boundaries not only of the individual masculine figure but of the nation as a whole."[17] The repeated imagery in *Angels in America* of the ozone layer disintegrating and skin being torn away demonstrates the connection between the attrition of boundaries and painful change, again connecting a conservative impulse, the rejection of change, to a need to shore up those boundaries at any cost. What is not accounted for in this ideological wormhole theory, however, is that neoconservatism in the eighties, on both a political and cultural level, explicitly rejected the policy of containment.

The central aspect of containment policy as it is taken up by Nadel in his theory of containment culture is the issue of borders: that a threat can be kept at bay through the establishment of impermeable boundaries through which the enemy cannot penetrate. This was established as U.S. foreign policy after the publication of George Kennan's "The Sources of Soviet Conduct" in 1947, which argued that "the main element of any United States policy toward the Soviet Union must be that of long-term, patient but firm and vigilant containment of Russian expansionist tendencies."[18] Not only Russian armies but also Russian ideologies needed to be contained; "hot" wars of the Cold War period did not involve the beating back of Russian troops from foreign soil but rather the prevention of the establishment of communist governments in countries from Korea to Vietnam to Nicaragua. The cultural weight that Nadel gives to containment in 1950s America stems from this aspect of containment; while physical violence against communists was limited, the defense against ideological contamination was everywhere, and various social and cultural mechanisms functioned to preserve the strong boundaries upon which a sense of American security depended.

The concept of containment also involves, however, the concept of coexistence, and it is this aspect of containment doctrine that was rejected by neoconservatives in the 1980s. Phyllis Schafly, who divided her time between military arguments and cultural ones, redefined Kennan as an "apologist for the Soviet Union" whose policy of necessary

coexistence with the USSR led to "a paralyzing dread of death by nuclear incineration" and thus to the establishment of mutually assured
destruction (MAD) as the only way to defend America against Soviet
threat.[19] Schafly, along with high-profile neoconservatives Daniel Gra-
ham, William Rusher, and Newt Gingrich, called for a defense of America that would be less passive than deterrence, which they described
as a "carefully constructed [by liberals] chamber of horrors" designed
to promote a liberal welfare state.[20] Reagan himself strongly rejected
the doctrine of containment. By the mid-1970s, Reagan had made it
known that, in the words of his secretary of defense, Caspar Weinberger, "it wasn't about containment; it was about winning the Cold
War."[21] In the first half of the 1980s, just as the American obsession
with the fifties reached hegemonic proportions, the ideology that created fifties culture appeared to have reached the end of its usefulness.

The technology that made the neoconservative rejection of containment possible was as conceptually elegant and entirely fictional as
the culturally constructed fifties themselves. On March 23, 1983, Ronald Reagan announced "a vision of the future which offers hope. It is
that we embark on a program to counter the awesome Soviet missile
threat with measures that are defensive."[22] Reagan proposed the development of a space-based antiballistic missile system that would shield
America from incoming missiles, rendering nuclear weapons "impotent and obsolete."[23] Although Reagan insisted that this would be a defensive weapons system and in no way offensively inclined, with such
a system in place, America would have essentially won the Cold War.
The balance of MAD would shift hugely in America's favor, creating a
world in which the United States could carry out a nuclear attack on
the USSR without fear of retaliation. The Soviet Union, in the face of
such a threat, would have no choice but to capitulate to American demands. The Strategic Defense Initiative (SDI), or, as it almost immediately became known, Star Wars, allowed Americans to imagine, for the
first time since the beginning of the arms race, a world in which they
did not have to coexist with their opponents but could vanquish them.
The concept of containing the Soviet threat was replaced with the
image of an impregnable shield or umbrella over the United States, restoring America to a state of nuclear security that had not existed since
the USSR developed the capacity for first and second nuclear strikes in
the early 1960s.[24]

As with the "fifties," the plausibility or potential reality of such a system is not my focus here (although the short version goes something like this: it was absolutely implausible, the technology for it did not exist and still doesn't, despite the fact that research for the program still continues at a cost of around $9 billion a year).[25] It is my contention, rather, that as an object of fantasy, the SDI, which generated an enormous amount of discourse from the moment of its announcement in 1983 to its relegation to back burner status by George H. W. Bush in 1989, both was produced by and changed the meaning of the intensely charged relationship between the 1980s and the 1950s. In proposing to make nuclear weapons "impotent and obsolete," Reagan was essentially promising a form of time travel, not to a future where nuclear bombs would no longer exist (after all, he rejected unilateral disarmament, the other obvious way of getting rid of nuclear weapons), but to a past where America was secure in its nuclear superiority. As a spatial defense infrastructure, SDI was, literally, full of holes. For all of the talk of umbrellas and shields, for all of the eighties' obsession with hard bodies, to predicate a national metaphor of defense on an impermeable boundary was no longer possible in the mid-1980s. Even if a perfect defense system over America were possible, there was no longer a Manichean Other to defend against on a huge scale. SDI could not protect against a nuclear weapon set off using the kind of guerilla tactics against which America had already lost in Vietnam, and increased international trade and more flexible borders led to imagined scenarios of nuclear bombs entering the country on the ground level; in a 1984 editorial cartoon titled *Modern Warfare,* for instance, Dick Locher juxtaposed a drawing of a giant space-based defense system bristling with missiles, lasers, and satellite disks, labeled SDI, with one of a stereotypically Middle Eastern–looking man crawling through a tunnel holding sticks of dynamite with a lit fuse.[26] The need to shore up Americanness with some kind of containment structure was no less strong in the 1980s than it had been in the 1940s and 1950s. Given the generally recognized impossibility of creating impermeable boundaries, however, if there were to be a fantasy of containment in the 1980s, then it would have to exist not on a spatial plane but on a temporal one.

The SDI thus encapsulates what I call, pace Nadel, a doctrine of retrocontainment. As a fictional technology, it was uniquely positioned to answer a broad range of American anxieties, from the decline of American technological superiority to the loss of American moral superiority after Vietnam (Reagan plants his flag firmly on the moral high ground when he asks rhetorically "wouldn't it be better to save lives than to avenge them?").[27] In a 1981 document titled "Space: The Crucial Frontier" written to persuade Reagan to take a more aggressive approach to conducting the Cold War in space, the Citizens Advisory Council on National Space Policy linked the establishment of military infrastructures in space with the restoration of all that this collection of Republican scientists and science fiction writers felt that America had lost: "A properly developed space program," they write, "can go far toward restoring national pride while developing significant and possibly decisive military and economic advantages. In exploring space we will rediscover frontiers and more than frontiers; we can rediscover progress."[28] SDI may have been an imaginary infrastructure, but it still brought with it all of the phantasmic benefits of other large-scale infrastructure projects that function to give humans a sense of mastery over time.[29]

In the case of SDI, this mastery would take the form of being able to establish a closed temporal circuit, which would make America strong not by strengthening its borders but by enabling it to destroy the threats against it before they could even get started. For Nadel, the inherent contradictions of containment culture eventually destroyed its ideological utility; by the mid-1960s, he argues, "the problems with the logic of containment... had started to be manifest in a public discourse displaying many traits that would later be associated with postmodernism."[30] As the rhetoric surrounding SDI demonstrates, however, it was precisely the postmodern sense that history was newly flexible that made containment in a different form accessible for a new generation: not as a shield but as the DeLorean through which, as Nadel argues in *Flatlining on the Field of Dreams,* America will be saved not by *making* but by *remaking* history.[31] In its new temporal guise, retrocontainment offered America a second chance at world domination.

The language of reversal pervades discussions of SDI and Reaganite foreign policy, which aimed to retroactively reverse the decision made in the late 1940s to contain rather than roll back communism. Historian Jeffery Cook quotes Russian commentator Yhuri Zhukov, who observed in *Pravda* in 1975 that "'the resurrected political dinosaur proposes a . . . policy of rolling back communism.' Most astonishingly, Zhukov noted that Reagan 'promises the restoration of the old system' in the countries of Eastern Europe."[32] The SDI was to provide the mechanism by which this "rolling back" could occur. In his SDI speech, Reagan offered what was essentially a do-over for atomic scientists: "I call upon the scientific community in our country, those who gave us nuclear weapons, to turn their great talents now to the cause of mankind and world peace, to give us the means of rendering these nuclear weapons impotent and obsolete."[33] Reagan's claim that he wants to make *all* nuclear weapons impotent is disingenuous; it took less than a year for Weinberger to clarify in front of the Senate Armed Services Committee that "if we can get a system which is effective and which we know can render their weapons impotent, we could be back in a situation we were in, for example, when we were the only nation with a nuclear weapon."[34] In 1985, E. P. Thompson drew out both the political and temporal aspects of SDI as an imaginary infrastructure when he argued that "in its ideological expression Star Wars is the ultimate decomposition of deterrence theory, and the attempt by US nuclear ideologists to return to the womb of Hiroshima. . . . It is out of that regression to an idealized golden sanctuary in the past that the ideological and political drive of Star Wars has come. Let us abolish the Other's Bomb!"[35] Retrocontainment is the iron fist of nuclear superiority in the velvet glove of fifties nostalgia; the relationship between the 1980s and the 1950s, far from being limited to Jamesonian pastiche or even to the cultural or aesthetic realm, is inextricably bound up with a shift in foreign policy and military spending priorities that was designed to restore America to a position of unstoppable global power.

The replacement of spatial boundaries with temporal ones was not limited to discourses of military defense in the 1980s but also characterized the ways in which a new threat to bodily/national integrity was imagined. The AIDS epidemic, as many critics have argued, was from the start understood in military terms of siege and invasion, even as Cold War militarism was itself described in the medical language of epidemic and quarantine. Indeed, Donna Haraway argued in 1989 that Star Wars and AIDS were linked as emblems of a broader immunological discourse that imagined both the body and the nation as seeking "the perfection of the fully defended, 'victorious' self . . . whether located in the abstract spaces of national discourses, or in the equally abstract spaces of our inner bodies."[36] A 1987 cartoon by Paul Conrad linked the defensive fantasies of sexual and nuclear barrier methods, juxtaposing phallic missiles labeled "Nuclear Weapons" with the title "Speaking of the need for condoms . . ."[37] Mediating between the distant environments of space and the intimate environments of the human body, immunology served as a crossover discourse that emphasized the importance of maintaining boundaries in the face of their apocalyptically threatening rupture.

The advent of AIDS, however, like the perceived Soviet threat, brought with it both the desire for containment and the recognition that spatial containment was impossible. In both the sexualized discourse of missile defense and the militarized discourse of AIDS, imagined boundaries are consistently evoked only to be ruptured. While the missile shield in space could be thwarted because "once in space, a Soviet missile might release ten or more warheads together with hundreds of decoys and quantities of so-called penetration aids such as chaff or clouds of infrared-emitting gases,"[38] the frequent description of the HIV virus as a "Trojan horse" invokes the potential for boundaries to be penetrated at multiple scales through "the concealment 'in the womb of the horse' that figures . . . viral action at the cellular level, infection at the level of the whole person, and the 'attack' of AIDS on the 'American homosexual community.'"[39] Both the proposal by secretary of education William Bennett and senator Jesse Helms that people infected with HIV be quarantined and the passage of the Helms amendment forbidding the spread of gay-positive educational material about AIDS operate through a boundary-obsessed logic that speaks more of its fears—gays walk invisibly among us! Reading about them can make you gay!—than of any effort to prevent the spread of the disease or to provide resources for those already infected. Even crossover allusions to the Maginot line in both SDI and AIDS discourses summon the image of a boundary that was doomed to fail.[40]

As with the SDI, the threat of boundary collapse in the discourse of AIDS carried a major affective charge. Jacqueline Foertsch describes how "the utopic desire for boundaries that hold ignites the rhetoric of the reactionary right throughout the cold war and AIDS eras, with destruction of these seen as equivalent to apocalypse";[41] I would add to this only that the desire for safety in boundaries is not limited to the reactionary right and that apocalypse is inconsistently defined and applied across different racial, socioeconomic, and sexual/gender identity groups in the 1980s (as Sarah Schulman's 1991 novel *People in Trouble* expertly delineates, "it was the beginning of the end of the world, but not everyone noticed right away").[42] Arthur and Marilouise Kroker, pursuing "the deep relationship between AIDS and Star Wars research," analyze them both in terms of boundaries and a spatial understanding of containment:

> The rhetoric surrounding both AIDS and Star Wars focuses on the total breakdown of immunity systems: AIDS can be perceived in such frightening terms because its appearance indicates the destruction of the internal immunological system of the body (the *crisis within*); while the rhetoric of Star Wars creates, and then responds to, generalized panic fear about the breakdown of the technological immunity systems of society as a whole (the Bomb as the *crisis without*). Both Star Wars and AIDS are theorised in the common research language of cellular genetics, where missiles are viruses and invading antigens body missiles. . . . Both AIDS research and Star Wars deal with ruined surfaces (the planet and the body), both operate in a common language of exterminism and suppression.[43]

While not explicitly referencing the doctrine of containment, the Krokers link this paranoid relationship with boundaries to earlier periods of the Cold War. In the 1980s obsession with bodily purity, they see "a *recyclage* of the McCarthyism of the 1950s which, this time on the terrain of bodily fluids rather than loyalty oaths, insists on the (unattainable) ideal of absolute purity of the body's circulatory exchanges as the new gold standard of an immunological politics."[44] In an inverse gesture to that made by Reaganite neoconservatives, the fifties function here as shorthand not for nuclear superiority and moral righteousness but for the oppressive state structures that mobilize the fear of boundary collapse to establish ever-greater disciplinary procedures. The fact that the Krokers call this mobilization "body McCarthyism" suggests a relationship between AIDS and SDI that is not exclusively spatial. With their backward look to the 1950s, they enter into the wider discursive arena of the intensely imbricated temporal relationship between the eighties and the fifties.

The strategy of retrocontainment was no less active in attempting to contain AIDS and homosexuality than it was in dealing with the atomic threat. The archetypal AIDS body, that of Rock Hudson, whose death from AIDS in 1985 brought the disease into the public eye, established the relationship between the fifties and the eighties as a privileged site upon which AIDS discourse would be constructed. According to Richard Meyer, the media depiction of the body of a 1950s leading man transformed into the AIDS-wracked body of a gay man "described the collapse of a particular fantasy of male containment and sexual safety—a fantasy once attached to Rock Hudson's body, a fantasy once embodied by Rock Hudson's closet."[45] If the neoconservatives of the 1980s imagined and worked toward a return to a state of nuclear superiority located in the fifties, then they also hearkened "back to an America of the past, when homosexuality was a taboo word and homosexuals were safely hidden in the closet . . . a mythical golden age in American history . . . the 1950s."[46] As Marlon Riggs wrote of the extraordinary measures taken by Reagan's government to silence queer voices in the 1980s, neoconservatism's "return to traditional values" was built on a more fundamental vision of the closet as national goal, of a forced return of queerness to "historic cells of solitude, shame, and silence."[47]

The shocking ease and even pleasure with which prominent Republicans imagined—and imagine—life after homosexuals has been documented and theorized by Eve Kosofsky Sedgwick, Leo Bersani, and Lee Edelman.[48] As with the SDI, however, what looks like a dream of futurity—"the fantasy trajectory toward a life after the homosexual," life *after* gays, when they and the bomb are "obsolete"—is also a dream of *return,* of rendering the enemy's atomic bomb or the gay man's phallus "impotent," as they were (in this imagination) before the arms race and the gay rights movement.[49] Even at the height of the Lavender Scare in 1950, when homosexuals were being purged from government positions at twice the rate of communists, the "threat" posed by them was curiously passive. Unlike communists, who worked actively to destroy the American way of life, homosexuals were dangerous because they were "vulnerable" to blackmail.[50] The AIDS language of "risk groups" and "passive" sex roles reflects both a continued aversion to "effeminate" men and a desire to go back to a time when "effeminate" was the only flavor of gay on the public menu; not that there would be no gays, as Bersani and Sedgwick suggest, but rather that gays remain exclusively effete, passive, and vulnerable in order that the heterosexual white male might have something against which to define himself.[51] Macho, active, and indestructible all need the other half of the binary if they are to signify anything at all; as Edelman writes in his 1993 essay "The Mirror and the Tank," "the popular homophobic discourse on AIDS that depends upon these apocalyptic conjunctions of narcissism, passivity, the anus, and death serves . . . to secure the ideological construction of the subject as heterosexual male."[52] The "neutral" subject cannot exist without his Other, but if his Other starts encroaching on his territory (say, by reappropriating "macho" as a homosexual fetish in the increasing visibility of the leather scene),[53] then it becomes imperative to put him back in his place—the place, in this case, being a 1950s holding cell where gay vulnerability is not, as it became in the age of AIDS, contagious.[54] Retrocontainment operates in 1980s AIDS discourse by restoring the equivalence of gay men and vulnerability in the public eye, allowing for a fantasy of forcible recloseting through a return to a 1950s definition of what it means to be gay.

Against the apocalyptic threats of nuclear and sexual vulnerability, retrocontainment serves its purpose—that of shoring up a straightened, whitened, seronegativized, and masculinized American national identity—in the Reagan era by functioning as a form of prophylactic time. Stepping in where spatial prophylaxes fail, it locates safety within a restricting and oppressive closed temporal loop in which the present is rendered safe by returning to a past that was, from the perspective of the 1980s, more secure. It matters not, from a 1980s point of view, that fifties America was wracked with nuclear terror; we know that nuclear war did not break out, and so the fifties can be retroactively constructed as a time of safety. The attitude to the future evinced by the Star Wars debate creates the same prophylactic time loop, moving everything forward thirty years but keeping the same shape. In the discourse surrounding the SDI, the secure past is able to be returned to because a future technology is debated as if it existed in the present; Reagan refused to sacrifice SDI in disarmament talks with Gorbachev, using it as a bargaining chip in the mid-1980s despite the fact that the technology itself did not yet exist. The temporal structure of retrocontainment thus aligns with that of anxiety, described by Tim Dean in the context of potential HIV infection as "a prophylactic against harm" that operates in the future anterior, "a gesture . . . that eclipses the uncertainties of the present by anticipating a future self with the capacity to retrospectively view its former state from a safe distance."[55] Treating SDI technology as real means that it is only a matter of time until we will have been safe, and imagining backward instead of forward means that we can close the "window of vulnerability" (to borrow a phrase from Reagan) between the future moment and now by replacing it with a past moment where safety is already imagined to reside.

Just as containment relies on the construction and policing of spatial boundaries, so retrocontainment establishes and defends temporal borders that come to define acceptable modes of existence. To be safe becomes equivalent to maintaining a singular timeline defined by a millennial, unchanging stasis, and a threat to that safety is met with extreme violence, as is suggested by the apocalyptic fantasies of an unstoppable AIDS plague or nuclear holocaust that were the dark underside of an American culture seeking comfort in a sanitized past: the severed ear in the grass of its perfect 1950s lawn.[56] The operations of retrocontainment point to the construction of a highly politicized historiography by the neoconservative state: a prophylactic temporal infrastructure that was used to determine what physical infrastructures should be prioritized (in this case, massive spending on SDI over any spending at all on AIDS research and treatment), construct and maintain a sense of American identity, and define who was or was not truly American and who should have access to the rights and benefits conferred on those who make the cut.

The militarization of history in the Reagan era produced historiography as a primary battleground for American cultural politics. In the midst of proliferating representations of American history from below that sought to construct multiple and contestatory versions of America's past, the doctrine of retrocontainment defended a privileged American identity from threats abroad and at home by establishing as state policy a historiography that was both closed and singular.[57] The extent to which this model of history became central to neoconservatism can be seen in Francis Fukuyama's high-impact article "The End of History?," which appeared in 1989 in the neoconservative journal *National Interest*. Fukuyama's claim that "we have already emerged on the other side of history" appeared after the heyday of retrocontainment but was nonetheless its product, based on the same millennial vision of static, retroactive time that defined the Reagan era.[58] Fukuyama's rhetorical strategy is a familiar one: the description of something that will occur in the future (the universal acceptance and practice of free market liberalism) is treated as if it already exists in the present. The essay is split evenly between assertions that liberalism has already won and *sotto voce* acknowledgments that in fact it hasn't really won anywhere; nevertheless, unfortunate facts like the existence of Black poverty in the United States and the nonliberal political and economic situations of most of the world are simply loose ends that we may as well treat as already trimmed and fastened. The end of history in Fukuyama's essay is not, as he claims, the world implementation of liberalism but a temporal structure that he takes straight from Reagan: the future is treated as if it were the present, while the present is transferred into a past (in this case, a sanitized French Revolution) that guarantees its safety. Even after the end of the Cold War, retrocontainment is the primary heuristic through which Reagan's heirs (including today's neofascist commitment to "Make America Great Again") imagine the relationship between American superiority and world history. The safety and the world-dominating position of America are contained within this historiographic circle; that history could crack wide open, in other words, becomes an act of treason and a national threat.

Will the Past Release Us? History as What Hurts
in *Angels in America*

The question of what history "means" in *Angels* has been a central one in its critical reception. David Savran's article "Ambivalence, Utopia, and a Queer Sort of Materialism: How *Angels in America* Reconstructs the Nation" has established both the position to beat on the play's historicity and that history would be the ground upon which the play's merits were debated. Savran situates his intervention within a field of critical responses to the play that had been uniformly positive—and uniformly insistent that the play itself was a historical turning point. He cites reviewers from the *New Yorker, Newsweek,* the *New Republic, Christopher Street,* and the *New York Times* who share the vision put forth by John Clum: that *Angels in America* "marks a turning point in the history of gay drama, the history of American drama, and of American literary culture."[59] Taking as his starting point the question of why such an apocalyptic and ambivalent play produced such a universally positive response expressed precisely in the terms of historical teleology, Savran argues that although *Angels* appears to operate through a Benjaminian dialectic of contradiction, in which binary oppositions function as "an oxymoron, a figure of undecidability whose contradictory being becomes an incitement to think the impossible—revolution," in fact Kushner always comes down on the side of the Enlightenment value of progress.[60] For Savran, this is a failure; *Angels* in this reading falls into "the pattern whereby the political is finally subsumed by utopian fantasies. . . . In the American way, contradiction is less disentangled than immobilized. History gives way to a concept of cosmic evolution that is far closer to Joseph Smith than to Walter Benjamin."[61] This opposition between utopianism and political efficacy has been central to critical responses since Savran's essay was published in 1995. For the most part, critics have agreed that the view of history presented by Prior in the epilogue is a nondialectical cop-out, that his assertion that "the world only spins forward" toward a time when "we will be citizens" reflects an antirevolutionary view of historical progress that maintains rather than challenges the liberal pluralist state. Charles McNulty argues that Kushner ultimately rejects Benjamin's view of history as catastrophe and "rushes headlong into a fairy tale of progress" based on "uncritical optimism," while Martin Harries writes of the ending that "the play blesses where, perhaps, it should curse."[62]

Angels in America is certainly shot through with history. Prior Walter begins the play at the very start of what Steven Kruger calls the "irreversible decline" narrative of AIDS; when he tells Louis that he has developed Kaposi's sarcoma, the revelation is framed by the story of his missing cat and the impossibility of time moving anything but forward: "I did my best Shirley Booth this morning, floppy slippers, housecoat, curlers, can of Little Friskies; 'Come back, Little Sheba, come back . . .' To no avail. Le chat, elle ne reviendra jamais, jamais . . ." (*MA* 21, ellipses original). Louis responds to this with his own historiographical approach; not only can he not deal with his lover's illness but he cannot deal with the historical decline narrative that it suggests: "maybe a person who has this neo-Hegelian positivist sense of constant historical progress towards happiness or perfection or something, who feels very powerful because he feels connected to those forces, moving uphill all the time . . . maybe that person can't, um, incorporate sickness into his sense of how things are supposed to go" (*MA* 25). When the Angel appears to Prior, she offers an end both to his decline and to history itself. History as change through time, we learn, is a result of God's creation of humans: "In creating You, Our Father-Lover unleashed / Sleeping Creation's Potential for Change" (*MA* 42); since God's abandonment of heaven and earth in 1906, the only story has been one of decay. The Angel demands of Prior that he become a prophet, telling the human race to "Cease to Progress" (*P* 45). Prior, like Jonah, runs from his calling; unlike his predecessor, however, he successfully rejects the Angel's demand, arguing that "we can't just stop. We're not rocks—progress, migration, motion is . . . modernity. It's animate, it's *animate,* it's what living things do" (*P* 130). The stasis of mass death by AIDS is rejected by Prior when he demands "more life"; this is carried out on earth when Belize acquires Roy's stash of AZT, allowing Prior to survive at least until the epilogue, when he asserts again that "the world only spins forward" (*P* 146). Articulations of different historical models and temporal infrastructures thus form the backbone of the play's thematic content, driving both character development and plot.

The debate over *Angels in America*'s historiographical structure has centered on Savran's diagnosis of the play as insufficiently dialectical. Critics trying to challenge Savran do so on his terms, either by rereading Benjamin to produce a model of dialectics more consonant with Kushner's or by arguing for the dialectical nature of hope or utopianism.[63] My own intervention is thus not aimed at casting a deciding vote on the question of whether the ending of *Angels* is revolutionary or antirevolutionary. In fact, the move I wish to propose is to suspend, just for a little while, the idea that the end of the play should be taken as its final word with regard to its model of history. This idea is central to the vast majority of the analyses of history in *Angels*; Prior's final speech in the epilogue, the commitment to "more life" that he demands as a blessing from the angels and then blesses the audience within the play's final moments, is taken as the play's argumentative conclusion as well as its narrative one, as if the purpose of the play were to rehearse the arguments in favor of progress or of stasis and then cast its vote at its conclusion. Such a reading is, in a word, apocalyptic: the complex ways in which history and temporality are represented and negotiated over the duration of this seven-hour piece are subsumed into a single meaning defined by what happens at the end. And since much of the play's conceptual apparatus revolves around the seductive but dangerous appeal of apocalyptic endings, it is important to approach Kushner's historical method not only through what is said about history in the epilogue but also through how history is structured and contested throughout the play.

Angels in America is in a strange position with regard to history. It situates itself specifically in the Reagan era; period detail includes the immediacy of Joe's investment in Reaganite ideals—"America has rediscovered itself. Its sacred position among nations. And people aren't ashamed of that like they used to be. . . . That's what President Reagan's done, Harper. He says 'Truth exists and can be spoken proudly.' And the country responds to him" (MA 26)—and the real-life illness and death of Roy Cohn (although, as Kushner points out in the introductory material, Roy died in August rather than in February 1986). Each act is carefully dated with the month of its occurrence; Perestroika opens with the announcement of the date (January 1986) by Aaleksii Antedilluvianovich Prelapsarianov (the world's oldest Bolshevik), and Millennium Approaches tells us in scene 2 that Cats and La Cage aux Folles are the hottest things on Broadway right now, situating it for any lover of a certain kind of camp somewhere in the mid-1980s (to make certain, Harper announces that it's 1985 in scene 3). In its dedication to period detail and the formal distinction between the mid-1980s, where most of the play is set, and the "present day" of the epilogue, Kushner establishes the body of the play within the genre of historical fiction: a world set in a period different from our own.[64]

This historical milieu was, however, in 1992—and still is, for some audiences—our milieu. The gap between then and now, them and us, that defines historical fiction cannot hold when the period being recreated is in living memory, even if, as Fran Lebowitz wrote in 1987, a world that feels like the present, that happened just a minute ago, is gone:

> The Impact of AIDS on the Artistic Community is that a 36-year-old writer takes time out at a memorial service for the world's preeminent makeup artist and a man worth any number of interesting new painters to get angry because the makeup artist's best friend and eulogist uses a story that she has for years been hoarding for her book which she can't write anymore anyway unless she writes it as a historical novel because it's about a world that in the last few years has disappeared almost entirely.[65]

History and living memory are intuitively opposed; the fact that fifties nostalgia was a novel phenomenon to critics like Shales and Jameson suggests that the possibility of thinking about a decade within one's own lifetime as open for commodification, qualitatively different from the present, arose no longer ago than the mid-1970s. But if the drive of retrocontainment allowed historical difference to be experienced within a single thirty-year generation in the early 1980s, then the devastations of AIDS were even more effective at creating a felt difference between a past of fewer than ten years prior and a present that could not envisage its own continuity with the years before it. If history is defined by its difference from the present, then *Angels,* a historical play about the very recent past, occupies a deeply paradoxical position within and in relation to time.

It is into this complexly constructed and contested set of ideas about history that Roy and Ethel arrive. Emphasizing the theme of continuity across historical periods, they, like the 1992 audience, trouble the distinction between the present and the past. As the only "real" historical figures in the play, they also occupy a different ontological plane to the fictional characters who populate the rest of Kushner's world. This enables them to signify more than naturalistic characters like Louis and Prior; the fact of audience recognition brings in a temporal fold: they are "old," they are "not new," they are "already there." They embody history, and two different models of history at that. Roy Cohn moves forward in time from the past to the present toward his death but also consistently refers back to the 1950s, both as a character who speaks often of McCarthy and as a historical figure from the McCarthy era; his temporality is that of retrocontainment. Ethel Rosenberg is a ghost who does not suggest the forward movement of time; she is "dressed modestly in a fifties hat and coat," as opposed to Roy, who, we learn, has changed significantly since they last met: "I haven't been that heavy since 1960" (*MA* 111). Ethel's temporality is discontinuous and uncertain; she appears and disappears until Roy's death, not impervious to calendrical time—she takes the 7:05 train to Roy's disbarment hearing, and tells him that "the Star of Ethel Rosenberg's Hatred . . . burns every year for one night only, June Nineteen" (*P* 112)—but not bound by it either. As these two characters maneuver around each other, their models of history both challenge each other and impact the historical structure of the play as a whole.

Roy Cohn is an iconic figure of the "wormhole" relationship between the fifties and the eighties, up there with Reagan and Rock Hudson. As Joseph McCarthy's right-hand man during the Red Scare, he became synonymous with the high Cold War era; after the downfall of McCarthy in 1954, he operated farther away from the spotlight until the late 1970s, when he returned to the public eye as "a rehabilitated celebrity of the New Right."[66] He functions as a bridge between the two eras; as Daryl Ogden argues, "in all of Roy's appearances in *Angels in America,* Kushner makes visible a Cold War political discourse that underlines the ideological similarities between the McCarthyite 1950s and the Reaganite 1980s."[67] He also, though, functions as a metonym: through his very iconicity he stands in for a backward turn toward the fifties. It is impossible to see Roy without also seeing McCarthy. While dependent on a linear model of history (the fifties always come before the eighties), the temporality associated with Roy is a backward one. Even at the moment of his death, the final forward step, he regresses, speaking in a childish voice and calling out for his mother to sing to him (*P* 113, even if he's faking). When Louis, horrified to discover that he has been sleeping with (in Belize's memorable terms) "Roy Cohn's buttboy," who carries the "GOP germ" (*P* 92, 93), he defends against possible ideological transmission in the language of the Army–McCarthy trials. Having learned that Joe has authored repressive and homophobic legal judgments in his role as clerk for a senile judge, he quotes Joseph Welch's famous attack on McCarthy: "Have you no decency, sir," he asks Joe. "At long last? Have you no sense of decency?" (*P* 106). When people see Roy in the 1980s, they see the 1950s too—and they go there, in his proximity or in proximity to his influence; the fight between Louis and Joe performs, literally restages, a crucial moment in Roy's career in the 1950s. Just as Roy's brand of neoconservatism seeks to return to the fifties to contain the threat of the eighties, so Louis returns to them to contain the threat of Roy. If the "GOP germ" isn't catching, retrocontainment, it seems, is.

If Roy Cohn functions in *Angels* both as a figure for the eighties–fifties loop of retrocontainment and as an instigator of that backward drive ("if you want to look at the heart of modern conservatism, look at me" [*P* 79]), then Ethel Rosenberg is a more uncertain figure. Like Roy, she is iconic, a metonym for a larger social imaginary, the mention of her name enough to summon images of anticommunist witch-hunts.

But while Roy exists as a connector between the fifties and the eighties by being famous in the first, living through the intervening decades more quietly, and then emerging again in the second, Ethel, dying in the first, enters time like a firefly against a dark sky. Her appearances and disappearances in *Angels* reflect a longer history of consistent but discontinuous representation; unlike Roy, whose first cultural representation is in the Reagan era, Ethel remains in the public eye after her death, becoming a figure for injustice who has "haunted the artistic imagination ever since."[68] In this temporal discontinuity, Ethel embodies a certain paradox in *Angels,* in which a millennial drive toward the stasis of mass death proposed by the Angel ("millennium approaches") is countered by the apocalyptic disintegration of the temporal structure upon which millennialism relies: "history is about to crack wide open." To be able to say that the millennium is approaching requires a linear chronology; history cracking wide open, in contrast, suggests that *past, present,* and *future* are about to become seriously confused terms.

Ethel articulates both of these positions as a prophecy directed at Roy in response to his claim that "I have *forced* my way into history. I ain't never gonna die." Roy's claim for immortality is based on the solidity of the past, its untouchability, that what he has done remains safe because it was done long ago. However, that Ethel and Roy, as embodied representations of the 1950s, are here at all refutes the idea that history will stay where you put it; as Nishant Shahani has argued, "the retroactive invocation of 1950s McCarthyism in the eighties disrupts what Benjamin calls the 'homologous, empty time' that informs the continuum of history."[69] The supercharged parallels between the fifties and the eighties constructed by neoconservatism are used by Kushner here to challenge the ground upon which retrocontainment stands: that the present is more in control than the past; that when you open a wormhole into the past, the ability to time travel only goes one way. If Roy embodies the time machine, Ethel is the ghost in that machine, proof that the past is not an empty space to be shaped at will but full of charged lines of resistance that will force their way into the present just as Roy tries to force his way into history. Ethel is the "play's prophet of liminality," but she also brings liminality with her: the world is revealed to be always already liminal, existing on an uncertain and unstable set of temporal boundaries, because she is there.[70]

As revenants of recent history, Ethel and Roy are to the world of 1986 as an audience alive in 1986 is to the world of 1992. Their status as corporeal history is reflected in the strikingly embodied terms in which critics have recorded their encounters with the play; Susan Knabe describes how writers, including David Román and Michele Sordi, "cite/site themselves in space and time, telling us where and when, and even what they were wearing and what the weather was when they first saw *Angels in America* before proceeding to generate a critical analysis of the text."[71] Whereas Knabe describes embodiment as an anti-apocalyptic encounter with revelation, my focus here is on how corporeality complicates ideas of historical periodization. In Román's account, published in the essay "November 1, 1992: AIDS/ *Angels in America*," he talks at some length about one of his companions, Michael Callen. The embodied experience of watching the play, the need for "water, fruit, candy, medications, and cigarettes," is framed in terms of the presence of Callen: "we wonder out loud how comfortable he will be sitting in the theater for such a long time."[72] Callen is the only one of four friends accompanying Román referred to by his full name in the piece; he is also, as Román points out, a reference point for surviving beyond what is considered to be your time: "consider Michael Callen, my November 1, 1992 theater companion, who, after being officially diagnosed with AIDS in 1982, introduced a different way of thinking about AIDS—most notably, the then radical and for many presumptuous concept of 'long-term' survivor."[73] The very possibility of being present to watch the premiere of *Angels* on November 1, 1992, was not by any means assured in 1986, not only for Callen but also within the apocalyptic narrative structure that had been written onto first GRID and then AIDS as news of the epidemic spread in the early 1980s. Steven Kruger defines the two narratives of AIDS as "irreversible decline" and "unstoppable spread"; for the gay community (and often, in certain strategic scare stories, beyond it), the governing narrative form was that everyone would get AIDS and that once you got it, you were done for.[74] The sense of historical estrangement produced by rewriting the recent past as the material for historical fiction in *Angels in America* reflects the broader temporal disjuncture represented by Michael Callen in Román's account: the audience has somehow lived into the present from a past that, according to the apocalyptic narrative of AIDS discourse, no one would escape. The breaking of the fourth wall in the play's epilogue when Prior addresses the audience directly underlines the coincidence of the play's time and its audience's, rupturing the distinction between the then and the now and foregrounding the audience's relationship to their own sense of history.

In casting the audience as unlikely survivors, Kushner aligns them with the two characters that also live beyond their period, Ethel Rosenberg and Roy Cohn. This produces a strange correspondence between audience and character: they're from the past/they're still here, on the stage; I'm from the past/I'm still here, in the house. Ethel and Roy do not only embody different models of history on the stage; rather, their presence in the play creates a historical paradigm through which to understand the play's own historicity and that of its audience. Kushner's play thus occupies a strange position with regard to Jameson's analysis of historical fiction in *Postmodernism*. Jameson offers two possibilities for historical fiction in the postmodern era. First is the "Pynchonesque" "real sewer systems with imaginary crocodiles in them" model, in which "you make up a chronicle (generational or genealogical) whose grotesque succession and unrealistic personnel, ironic and melodramatic destinies, and heartrending (and virtually cinematographic) missed opportunities mime real ones, or to be more precise about it, resemble the dynastic annals of small-power kingdoms and realms very far from our own parochial 'tradition.'"[75] The complex, anarchic adventures in real historical space of something like *Gravity's Rainbow* seem to be Jameson's target here; his interpretation of this mode defines it as a compensatory fantasy of historiographic empowerment: "the making up of unreal history is a substitute for the making of the real kind. It mimetically expresses the attempt to recover that power and praxis by way of the past and what must be called fancy rather than imagination."[76] For Jameson, the desire for praxis is commendable, but the best thing that can be said about this kind of aesthetic engagement with history is that it affirms a desire for historical agency.

Jameson's second option is "in some ways the inverse of this one. Here, the purely fictional intent is underscored and reaffirmed in the production of imaginary people and events among whom from time to time real-life ones unexpectedly appear and disappear"; "the toads again become 'real' while the gardens grow imaginary."[77] This version

of historical fiction is the literary equivalent of Jameson's description
of postmodern architecture, an edifice with randomly selected Geor-
gian columns and minarets sprouting from it—"every atom of history
becomes disconnected and free-floating, recombinatory."[78] Both of
these, in turn, differ from nostalgia film, in which the referent era itself
becomes "the central character, the actant and the 'world-historical individual' in its own right."[79]

Jameson's account of postmodern historical fiction emerges from
the same moment as does *Angels in America*—a moment that was, in
the words of historian Jessie Swigger, "pivotal in altering the relationship between the public and the past."[80] Both texts are concerned with
the backward temporality that I have described as retrocontainment;
both use the relationship between the fifties and the eighties as their
privileged example. The sense of history produced by this relationship
in *Angels,* however, challenges Jameson's understanding of the relationship between the present and the past as producing either nostalgia for a time when historicity was possible or desire for the vanished
possibility of political praxis.[81] Jameson's theory may be predicated on
the idea that the contemporary subject is no longer empowered in relation to history, but it also requires that the past be understood as
subject to the constructions of the present, ready to be picked up and
rearranged, moved around like Tetris blocks. One of the contributions
of a ghost theory stemming from Derrida's 1994 *Specters of Marx* has
been to challenge this understanding of the past, looking instead at
the ways in which the past resists interpretation, challenges the present, and haunts it beyond our control.[82] *Angels in America,* poised mid-
way between *Postmodernism* and *Specters,* falls neither on the side
of "history-as-virtual-modeling-clay" nor on the side of "history-as-
desired-but-feared-ghost." Indeed, it challenges the idea of a text having to operate through a single kind of history. *Angels* features both
imaginary crocodiles in real sewers and real toads in imaginary gardens; Joe works in a real court and authors real court decisions, while
Roy offers to represent God from the depths of hell. When the fifties
return to the eighties here, they are neither exclusively conjured nor
exclusively ghosts; Ethel may fall into the tradition of ghost of historical injustice troubling the present, but Roy simply survives into the
present day. Furthermore, the focus of *Angels* on the corporeality of
history, aided by the necessarily embodied experience of performance,

puts its historical characters on the same ontological plane as its audience. In conjunction with the temporal parallels between Roy/Ethel and the audience, this works to privilege the audience's relationship with history over their relationship with fiction. While it is much easier to identify with Prior or Belize or Harper as sympathetic characters, the play aligns us structurally with Roy and Ethel, the embodied representations of historical experience.

Angels in America thus foregrounds the uncanny experience of survival, of living through. It makes us aware of our own existence as "future dead people" and at the same time refuses to accept that the future, endings, and death are synonymous.[83] Prior lives, and death is not the end for Ethel or for Roy, who, even after his big death scene and the pivotal moment when Belize, Louis, and Ethel recite the Kaddish prayer of forgiveness over his body, turns up again in ghostly form to act tenderly toward Joe. It is precisely this future orientedness, however, that has proved a sticking point for Savran et al. If Enlightenment conceptions of progress are inextricably bound up with the maintenance of a capitalist world system; if Louis's belief in a "neo-Hegelian positivist sense of constant historical progress towards happiness or perfection or something" leads him to abandon his lover upon his AIDS diagnosis; if, as Savran claims, in the peculiarly American form of millenarianism with which *Angels* engages, "the political is finally subsumed by utopian fantasies," then this insistence on futurity even in the face of death seems like a naive refusal of political reality. In Janelle Reinelt's analysis, the undialectical or not Marxist enough nature of the play means that "the replacement of class analysis by other identity categories . . . leaves the play with no other foundation for social change than the individual subject, dependent on an atomized agency. Since this subjectivity is contradictory and collapsed, the only horizon of hope must be transcendent."[84] Lacking the negative side of the dialectic, Kushner's optimism is read as blinded by an imagined light coming from a future where everything is OK.

The debate about optimism in *Angels* is paralleled by the debate about optimism that has circulated through queer theory in recent years. The question of how an oppressed past relates to an oppressive present and how to manage both of these in the fight for a less oppressive future has been recoded in historiographic, relational, and affective terms: how do we write history, how do we relate to society, and what should we feel toward the future and/or the past? The ground-work for this movement was laid by Leo Bersani in his 1987 essay "Is the Rectum a Grave?," which essentially answers yes: the association of gay men with passivity and death should be celebrated because it helps us to think beyond the association of sexuality with "proud subjectivity" and the oppressive social structures that stem from the equivalence of sex and proud subjecthood with masculinity, power, and agency.[85] Lee Edelman builds on Bersani's antisocial thesis by extending it into the temporal dimension, arguing in *No Future* that queerness is structured in opposition to a heteronormative orientation toward the future that he calls "reproductive futurism." Like Bersani, he argues that queers should embrace rather than fight their enforced occupation of a posi-tion of negativity as an apolitical (because politics always takes place in the time of reproductive futurism) resistance to the privileging of the future over the present, a privileging that always works to perpetuate the oppression of those who are already seen as having no future.[86] The argument that queerness is intrinsically opposed to what Tom Boellstorff calls "straight time," linear and forward looking, has been both popular and generative.[87] Arguments about the affective intensity of a queer relationship to the past have been made by, most canoni-cally, Carla Freccero, Carolyn Dinshaw, Elizabeth Freeman, Heather Love, Christopher Nealon, Kate Thomas, and Ann Cvetkovich.[88] Fac-ing in the other direction, the question of what a queer relationship to the future should look like has been more divisive, falling into those who follow Bersani/Edelman's antisocial, antifutural stance and those who insist that it is possible to conceptualize a queer relation to the future that offers hope instead of the deathly maintenance of current conditions.[89]

This is a schematic outline, and the sketch of the field that I have presented here does no justice to the complexity of the picture in all four of its dimensions. It is also important to note that the assump-tions that queer time is automatically less normative than straight time and that there is such a thing as a single linear temporality anywhere have been challenged. As Valerie Rohy argues, "the alignment of queer-ness with aberrant temporalities, and such temporalities with chal-lenges to heteronormativity, also merits question. Whatever form it may take—*Nachträglichkeit*, discontinuity, belatedness—anachronism has no essential politics. Temporality studies . . . cannot assume that

STAR WARS, AIDS, AND QUEER ENDINGS

non-normative time will ally itself with perversion against the Law."[90] Even reproductive time, the straw man metonymy for a brutalizing heteronormative futurity, is not, as Ben Davies and Jana Funke point out, linear; the rhythmic disruptions of pregnancy and life with a new-born challenge both linear time and the sense of agential subjectivity that conceptually attends it.[91] When Harper reaches her limit with the empty heteropatriarchal repetitions of her married life with Joe in *Angels,* she flees to an imaginary Antarctica and an imaginary pregnancy, a protective circular time: "Maybe I'll give birth. To a baby covered with thick white fur, and that way she won't be cold. My breasts will be full of hot cocoa so she doesn't get chilly. And if it gets really cold, she'll have a pouch I can crawl into. Like a marsupial. We'll mend together" (*MA* 103). Reproductive futurity can be as much a utopian vision of escape from oppression as it is oppression's tool.

The debate about queer futurity is fervent, complex, and ongoing, and my intention is neither to adequately summarize it nor to resolve it here. I do, however, want to follow Christopher Castiglia and Christopher Reed in asking where AIDS has gone in all of this. "Is the Rectum a Grave?" is Bersani's response to the AIDS crisis, and *No Future* elaborates on concepts first formulated by Edelman in his own AIDS essay "The Mirror and the Tank." And yet there is very little mention of the epidemic in the field of queer temporality studies, especially in the debate regarding futurity that stems directly from Bersani's and Edelman's work. While I do not necessarily agree with Castiglia and Reed's argument that the elision of AIDS from queer theory is a form of universal posttraumatic stress syndrome evinced by the academy, their analysis of a prophylactic "unremembering" in both gay and mainstream culture is astute. The AIDS crisis, they argue, "became an occasion for a powerful concentration of cultural forces that made (and continue to make) the syndrome an agent of amnesia, wiping out memories not only of everything that came before but of the remarkably vibrant and imaginative ways that gay communities responded to the catastrophe of illness and death and sought to memorialize our losses."[92] Concentrated amnesia becomes in this analysis a route toward mainstream acceptance; following the constant reading of AIDS by both gay and straight commentators as a punishment for the abandoned promiscuity of the 1960s and 1970s, the disavowal of the gay past and an assertion of difference from it becomes a way to position the homosexual as no longer an adolescent but an adult worthy of "a place at the table."[93] In queer theory, the affective turn toward analyses of "psychic disaggregation," while productive in many ways, also served to "dehistoricize the queer psyche along with the socially located affects of shame, anxiety, and depression generated by the deaths, violence, and social stigma arising from AIDS."[94]

The elision of AIDS in discussions of queer temporality produces a strange absence located in the recent past. With the recent exception of Dagmawi Woubshet's powerful *The Calendar of Loss: Race, Sexuality, and Mourning in the Early Era of AIDS,* a queer past is either located pre-Stonewall, as in the work of Nealon and Love, or as coterminous with the present; even Cvetkovich's *Archive of Feelings* and Halberstam's *In a Queer Time and Place* engage with AIDS only to argue that the fragility of queer life and culture means that we should be creating our own archives of the present to maintain queer connections with historians in the future. How AIDS itself led to radically distorted experiences of time is rarely factored in even to scholarship emerging from that radically distorted time itself, and queer theory finds itself able to conceptualize a long queer history more coherently than it can describe its own living memory. Looking toward the future, its discourse becomes strangely catachretic: when Edelman calls on us to embrace a world with "no future" for us, when Abigail Rine asks "is there a future for the queer?," the concept of questionable gay futurity is abstracted from the conditions that produced it when the answer to Rine's question was "probably not."[95]

The question of queer futurity thus becomes inseparable from that of a queer past, located not in the moment of the emergence of a recognizable homosexual identity category but at the moment that threatened its disappearance.[96] This temporal confusion is itself typical of AIDS discourse; as Marlon Riggs invoked with his ritual repetition of the question "what time is it?" in his 1990 address to the Fourth Annual Lesbian, Gay, and Bisexual Studies Conference, AIDS is never quite on time. The untitled poem in Eve Kosofsky Sedgwick's *Fat Art, Thin Art* referred to as "Guys who were 35 last year are 70 this year" describes AIDS as "this rack of temporalities," upon which time is stretched ("they've ambled into the eerie slow-mo / extermination camp the city sidewalks are"), sped up ("a killing velocity"), collapsed ("Guys who were 35 last year are 70 this year"), and shockingly repetitive and everyday ("every morning / we have to gape the jaws of our unbelief").[97] Woubshet's *The Calendar of Loss* similarly reckons with what he calls "a poetics of compounding loss," an aesthetic response to the new temporality of an epidemic whose "grammar of loss is at once behind and ahead of time," in which deaths accumulate too fast to reckon with and in which one's own future death remains insistently present.[98] AIDS accumulates temporalities like it accumulates bodies, stacked times palimpsesting onto each other.

In addition to the multiple temporalities of AIDS, the epidemic brings into confusion the linear temporalities of past, present, and future. The official response to AIDS has long been, as Bersani writes, "to think of AIDS as an epidemic of the future rather than a catastrophe of the present"; at the same time, the emergence of an incurable virus at the end of the twentieth century came as an unwelcome *revenant,* "an unannounced visitor from the past, a reminder that even half a century of triumphant medical progress could not promise immunity from transmissible disease."[99] Steven Bruhm argues that AIDS brings the future into the present, in that "in the age of AIDS, [the] distinction between 'anticipation of loss' and 'unabashed grieving' for a loss already experienced has always been a difficult one to sustain"; even the nature of grief itself becomes temporally confused, "for this ultimately is—or was—grief in the age of AIDS: to move forward is to carry the past, to have one's present and future continually inflected by the past, and to have the past continually inflected by the present and the future—at least until a cure for HIV could be found, until gay men and others stopped dying from the syndrome."[100] Collapsing the boundaries between past, present, and future, the temporalities of AIDS are multiple and heterogeneous. It thus occupies an uncertain and shifting position with regard to the three models of temporality addressed in this chapter so far: the linear, backward stasis of neoconservative retrocontainment; the insistent forwardness of survival; and the disruptive, discontinuous temporality created by Kushner in his juxtaposition of different modes of historical experience. It also challenges the temporality most frequently associated with AIDS itself: the apocalyptic foreclosure of any kind of future at all.

If we attempt to see AIDS as a part of queer's past, then its impact on the present and on the present's understanding of futurity is uncertain precisely because it calls into question the possibility of being certain in relation to time. It both creates and disrupts timelines, often the same timelines at the same time. The many conflicting models of history in *Angels in America,* produced but not determined by the apocalyptic setting that cracks history "wide open," can thus be read not as coming together to point toward a utopian future with a blind or naive optimism but rather as a way of incorporating the temporal disruptions of AIDS into a form that stands against the singular timelines of the nuclear state that would rather see queer bodies consigned to the past. The play is full of formal challenges to a linear temporality. Its most unusual theatrical technique is its use of split scene, where two scenes take place simultaneously on stage. This technique, described by Art Borreca as demonstrating "theater's capacity to evoke simultaneity," is a challenge to the linear temporality of theater, a medium that tends to present a sequence of moments one after the other, however radically disparate these moments might be in their intradiegetic time.[101] In Kushner's split scene, two moments occur at the same time, creating a temporal density that crowds the stage with coexisting histories. This is not the only way that temporal space gets crowded in *Angels.* Narratologically, the use of flashback as the only way that we gain access to Prior's first conversation with the Angel places the central episode of the play—the one to which the entire first part of the play builds up—in a strangely atemporal location: while it is shown in the second part, it "actually" happens between the play's two halves. This creates its own simultaneity, an impression that what we are seeing has already happened in an extratheatrical space. It folds time over and brings the time outside of the play's running time into the narrative time of the play.

These techniques perform the rupture of any coherent, singular temporal structure; the play's content may dedicate itself to futural optimism at the end, but its form suggests that this temporal orientation will not—indeed, cannot—remain uncontested. Even the epilogue itself, read so often as containing only the linear temporality of progress, contains within itself multiple modalities: we have jumped forward in time from the end of the play proper and must reorient ourselves to the new situation; Louis gives us an update on the recent past, letting us know that "the Berlin Wall has fallen" and that, in the present, "the whole world is changing" (*P* 143); an apocalyptic temporality is still haunting the space in the reference to how "when the Millennium comes . . . the Fountain of Bethesda will flow again" (*P* 145); and Prior delivers a more immediate prophecy when he declares that "this disease will be the end of many of us, but not nearly all, and the dead will be commemorated and will struggle on with the living, and we are not going away" (*P* 146). This is not straight time or queer time so much as crowded time, a time that cannot be thinned out without doing violence to the living and the dead.

The futurity proposed by *Angels in America* is thus not only utopian or optimistic, a fantasy of security projected into a future guaranteed by an Enlightenment idea of progress and a naive faith in the perfectible nature of democracy. It is also an assertion that limiting and limited temporalities can be broken through without, as they threaten to do, taking the whole world with them when they go, negating the apocalyptic threat to the fixed future that subtends retrocontainment's fantasy of temporal safety. In foregrounding the historical experience of the audience within the play, *Angels* makes us aware of our own existence in time; in refusing to accept a single prophylactic temporality, it fills that experience of time with other possibilities, other histories, other temporalities. It negates the lethal singularity of nuclear retrocontainment by making visible that which retrocontainment must deny: a past that is unsanitizable and continues to act in the present; a contingent present that is full of different ways of being in time; and a future that contains no guarantees, with no possibility of immortality for anyone.

In Your Blood We Write: The Angel of History

When Prior declares that "the dead will be commemorated and will struggle on with the living, and we are not going away," it does not necessarily serve to further the optimism of the play's ending (*P* 146). There is something slightly chilling about the "we" who are "not going away"; the pronoun can refer to the dead or to the living, and in many of the possibilities inhabiting us at that moment, "we" are already dead. Roy stakes his claim—"I ain't never gonna die"—but his is the only onstage death that we see, challenging the neoconservative claim to perfect security that seeks to deny the inherent futurelessness that is the condition of human vulnerability. This is not, I think, an accident on Kushner's part. His engagement with Walter Benjamin's historiography has been extensively documented and debated, and I do not wish to rehearse that debate here. But there is an aspect of the angel in *Angels* that has not been mentioned and that also touches upon the debate surrounding queer futurity more generally.

Benjamin's Angel of History appears in his "Theses on the Philosophy of History," where he describes Paul Klee's painting *Angelus Novus*:

> His face is turned toward the past. Where we perceive a chain of events, he sees one single catastrophe which keeps piling wreckage upon wreckage and hurls it in front of his feet. The angel would like to stay, awaken the dead, and make whole what has been smashed. But a storm is blowing from Paradise; it has got caught in his wings with such violence that the angel can no longer close them. This storm irresistibly propels him into the future to which his back is turned, while the pile of debris before him grows skyward. The storm is what we call progress.[102]

The combination of a yearning, reparative drive toward the past even as progress drives the angel irresistibly forward has made this passage a key text for queer historicism, which must account for a past so full of wreckage and a future so clouded and uncertain.[103] The image of the angel standing helplessly as the world collapses into rubble is also mirrored in Kushner's presentation of the angels in *Angels,* whose heaven "has a deserted, derelict feel to it, rubble is strewn everywhere" (*P* 118). Kushner has stated that Benjamin's "Theses" are a major influence on *Angels,* and the prevalence of critical work drawing out connections between the two reflects this. In both queer theory and *Angels* criticism, however, there is a shared assumption that does, I think, bear questioning: that in this scenario, the angelic perspective is a human one.

In queer theory, it is the historian or the theorist who is the angel, forever reaching out to a vanished past; in critical writing about *Angels,* Kushner is positioned as the angel, trying to hold everything together, gearing up to blast holes in the continuum of history in the requisite manly fashion. This is, fundamentally, an agential and sequential view of history that assumes that the writer in the present is qualitatively different from the wreckage that she beholds. But it is not one that *Angels* supports. Indeed, the character who comes closest to wielding the continuum blaster in the play is Roy, who has "*forced* his way into history," and his pretensions to historical mastery are given the lie by the return of Ethel, his disbarment, and his death. The line that divides "same" from "different" in the play does not fall between past and present; the ways in which the play troubles the historical periodization that usually divides the then from the now actively work against this. Instead, it falls between humans and angels. Angels are immortal. The "we" in Prior's final address to the audience, the one that positions us so uncertainly between the living and the dead, cannot include them, who will never die. In this context, the angel of history cannot stand in for a human perspective. When the Angel crashes through the ceiling "like a missile" in *Millennium Approaches,* she flies spectacularly above the stage while Prior sits in bed, surrounded by and a part of the chunks of plaster and wood that the arrival of the Angel has produced.[104] If we seek a place for ourselves in Benjamin's image, it must be as the wreckage, the ever-accumulating pile of rubble. Seeing ourselves as what is left behind renders everything more uncertain. The world, it is true, only spins forward, but we do not.

There is certainly optimism at the end of *Angels in America,* faith in progress, a fantasy of democracy, and a utopian impulse. But I do not believe that, as Savran and McNulty argue and as Edelman's antifuture argument would imply, this optimism is blindly naive and acquired at the expense of an acknowledgment of loss. In separating the world that spins forward from the human perspective that cannot accompany it, Kushner registers the massive losses of his generation and from them produces a stubborn commitment to a temporary but innately futureless survival that, far from refusing to acknowledge history, sets itself against the perpetuation of that history in the future. Futurelessness here is the ground on which we fight. Harper's assertion at the end of *Perestroika* that "nothing's lost forever" positions the materiality of the histories that are excluded by the weaponized white picket fences of retrocontainment as the cause of its inevitable failure (*P* 142). Wreckage can't do much; it can't change history, it can't reproduce, it can't blast its way through anything. But it accumulates, and it changes the nature of what is by its existence; and it is difficult, perhaps impossible, to build a white picket fence—or a nuclear umbrella—upon a ruined foundation.

4

Nuclear Waste, Native America, Narrative Form

> Where one violence occurs, the smoke caused obscures
> another somewhere else: bombs, borders, the border as
> a bomb dropped into people's lives, and all the deadly
> effects lingering, lingering.
>
> —Lou Cornum, "The Irradiated International"

THIS BOOK HAS BEEN CONCERNED with the impact of the nuclear-military–industrial complex on everyday life, on how we experience sovereignty, race, environment, illness, sexuality, time. In the preceding chapters, apocalyptic forms have woven together the material and narrative elements of the nuclear age in its second-order infrastructures: the new bureaucracies, cities, and bodies that have emerged within a nation structured around nuclear weapons. This chapter remains attentive to the dialectical relationship between the material and the cultural as it returns to the first-order materiality of the nuclear age: the yellow rock, the exploded atom, its isotopes and their mutated cells; the gloves, paper cups, and hair nets in which they will reside long after the end of the human history that produced them; and the infrastructures that seek, imperfectly, to manage them.

The dangerous materials of the nuclear complex have been perceived differently at different points in space and time. Broad scientific and public concern about the environmental consequences of at-home nuclear weapons testing was evident in the United States at multiple points during the Cold War; the chilling discovery of strontium-90 in children's teeth, for example, led to a public outcry and the 1963 signing of the Limited Test Ban Treaty banning the detonation of nuclear bombs in the atmosphere, under water, and in space. Once testing went underground, the fear of fallout diminished within the American mainstream.[1] After 1989, however, the light of the post–Cold War dawn came up on the landscape that had been overshadowed by the imagined future disaster of atomic war: the toxic rivers and groundwater, the tons of uranium pilings and lethal slurry, the many more tons of mid- and low-level waste composed of the everyday objects of nuclear production (the gloves, paper cups, hair nets) that could now kill, if not dramatically and suddenly, then over time and no less surely.

Many people in what is currently the United States—in particular, the residents of the communities downwind of the Nevada Test Site and the Western Shoshone, Hopi, Navajo, Zuni, Ramah Navajo, Acoma, Laguna, Isleta, Canyonlita Navajo, San Felipe, Santo Domingo, Cochiti, Zia, Jemez, Pajoaque, Santa Clara, San Juan, San Ildefonso, Tesuque, Jicarilla Apache, Ute Mountain, Taos, Wanapum, Yakama, Nez Perce, and Umatilla nations—had long been aware of the devastation of the land and its inhabitants as a result of the nation's disproportionate commitment to nuclear technology. This devastation had, however, been denied as a matter of official policy throughout the Cold War. At the Hanford nuclear facility adjacent to the Yakama reservation in Washington State, for example, public concern over the toxic products and by-products of plutonium manufacturing was defused by the Department of Energy with, essentially, lies. Even after the plant had been closed down as a potential safety risk in 1987, Hanford was described by federal officials as having operated in a "safe and essentially accident-free fashion" throughout its operational existence. What this meant, exactly, emerged in July 1990, when "government spokespersons admitted that the weapons facility had been, since the early '50s, secretly dumping radioactive wastes into the environment at a level at least 2,000 times greater than those officially deemed 'safe.' . . . A year later, in April 1991, this was spelled out as meaning that 444 billion gallons of water laced with plutonium, strontium, tritium, ruthenium, cesium, and assorted rare earth elements had simply been poured into a hole in the ground over the years."[2] Official discourse slams into lived experience: for the federal official, as for the scientists who defused the repeated disasters of nuclear detonations by labeling them "tests," Hanford was "safe" because it was "accident-free." For local residents, conversely, the fact that eighty square miles of land, the Columbia River, and almost all of the local groundwater have been irreparably contaminated is no less threatening because it was done on purpose.[3]

With the post–Cold War declassification of previously secret files and new legislation requiring the assessment and remediation of toxic sites, the environmental catastrophes of the nuclear age became newly visible as such within the public sphere. As a result of these revelations, and of the unimaginable-until-it-happened meltdown at Chernobyl in 1986, the nature of the perceived nuclear threat changed considerably in the late 1980s and 1990s. Rather than a single missile poised to take out your city or nation, the nuclear complex itself held the potential to kill anyone, anywhere, at any time. And this threat was poised not in the silo of the future, waiting to be deployed, but within the air, soil, water, and cell of the present, already fallen out, albeit quietly and without spectacle.

This period thus saw a radical reevaluation of nuclear threat as a phenomenon in both space and time. As we have seen, the Cold War United States held fast to an ideology of containment in both, but at the end of the Cold War, it was not communist ideology but the equally invisible and insidious matter of radioisotopes that breached both physical and conceptual boundaries. In part, this conceptual leakage became possible due to an unexpected by-product of the nuclear complex: an ecological science based on ecosystems theory, which produced an understanding of the natural world not as a collection of objects that might be contained from each other but as a set of interlocking processes and flows that looped around each other in intricate feedback. While the term *ecosystem* was coined in the 1930s, the "Age of Ecology," Joel B. Hagen notes, coincided with the "Atomic Age."[4] The reasons for this overlap were twofold. First, the introduction of radioactive isotopes into ecosystems allowed radioecologists to track the movement of matter and energy through an ecosystem for the first time, making visible the food chain and other system linkages as the traceable atom circulated through them. Second (and there would have been no first without this second), the burgeoning field of ecology received massive institutional support from the nuclear complex.[5] As Valerie Kuletz demonstrates, post–World War II ecologists received much of their funding from the Atoms for Peace program, a program established by the Atomic Energy Commission (AEC) to assuage public fears about the atom. AEC-funded ecological experiments relied on, while simultaneously helping to justify, ongoing military irradiations of various parts of the world; crucial ecosystem data were gathered at the Nevada Test Site, Hanford, and Eniwetok Atoll, while other irradiations were led by ecologists but still provided important data to the military about the long-term impact of radiation.[6] Between 1963 and 1967, for example, more than one hundred ecologists worked on an AEC-funded radioisotope project that continuously irradiated a section of the El Verde forest in Puerto Rico for three months.[7] An experiment that might have been decried in the name of war was, in the technologically focused mind-set of the Cold War United States, ideologically neutral as long as it was conducted under the aegis of science.[8]

If the field of ecology provided neutral cover for many of the most appalling acts of violence performed by the nuclear complex, then it also provided some of the first irrefutable evidence that the nuclear complex was damaging the planet and its inhabitants in ways that might be uncontrollable and irreversible. As early as the 1950s, "the energy flow diagrams produced by way of observing radioisotope movement began to show that radionuclides from fallout, waste, and pollution could not be defused safely within the system, posing no threat to organic life forms. Instead, they could become concentrated, magnified, and very dangerous."[9] E. P. Odum, who, along with his brother H. T., was one of the leading ecosystems ecologists of the nuclear age, was forced to conclude that "we could give 'nature' an apparently innocuous amount of radioactivity and have her give it back to us in a lethal package."[10] No longer a set of relations between things that can be mapped and controlled, nature is now a personified figure of vengeance who returns our own poisons back to us, gift wrapped.

Contemporary ecocriticism tends to tell the story of environmental awareness after 1945, and particularly of awareness that the environment is becoming increasingly toxic due to human actions, as one in which the threat moves from nuclear materials to chemical and biological ones. Laurence Buell, for example, the originator of the influential term *toxic discourse* to describe the language of environmental risk, argues that the impetus of ecocatastrophic novels "devolves, just as [Rachel] Carson's diagnostic does, from Cold War–era nuclear fear." The apocalyptic vision of an uninhabitable planet slides metonymically from the nuclear threat to the destruction of the environment, taking upon itself the jeremiadic urge to reform that Carson typifies.[11] While Buell demonstrates how ecocatastrophe rhetoric took up the language of the nuclear threat in the 1960s and 1970s to make itself comprehensible, Heather Houser asserts that in the 1980s and 1990s, environmentalism left the nuclear behind, arguing that "if, immediately after World War II, environmentalism targeted nuclear energy as the greatest technological threat, turn-of-the-millennium environmentalism shifts focus to biotechnologies that permeate the quotidian."[12] The fear of a toxic world, in these accounts, may take its shape from an earlier nuclear threat, but it no longer takes its primary orientation from it.

Evacuating the nuclear from ecocritical analysis, however, not only risks dehistoricizing the field from within but also excludes alternative ways of thinking about risk that might come from a nuclear perspective.[13] The perception of the world and its inhabitants as subject to various forms of risk has produced the new para-ecocritical field of risk theory since the 1970s, emblematized by Ulrich Beck's *Risk Society: Towards a New Modernity* (Ger. 1986; Eng. 1992). In Beck's influential description of the risk society, "dangerous, hostile substances lie concealed behind the harmless façades. Everything must be viewed with a double gaze, and can only be correctly understood and judged through this doubling. The world of the visible must be investigated, relativized and evaluated with respect to a second reality, only existent in thought and yet concealed in the world."[14] The traumatic nature of living in a world of risk, exemplified in the canonical toxic-world novels *White Noise* (DeLillo 1985) and *Gain* (Powers 1998), lies in the way that the real world is no longer accessible to perception. Risks become perceptible only when they are already no longer threats but events, a condition that makes risk itself appear in a fundamentally literary mode; as Susan Mizruchi writes, "when improbable risks are actualized in catastrophe, the familiar becomes the uncanny."[15] What Mizruchi calls the uncanny Laurence Buell describes as the gothic; in both cases, Beck's description of a second, more real world beneath the phenomenological one finds a strong descriptor and a place in literary history as critics connect risk fiction to more established genres that account for what we cannot perceive and cannot understand. No longer haunted by falling helmets or animate dolls, the risk novel tries instead to theorize the connections between tumors and the factory that closed down two generations ago, between what we know of bioaccumulation and what we feel when we look at a carrot.

The risk posed by nuclear materials, and its challenges to perception and orientation, overlaps considerably with the kind of risk described here. Joseph Masco also draws on the language of the uncanny to describe the effects of radiation: "radiation," he argues, "fundamentally distorts how people experience an orientation in time and space. . . . This temporal ellipsis between radiation exposure and radiation effect is a specific aspect of the nuclear uncanny, one that can generate a proliferating psychic anxiety as potentially exposed individuals realize their inability to evaluate risk in everyday life."[16] The nature of nuclear waste, however, poses different epistemological questions than the global toxicity of the risk novel does. The epistemological challenges of risk, as described earlier, produce a particular kind of mind-set that Peter van Wyck characterizes as paranoid:

> Contemporary ecological threats can come to make ecological thought itself look like a particularly advanced form of cultural paranoia. I mean this in the sense that once we say that everything is connected in this fashion, we mean that everything is, if not already, then at least potentially integrated into a framework of understanding. And it isn't. To make everything connected is to see the fissures and cracks rendered by ecological threats— whether the threats posed by wastes or the threats retroactively discovered through accidents—as a kind of recompense for a failure to have properly understood the connections. *The real punishing the epistemic for its sins of omission.*[17]

Whereas van Wyck sees the paranoia of ecological thought as contiguous with that produced by nuclear waste, I propose that nuclear waste occupies the limit point of such an epistemological urge. Nuclear waste brings us face-to-face with the sheer impossibility of the kind of paranoid completion that van Wyck describes here, the paranoia that insists, as Eve Kosofsky Sedgwick writes concurrently with van Wyck, that "there must be no bad surprises."[18]

The differentiating factor here is time. When risk theorists describe

the temporal confusion of risk, they do so in terms of decades or generations; a local dioxin spill might give us cancer twenty years from now
or cause our offspring to have birth defects. While we might never, as
Beck argues, be absolutely certain that the spill was the cause of these
events, they are close enough that the paranoid urge for connection
can seek to reach across the gap. The tons of transuranic waste that
have been produced by the global nuclear complex, however, present us
with a temporal disjunction that is so much larger than even our most
practiced paranoids can imagine that it becomes qualitatively different from other kinds of risk. The half-life of plutonium-239, the most
common by-product of nuclear weapons and power, is 24,100 years;
that of uranium-238 is 4.47 billion years. Ten thousand years ago, the
first human settlements were coalescing around the newly developed
technologies of seed planting and animal husbandry. Two and a half
times that length of time from now, one-half of the plutonium created
and discarded in the last seventy years will have decayed to a nontoxic
level. Since the abatement of radioactive materials is estimated at ten
half-lives, we can expect the plutonium elements of nuclear waste to
have settled down in approximately 241,000 years. How can a human
perspective position itself on such a timescale? In the twenty-first century, the nuclear age often feels behind us, secured in the atomic kitsch
of the mushroom cloud and the duck-and-cover drill.[19] From its own
perspective, however, the nuclear age makes a mockery of any periodization beneath the level of the species or the rock.

Nuclear waste thus dwells less in the economy of risk and more
in the blown-out realm of deep time. Inhabiting the temporal scale
that has recently been christened the Anthropocene, the geological era
defined by the impact of human activities on the world's geology and
climate, nuclear waste unsettles any attempt at literary description,
challenging human imagination at every turn.[20] The question posed by
nuclear waste is simultaneously historiographical and narrative. How
do we understand history when we are no longer the sole recognized
agents of change, when history does not proceed in our understood
frameworks of agency and duration? When we might not be in it? Or
in a different frame, how might we write a novel—that most humanist
of genres—that lasts a million lifetimes or that has a nonliving agent
as its protagonist?[21]

In what follows, I examine how three quite different texts address the relationship between writing and nuclear waste precisely as a problem in and of deep time. I begin with an analysis of a somewhat obscure and extremely strange moment in U.S. governmental history when fiction was deployed as an analytic tool in the creation of a nuclear waste dump site. I then read two novels published in the 1990s, David Foster Wallace's *Infinite Jest* (1996) and Leslie Marmon Silko's *Almanac of the Dead* (1991), as novels that approach the fundamental question of the risk society—*"how do you live when you are at such risk?"*—from a nuclear perspective.[22] By analyzing the risk society through a heuristic of nuclear waste, these texts offer a critique of settler colonialism and environmental racism. At the same time, however, their use of the apocalyptic mode in deep time allows them to move beyond the paranoid logic of risk. In the flattened world of deep time, all that *might* come to pass *will* come to pass, sooner or later. The endless *maybes* of risk become certainties. The impossibilities of our own deaths and the deaths of everything else *will* come. But so, too, will other impossibilities: talking macaws and weaponized videotapes; the end of the colonial occupation of North America, perhaps, or a sudden human determination to let the world live. The end of capitalism may yet become more thinkable than the end of the world. Just wait long enough. Stranger things will happen.

Radioactive Realism at the Waste Isolation Pilot Project

In his 2003 book *From Apocalypse to Way of Life: Environmental Crisis in the American Century,* Frederick Buell proposes that genre is the key to both perceiving and, possibly, correcting environmental crisis. As his title suggests, Buell tells the story of a discourse that began in the apocalyptic mode in the 1960s and 1970s, when discussions of "the immanent end of nature" most commonly took the form of "prophecy, revelation, climax, and extermination" before turning away from apocalypse when the prophesied ends failed to arrive.[23] Buell offers his suggestion for the appropriate literary mode for life lived within a crisis that is both unceasing and inescapable: new voices, "if wise enough . . . will abandon apocalypse for a sadder realism that looks closely at social and environmental changes in process and recognizes crisis as a place where people dwell."[24] In a world of threat, Buell demands a realism that might help us see risks more clearly and aid our survival.

Buell's argument has become a broadly held view in contemporary risk theory and ecocriticism. For many critics, as for Buell, the gothic terror of a world of risk produces apocalypticism as a symptom and realism as a solution.[25] Even when apocalypse is recognized as a potentially valuable tool for approaching risk, as in Ursula K. Heise's insight that in a world of world-threatening danger, "apocalyptic narrative . . . can appropriately be understood as a form of risk perception," the potential benefit of apocalypse is as the most realistic genre for representing a scenario that is genuinely apocalyptic (as in the exponentially increasing flood of contemporary apocalypse novels depicting climate change).[26] Such an opposition between realism and apocalypse presupposes several things: that apocalypse cannot exist in the present or accurately describe the real; that realism does accurately describe the real; and that it is a neutral tool for epistemological clarity. As this project has shown, however, apocalypse as a form has nonrealist uses in addressing the present-day dangers of everyday life, while in the nuclear context, realism has played an important role in maintaining the nuclear complex and the settler-colonial systems of power that produced it and which it in turn upholds. This role can be seen nowhere more clearly than in the governmental experiment with realism that goes by the unglamorous name of the Waste Isolation Pilot Plant (WIPP).

The story of the WIPP is convoluted and full of acronyms. By the end of the Cold War, nuclear waste storage had reached a point of crisis that threatened to shut down the nuclear industry if the issue could not be resolved with safe, long-term facilities for storing radioactive materials. The Department of Energy (DOE) therefore charged Sandia National Laboratories (SNL) with proving that burying waste in the 250-million-year-old salt flats of New Mexico would provide an adequately secure disposal method. To comply with section 191.14(c) (the Assurance Requirements) of the 1985 Environmental Protection Agency (EPA) regulation 40 CFR 191 (the Standard), SNL was required to address the security of the WIPP and its future human coinhabitants not only in space, by containing radioactive materials, but also across time. In the Standard, the U.S. government takes responsibility for ensuring that the probability of inadvertent human intrusion into the WIPP is less than 1 in 10,000 for the next ten thousand years. To calculate this probability, SNL convened the Futures Panel, whose work was published as Hora et al., *Expert Judgment on Inadvertent Human Intrusion into the Waste Pilot Plant,* in December 1991. Four teams of experts spent months imagining potential futures for the WIPP site. The teams then assigned a numerical probability to the likelihood of intrusion into the site over the next ten thousand years to each of the scenarios, which were added together to produce a scale model of the deep-time future of the WIPP.[27]

The statistical model used to map out the WIPP's potential futures, however, produces specific restrictions on what it means, in this state imaginary, to model deep time. The Standard requires that "the performance assessment will be assembled into a complementary cumulative distribution function (CCDF)."[28] The choice of the CCDF as the required output determines how the various dangers facing the WIPP must be conceptualized. For such a graph to emerge, "the procedure for developing scenarios must produce a comprehensive set, so that no important scenarios are omitted. In addition, the scenarios must be mutually exclusive, so that the cumulative releases and the probability of occurrence can be combined in a CCDF."[29] Since the probability in a CCDF cannot equal more than 1, overlapping or impossible or incomplete scenarios might produce unmappable probabilities and thus must—in this particular method of predicting the future—be ignored. Scenarios are defined for the Futures Panel "as sets of naturally occurring and human-induced events and processes that represent *realistic* future changes to the repository."[30] The list of futures produced is then organized to establish its completeness, before being "screened to eliminate those that are not pertinent"; the screening criteria are "physical reasonableness, probability of occurrence, and consequence."[31] At the WIPP, any event that was determined to be unlikely or impossible is excluded from scenario development.

The mathematics of the WIPP are therefore based on a probability model that requires certain assumptions of reasonableness, likelihood, and causality. If we can establish a consensus reality, this model suggests, then we can foresee how the future will play out by calculating the different probabilities of chains of events extending forward in time from the information that we have. This has long been the structuring logic behind theories of probability; statistical pioneer Pierre Simon Laplace writes in his 1795 *Philosophical Essay on Probabilities* that "given for one instant an intelligence which could comprehend all the forces by which nature is animated and the respective situation of the beings who compose it—an intelligence sufficiently vast to submit these data to analysis— . . . for it, nothing would be uncertain and the future, as the past, would be present to its eyes."[32] For this kind of statistical realism, a sufficiently detailed description of reality allows a viewer with enough computing power to model the future with perfect confidence along various chains of probability. Surprise becomes impossible, and the paranoid's ultimate fantasy is fulfilled.

The problem that SNL runs into with the inadvertent human intrusion requirement is one of data: it, like Laplace's statistical deity, needs certain data points from which to extrapolate. Data are available from decades of nuclear testing about the effects of radiation on salt and metal and from other sciences about the likelihood of tectonic plates shifting or rivers rerouting. What the performance assessment lacks is data about the future of humanity. This lack of data about the future is understood by the Standard, and by SNL, as itself a specific kind of risk. Section 191.14(c) was passed into law "to reduce the potential harm from some aspect of our uncertainty about the future."[33] The state is confident, as it lays out its regulations for environmental protection, that it can control risk by modeling what is likely to happen in the present and the near-future. It is thrown into a spin, however, by its own ten-thousand-year requirement: it does not have the data to feed into the assessment, and so uncertainty haunts the model, exposing the Standard to the risk of failure resulting from its inability to include all potential scenarios in its model, to add up to 1.

This is where the Futures Panel comes in: to provide data that will structure the uncertainty of the deep future and minimize risk to within acceptable boundaries. Its role is to translate the unknown unknowns of the distant future into known unknowns that can be contained within a probability model. This task is understood by Hora et al. to be an aesthetic one; "in the present study of future societies . . . the experts are required to employ substantial creative effort in structuring their analyses."[34] The Futures Panel is asked to compose realistic narrative fictions that will become data within a probability function: "six futures [that] could be considered as exhaustive for most practical purposes."[35] The kinds of fictions that are produced under this rubric work hard to give even their least likely-sounding scenarios an air of plausibility. The scenario "A Feminist World, 2091" written by the

Boston team, for example, is written not in the future tense or sub-junctive mood that would more properly denote speculation but rather in the descriptive past tense, while each of its details is carefully tied to a recognizable condition in the present: the outlines of the "feminine mystique" that defines the new canons of science, art, and literature in the feminist future "were visible as early as the late 1960s," while the prediction/description that scientific "knowledge" (scare quotes in the original) would be understood as "erroneous masculine definitions, constructions, and representations of reality" is carefully backed up with citations from contemporary feminist thinkers.[36] The future may be different in such scenarios, but it is not so different that it cannot be known, understood, and predicted by the present; as Daniel Grausam argues in his analysis of the Boston Team's scenarios, the team forecloses any sense of surprise that might be associated with imagining distant futures.[37] By imagining the future in a way that is consonant with our beliefs about the present such that the imagined future passes a kind of verisimilitude test, a test of its realism, the Futures Report thus tames the uncertainty of risk, of the unknowable future in deep time.

The argument made by SNL here is that fiction written in a realist mode is functionally equivalent to probability modeling: that realism represents the real world and that verisimilar depictions of the future can provide a totality of representation that will cover all *realistic* scenarios.[38] Such an equivalence may seem counterintuitive at a moment when literature and science are generally conceptualized as opposites. But as Rüdiger Campe has demonstrated in his transformative intellectual history of probability, both mathematical probability and realist fiction develop from the same origins in Greco-Roman poetelogical and logical theories and undergo related trajectories of change in the Enlightenment. In its original rhetorical form, probability was opposed to the "true knowledge of science."[39] "Between 1660 and 1800," however, "probability constituted itself as a measurement of scientific knowledge and as a theory of aesthetic semblance."[40] These two reconstitutions were bound up with each other in the concept of verisimilitude. As Campe writes, "the traditional rhetorical and poetical concept of the -*similis* in *verisimilis* can be understood as a kind of likelihood that implies the semblance of truth. Eighteenth-century aesthetic thinking increasingly begins to conceptualize the -*similis* instead as appearance, an appearance that may be either false or true but that is seen as the way things manifest themselves."[41] Mathematicians and aestheticians took from the ancients the idea that probability was conceptually indistinguishable from verisimilitude, but they reinvented both concepts: both probability and verisimilitude would no longer *seem* like reality but rather would be reality *appearing* in aesthetic or mathematical form. Thus can the Hora report operationalize realist fictions into data: under the post-Enlightenment logic of probability, plausible representations (fictions with enough verisimilitude) can be taken as manifestations of reality and used to make calculations about the real world and its future.

In its orientation toward the far future, the Futures Panel combines early realism's commitment to verisimilitude with a later, Lukácsian theory of realism: the Hora report, like the realist novel, "is the epic of an age in which the extensive totality of life is no longer directly given, in which the immanence of meaning in life has become a problem, yet which still thinks in terms of totality."[42] The ability of fiction to represent complete realities is no longer assumed, but it can certainly be strived for—and, in the case of SNL, achieved through probability modeling that successfully accounts for uncertainty, that includes the unknown in the totalizing remit of the known. The probability model's Laplacian ability to predict the future from a fully accurate account of the present provides a mathematical analogue of Lukács's later theory of realism as prophecy: true realism, a total realism that portrays "man in the whole range of his relations to the real world," "captures tendencies of development that only exist incipiently and so have not yet had the opportunity to unfold their entire human and social potential."[43] Realist fiction and probability modeling share a function as well as a history here: to describe the present with a large enough degree of verisimilitude that the future may be extrapolated from the description. In SNL's literary theory, expressed in the statistical realism that defines its epistemological battle against the future and its unknowable dangers, realist fiction is the equivalent of the CCDF graph, and both narrative forms fulfill the paranoid desire for risk control: with the present and the future and the unknown drawn into the total description, there will indeed be no bad surprises.

If the history of statistics reveals the conceptual underpinnings of SNL's statistical realism, however, then it also discloses the limits of its claim to descriptive totality. The pronoun used to refer to "La-place's Demon," *it,* manifests the relationship between statistics and state building that began with the birth of statistics and continues to operate at the WIPP. Campe indicates that the knowledge-producing subject for Laplace is no longer the individual, who could never hope to accumulate and process the required amount of data, but rather the state-run statistics bureau.[44] Throughout the eighteenth century, European nation-states increasingly combined diachronic histories of their own development with synchronic statistical representations of their current situations to define national identity. States gathered statistics about themselves to define the nature of their statehood, and in so doing, they defined the object of statistical representation as the state; in such a situation, "no statistics are possible without reference to a political unity, whose reflection it is supposed to provide in high resolution."[45] The abjected other of the territorial state, in statistics as elsewhere, becomes those peoples whose social organization is not recognized as a nation-state: according to Johann Christoph Gatterer in his 1773 *Ideal of a Universal World Statistics,* the fourth world "savage," as well as "subject" or "tributary" peoples, could not be the object of either statistics or history because they "do not constitute any particular body politic themselves."[46]

The history of the nuclear complex in North America demonstrates the continued power of the conceptual relationship between statistics and state sovereignty to determine what can be accepted as knowledge. Even when Indigenous nations have produced their own statistical data to counter the DOE's analysis of reality on its own terms, the U.S. state remains the final arbiter of whose statistics can count as truth.[47] In the ongoing struggle over the remediation of the Hanford plutonium plant, for example, the Yakama and Umatilla nations have countered EPA risk assessments, which use aggregated data based on a white suburban lifestyle, with their own statistical models based on more accurate accounts of their likely exposure to radioactive waste. In an interview with geographer Shannon Cram, however, an EPA staff member explains that "for us, we can't choose [the Umatilla scenario] because it's not *credible.*"[48] For the U.S. nuclear state, as for Gatterer, statistics only count when they are produced by the state to represent itself. The plausibility that subtends statistical realism is born out of and defined by the operations of colonialism, as the state becomes that which can authorize statistics as credible truth, while the colonized subject can be counted but can never be significant, can be described but can never be data.

SNL resolves the apocalyptic threat of nuclear waste by turning to a probabilistic realism that provides the plausible illusion of a knowable future, but the stakes of its verisimilitude are high and are deeply bound up with the settler-colonial state. At the WIPP, the future can only be imagined in terms of the colonial state's present, a present that would have to continue unchanged for the state's statistical self-description to continue to signify; it is the perfect neoliberal waste disposal technology, foreclosing futures of possible difference, including decolonial futures, into an ongoing, unchanging *now*.[49] Imagining a future, even ten thousand years from now, that is not qualitatively different from the present contains the epistemological challenges posed by deep time. In this version of living in risk, the past in which the waste was produced and the future in which it kills us are transformed into pillars of salt, frozen in place as we watch the present burn, forever.

Apocalypse Where? *Infinite Jest*

At the end of the Cold War, then, the official discourse of nuclear risk and its environmental dangers seems to have made the switch recommended by F. Buell: it has transitioned from a discourse of apocalypse, of imminent, global destruction, to one of sober realism, addressing the long-term residues of a nuclear apocalypse that failed to arrive as predicted. The realism of probability modeling, however, while it successfully manages the *risk* of nuclear waste as it is felt and perceived, does little to manage its *danger*. The fantasy of the ancient salt beds, frozen in time, that might metonymically impart the same stability to the transuranic waste interred therein is a powerful one; it was certainly powerful enough to make the WIPP plausible to legislators, and the facility received its first shipments of waste in 1999. And yet in February 2014, some fifteen years into that ten-thousand-year future, the WIPP was closed after radiation was found to be leaking into the atmosphere from two of its storage chambers. An SNL employee and docent at the Museum of Nuclear Science and History in Albuquerque tells me in early 2015 that word is going around that the leak contained plutonium ions, which is interesting, he says, because plutonium waste is of a higher grade than is legally allowed to be stored at the WIPP. The totalizing power of the probability model makes everything not entered into its initial data-world unthinkable; when the unthinkable happens, it punctures the boundary of the reality-effect and transforms science into—or reveals it to have been—less of an absolute descriptive power than a rumor mill. During my time in Albuquerque, the irradiated chambers of the WIPP were too hot to be approached; they could not be seen or described in ways that are understood to be realistic. "What happened" at the WIPP was, in that 2015 moment, unknowable through observation or inference. Instead, scientists speculated about unforeseen interactions from the surface. Nuclear telemetrists gossiped with women in museums.[50] When risk turns into danger, nuclear materials challenge the terms of their confinement, exposing the limits of probabilistic risk analysis as the epistemological basis for dealing with threat.

The use of statistical realism to manage the risk of nuclear waste must thus be seen as an operation of force in the present rather than as a means of protecting the future; as Charles Perrow writes of risk assessment more broadly, "the issue is not risk, but power."[51] The language of risk is a rhetorical one whose function is to distribute danger unevenly across bodies and spaces; discourses of acceptable risk frequently lie behind decisions whose outcomes become visible as environmental racism, the massive weighting of toxic exposure toward the third and fourth worlds, people of color, and the poor across the globe.[52] The officially established 10^{-8} percent chance of the WIPP leaking did not stop the leak from happening, but it allowed billions of dollars to be spent on researching and opening the facility, millions of tons of salt to be moved, and the ongoing operations of the global nuclear complex to continue.

If realism has historically been press-ganged into supporting the logics of risk assessment, however, literature at the close of the Cold War took up the relationship of aesthetic form to risk and power as an object of critique. The relationship between risk, power, nuclear waste, and narrative form is a central concern of one of the most canonical novels to have emerged from the post–Cold War moment, David Foster Wallace's *Infinite Jest*. Published in 1996, *Infinite Jest* was written primarily from 1991 to 1993 and is situated squarely in the period in which the problem of nuclear waste was entering public consciousness through debates about the WIPP, the remediation projects at sites such as Hanford and Rocky Flats, and the ill-fated but heavily invested-in plan to store high-level waste in a hollowed-out Yucca Mountain repository. Representing a world that has been remade by nuclear waste rather than one that is threatened by nuclear war, Wallace models a different kind of nuclear literature from its postmodern ancestors: a literature that exists not in relation to its own future destruction but that rather depends on an understanding that in fact the worst has already happened, that the will-have-been of the future anterior is exactly the same as the how-it-is of the present tense.[53]

Recalling the intertwined histories of ecosystems ecology and the nuclear complex, *Infinite Jest* depicts a fully Anthropocenic near-future in which nuclear waste operates as an ecosystemic force. Its counterfactual departure from our own history begins with the arrival on the political scene of Johnny Gentle, an ex–lounge singer whose history of union busting and Strategic Defense Initiative–style fantasies of dealing with America's waste crisis ("Let's Shoot Our Wastes into Space") position him as a Reagan figure.[54] Unlike Reagan, however, Gentle and his "Clean U.S. Party" (CUSP) make themselves indispensable into the 1990s to an American electorate that, in a time when "all landfills got full and all grapes were raisins and sometimes in some places the falling rain clunked instead of splatted" and U.S. victory in the Cold War has led to the absence of clearly defined enemies, "sort of turned on itself and its own philosophical fatigue and hideous redolent wastes with a spasm of panicked rage" (382). Orchestrating "the strange-seeming but politically prescient annular agnation of ultra-right jingoist hunt-deer-with-automatic-weapons types and far-left macrobiotic Save-the-Ozone, -Rain-Forests, -Whales, -Spotted-Owl-and-High-pH-Waterways ponytailed granola-crunchers" (382), CUSP transforms an America that experiences itself as a clogged ecosystem into an energy-independent nation that has no waste, anywhere.

Energy independence is achieved in Gentle's America through the new nuclear technology of annular fusion, an evolution of nuclear fusion that brings both "hellacious amounts of highly poisonous radioactive wastes" and other "massive poisons" into its energy-producing feedback cycle (571). Such a technology evokes the fantasies of early nuclear ecologists, who assumed that nuclear waste could be absorbed and dispersed by nature's feedback loops; Odum's horror over the bioaccumulation of toxic materials marks the moment at which this fantasy failed.[55] At the other end of the Cold War, annular fusion deals with the problem of a nuclear waste that can be neither used nor disposed of by finding a use for it that also disposes of it, using toxic waste to transform nuclear waste into energy, which process produces more nuclear waste that can be so converted, and so on. The dream of sustainable energy comes true here, with the immense toxicity of the process a minor concern.[56]

This set of energy infrastructures, however, both requires and produces a huge amount of highly radioactive waste that "all but necessitates the second-tier option of transforming certain vast stretches of U.S. territory into uninhabitable and probably barbed-wired landfills and fly-shrouded dumps and saprogenic magenta-fogged toxic-disposal sites" (402). The paradox created by a "Clean U.S. Party" that commits to such an action is resolved by an act of "ecological gerrymandering" (403): CUSP seeds the greater part of New England with highly toxic and radioactive waste, declares an ecological emergency to evacuate its inhabitants, and then forces Canada to annex the toxic territory by threatening to implode thermonuclear weapons in American silos and fan the resulting radiogenic clouds across the border (393). This act of "territorial reconfiguration" creates the monstrous ecosystem known as either the Great Convexity or the Great Concavity (depending on whether you take an American or a Canadian perspective) that absorbs America's waste and produces America's power without America having to deal with the environmental devastation that leads to, among other things, an enormous rise in birth defects in communities that now live alongside a highly radioactive area. Giant fans blow the toxic waste away from the American border toward Quebec, resulting in babies being born with massive congenital deformities, the most consistent of which is having no skull. The result of these "paper atrocities" is a violent insurgency of Québécois separatist radicals, the most extreme of whom, in one of the novel's main plotlines, want to destroy the United States from the inside by distributing a film (titled *Infinite Jest*) so addictively pleasurable that no one who watches it can survive (776).

U.S. imperialism, which extracts resources and brings them home, is thus converted in *Infinite Jest* into "experialism," in which the nation exports the unwanted by-products of its consumerist lifestyle to less powerful countries. That this ecological gerrymandering begins with the signing of NAFTA-esque treaties with Canada and Mexico to create the Organization of North American Nations (ONAN) has led most critics to read experialism as an analogue to the neoliberal practices of late capitalism; think, for example, of the environmental and human damage inflicted in northern Mexico by U.S.-owned *maquila* factories.[57] Other critics have read the novel from a more ecocritical position. N. Katherine Hayles describes the text as reinforcing an ecological perspective that CUSP, with its desire for "sending from yourself what you hope will not return" (1031), would rather deny, as Wallace teaches us to "see [the novel], as well as the world it describes, as a complex system that binds us into its interconnections, thus puncturing the illusion of autonomous selfhood."[58] On a more concrete level, Heather Houser recognizes that the specific ecologies of the novel are more familiar than counterfactual to many of its readers: "imagining territorial reconfiguration, toxification, and energy production, Wallace presents a predicament that is acutely familiar to twenty-first-century Americans: consumer and industrial growth fuels the demand for energy, the production of which alters the environment irremediably."[59] On either a geopolitical level or an ecological one, the territorial reconfiguration that motivates much of the action of this epic novel is read as a commentary on the relationship between the United States and the land beyond its borders, its protected and nurtured communities and its abjected outside.

As an act of what Joseph Masco has called "radioactive nation building," however, the territorial reconfiguration of North America carries a different historical valence—one that Wallace evokes by placing the inverted nukes that Gentle is all too happy to fire into American soil within the "Turtle Mtn. Indian Reservation" (392). Radioactive nation building is a concept developed by Masco to describe the reorientation of national priorities around atomic technologies in the nuclear age.[60] However, as his use of the term *nation building*—a term more usually used to describe the efforts required to create the nation as an imagined community in less stable times, such as the early colonial period or the Civil War—suggests, the territorial and imaginative resources required to promote the atom were far more continuous with earlier forms of violent national autopoiesis than they were different.

From its earliest days, the U.S. nuclear complex has been a colonial project. Its status as such is the outcome of some 450 years of settler colonialism on the North American continent. Centuries of signed treaties, broken treaties, Supreme Court decisions, eugenic state practices like the blood quantum, and federal determination of tribal governance have produced vast reservation territories with precisely the kind of indeterminate national status that defines the Concavity/Convexity: simultaneously sovereign nations and "domestic dependent nations," the "nations within" the United States that both do and do not belong to it.[61] These territories have been central to the nuclear complex for several reasons. First, they offered in the 1940s and 1950s the kind of minimally populated, remote, and ecologically undamaged locations that were required to develop and test the bomb in secret.[62] Second, they contained (and contain) nearly two-thirds of the nation's uranium ore, and so the rapacious resource extraction conducted by industry and enabled by the federal government that has defined the colonial position of Native nations ever since the reservation system was established in the nineteenth century has continued into the nuclear age.[63] Finally, the ecological devastation of land and human and animal life that has resulted from the United States' commitment to nuclear weapons has fallen heavily on Indigenous communities, both within North America and beyond it.[64] The logic behind the positioning of the Nevada Test Site was openly colonial/capitalist: by placing the site close to reservation lands and only testing when the wind was blowing toward the Pueblos, officials at Los Alamos calculated that radioactive damage would be limited to "low-use segments of the population."[65] Even when uranium is not extracted from Native land, the ecologically disastrous processing is carried out there; at the height of the uranium boom in the 1970s, "100 per cent of all federally controlled uranium production accrued from the contemporary reservation land base."[66]

Thus it is not entirely accurate to argue, as does John Beck, that the Second World War transformed the Southwest from an extraction-based colonial economy to what Gerald D. Nash has described as "a technologically oriented and service economy."[67] Rather, the arrival of Los Alamos in New Mexico triggered a new phase of settler colonialism in the Southwest as well as in other locations in the United States, one that Ward Churchill and Winona LaDuke would later define as "radioactive colonialism."[68] Under the new regime, the occupation of

Native land by the United States and the expropriation of its natural resources (internal colonization) shift into a form of nuclear colonization that depends on land occupying a specific relationship to the U.S. nation: both internal enough to the nation that the nation can use it as it wishes and external enough that the nation can comfortably use it as a dump site.[69] The reservation land base, in but not of the United States, is perfectly positioned to become the space that, in Michelle Ty's analysis, all national waste dumps require, whereby "infrastructures of waste must contain . . . a node of non-belonging, a place that is contiguous to the network but categorically severed from it."[70] This form of colonialism produces a kind of quantum geography in which territory belongs simultaneously to a Native nation and to the United States, becoming definable as one or the other only from a specific position that will, following Heisenberg's principle, itself influence the determination.[71]

In *Infinite Jest,* Wallace re-creates this phasing geography through both the novel's content and its form. Like the areas of the Southwest that are simultaneously the Nevada Test Site and Newe Segobia, the unceded homeland of the Western Shoshone described by geographer Bernard Nietschmann as "the most bombed country in the world," the Convexity/Concavity both is and is not the United States—not only within the world of *Infinite Jest* but also in the counterfactual gap between the novel's reality and our own (a gap that we experience when our knowledge that New Hampshire is in the United States bumps up against the novel's geography in which it is a part of Canada).[72] Wallace thus allegorizes the history of the nuclear complex in the fourth world by constructing a counterfactual version of the first world. This allegory works on several fronts and has gone mostly unacknowledged. When Daniel Grausam describes the territories of the Convexity/Concavity in passing as "national sacrifice zones," the reference seems catachrestic, as no context is given for the phrase.[73] The context, however, is crucial: the creation of "national sacrifice areas" was proposed by the National Academy of Sciences to the Nixon administration in 1972 as a way of dealing with both the ecological disasters of the nuclear complex and the growing backlog of unstorable nuclear waste.[74] The proposed solution was to remove the human inhabitants of the already-poisoned territories that had hosted most of the nuclear industry and turn the territories into dumping grounds for nuclear waste, a circular logic of sacrifice that surely provides the model for the Gentle administration's closing of the waste–energy circle through annular fusion in *Infinite Jest*. Such a policy would also have involved destroying a large percentage of remaining reservation land, making Native Americans into "national sacrifice peoples."[75] More recently, the enforced gifting of poisoned land to Canada finds a referent in the strategy that the DOE has pursued since the early 1990s "in which new recognition of the sovereignty of indigenous nations is quickly followed by invitations from federal bureaucracies and corporations for politically unpopular, environmentally dangerous projects."[76] These nations, having been rigorously impoverished by the United States, are often in no position to refuse the cash payments that would accompany the radioactive materials to be stored. Looking beyond the borders of the continental United States, the babies born without skulls in Wallace's Québécois territory also have a fourth world referent in the kinds of congenital deformities still occurring in the Marshall Islands as a result of U.S. nuclear testing, where "well into the 1980s [the] history of nuclear colonialism, long forgotten by the colonizers, was still delivering into the world 'jellyfish babies'—headless, eyeless, limbless human infants who would live for just a few hours."[77]

It is precisely this forgetting that the novel delineates in its allegorical treatment of nuclear colonialism. For while the referential relationship between the "territorial reconfigurations" of *Infinite Jest* and the history of nuclear colonialism is obvious from a fourth world or decolonial perspective, the lack of critical or readerly recognition of this relationship suggests that from a first world perspective, it does not exist.[78] This is an allegory, in other words, that performs its function by failing: when readers fail to recognize it, that very failure recreates the relegation of Native national sacrifice zones and peoples into what Rob Nixon calls "unimagined communities."[79] Nixon uses this phrase to refer "not to those communities that lie beyond the national boundaries but rather to those unimagined communities internal to the space of the nation-state, communities whose vigorously unimagined condition becomes indispensable to maintaining a highly selective discourse of national development."[80] The technological supremacy of Cold War America relied on a narrative of national progress; for that narrative to obtain, the communities who were sacrificed to it had to be "vigorously unimagined" by those who occupy a position within the imagined communities of the nation. When we read *Infinite Jest* without recognition of its real-world Indigenous referents, we perform the unimagining that allows the narrative of national progress and the practice of radioactive colonialism to continue unimpeded. The exclusion of specific histories, Wallace suggests within the novel, is the condition of possibility for the territorial reconfiguration; as CUSP's political mastermind Rodney Tine declares while outlining the plan to the cabinet, "President Gentle's decided we're going to reinvent not just government but history. Torch the past. Manifest a new destiny" (402-3). The irony of Tine's claim that the United States will "manifest a new destiny" by "torch[ing] the past" lies in its use of the historical language of settler colonialism in a context that demands the evacuation of history from the present. Nuclear colonialism in this setting becomes a particular kind of historical forgetting, a desettling or unsettling colonialism: "eminent nondomain: yes. Renewal-grade brand of sacrifice: you bet. Heroes, new era's breed of new pioneers, striking in bravely for already-settled good old settled but unfoul American territory: bien sûr" (403). Torching the past here means separating language from its historical referent: the language of settler colonialism exists only as its own undoing as eminent domain becomes undomain and the meaning of *pioneer* is amputated from its form. That we encounter this scene, itself constituting the history of the novel's present, as a postmodern documentary combining real and fake newspaper reports with imagined puppet show re-creations of cabinet meetings underlines the failure of historical consciousness as a central theme of the novel, as it enables both the nuclear colonization of New England and Quebec within the text and the unimagining of nuclear colonialism in the United States beyond it.

The approach of the Gentle administration, heavily mediated appearances as finger puppets and all, thus provides an analogue within *Infinite Jest* for the kind of risk management that we saw in action at the WIPP: they manage the risk of nuclear waste by unimagining the communities that will be affected by nuclear materials, strictly delimiting the data that can be accepted as relevant to the calculation, torching the past, and fixing the future into an eternal present. The territorial reconfiguration also leads to the end of linear time in the world of the novel, as the massive cost of evacuating New England is met by establishing "subsidized time" in which years are no longer numbered but are sponsored by corporations. Thus Year of the Depend Adult Undergarment, Year of the Perdue Wonderchicken, Year of Dairy Products from the American Heartland.[81] This eternal present both signifies the loss of historical consciousness as a crucial aspect of nuclear colonialism and re-creates this experience in the reader; given that most sections of the novel are dated in the new system, it is strikingly difficult to follow the sequence of events without continually checking whether the Year of the Trial-Sized Dove Bar comes before or after the Year of the Whisper-Quiet Maytag Dishmaster.[82] The reader is trapped in the world that nuclear waste made, as annular fusion begets annular time.

This is, crucially, not an unrealistic world; as Houser notes, the novel is heavily descriptive, and its descriptions are given in a series of matter-of-fact narrative voices that foreground the continuities between our world and this one rather than the differences.[83] Its insistence on verisimilitude, in other words, is disproportionate to the reality of the world that it depicts. The world that is brought forth by nuclear waste and nuclear colonialism here is the world of statistical realism, accumulating data and projecting a future for the nation-state that remains resolutely the same as the present. In the novel's closing image, the gruesome torture of Don Gately's friends gives way to an endless gray vision: "when he came back to, he was flat on his back on the beach in the freezing sand, and it was raining out of a low sky, and the tide was way out" (981). Bradley Fest takes the final scene of the novel as an example of the open ending that Wallace, in Fest's argument, wants us to find in place of the apocalyptic endings of the Cold War.[84] Purely descriptive, resolutely anti-apocalyptic, this closing sentence does indeed privilege an ongoing realism above an apocalyptic ending. Yet it cannot be read out of context, and it carries with it the extreme violence of the pages that lead up to it. This unchanging, realist present is saturated with violence, and its seeming unchangeability should not, I suggest, be taken as a good thing. *Infinite Jest* shows us the colonial violence that undergirds the real and its future in the nuclear age, as both land and history are sliced and diced to allow for the perpetuation of the nuclear complex and the United States itself. As we will see in this chapter's final section, apocalypse may yet be a necessary resource here, when the real is built to unimagine communities and the unending present offers only the annular repetition of the same.

Thinking the North American Unthinkable: *Almanac of the Dead* and Nuclear Decolonization

Leslie Marmon Silko's 1991 epic novel *Almanac of the Dead* describes in detail what *Infinite Jest* can depict only as absence: the history of settler and nuclear colonialisms in the New World, and a sense of historical time that stretches for millennia into the past and the future. Here the accumulation of "paper atrocities" in countless descriptions of torture, rape, and murder in addition to centuries of U.S. legal malfeasance produces a fully fledged "paper apocalypse."[85] Set primarily in the areas around Tucson and Tuxtla Gutierrez, the novel follows an interweaving cast of more than seventy characters as they negotiate turn-of-the-millennium North America. While the wealthy and well connected continue to extract as much value from the land and its inhabitants as possible, finding erotic pleasure in the despoliation of environments and economies as well as bodies, the poor and disenfranchised organize against their exploitation in increasingly interconnected ways. The novel ends with an Indigenous army walking north from Mexico, promising to retake the land peacefully in fulfillment of the ancient prophecies written in the Almanac of the Dead, a fictional fifth Mayan codex circulating within the novel that foretells the end of Euro-American domination in the Americas. Juxtaposing a secular vision of an earth apocalyptically destroyed through the activities of a Euro-American culture devoted to exploiting resources in every possible way with an equally apocalyptic, sacred vision of the inexorable destruction of the fourth world (the age of the Destroyers) by the arrival of the fifth world, in which the culture of destruction will pass away, Silko depicts a world in which apocalypse saturates the everyday, undoing the realism of the nuclear complex by positioning it in a different timeline that has a different past, a different future, and a different present to anything that the nuclear state might think to contain in even its most totalizing attempts to model the world.

Silko's first novel, *Ceremony* (1977), is a canonical text in both Native American studies and ecocriticism, where it prompts valuable discussions of the environmental impact of the nuclear complex and the unevenly distributed violence that links Indigenous and racialized communities in the nuclear age.[86] *Almanac of the Dead,* on the other hand, is rarely read as a nuclear novel. While the downgrading of the nuclear in *Almanac* criticism is partly a reflection of the exponentially larger scale and scope of Silko's second novel, which offers a panoramic vision of destructive technomodernity within which the nuclear occupies a proportionally smaller space, this shift in critical attention also reflects the tendency in nuclear criticism more generally to magnify the conditions of the atom bomb's use in wartime over those of its production and disposal. *Ceremony,* which connects the Pueblos of the Southwest to Japan through uranium mining and the detonation of the atom bomb, is more appealing as nuclear literature than is *Almanac,* which connects the Pueblos to Africa through a shared experience of uranium mining and nuclear waste. Given the centrality of anticolonialism to Silko's thought and aesthetics, however, it seems important to resist such a tendency; Kyoko Matsunaga makes the stakes of this resistance clear when she argues that in both novels, "during the Cold War period, when other literary works portrayed nuclear fear, nuclear anxiety, and nuclear apocalypse, Silko challenged colonial nuclear discourse in the American Southwest."[87] As I argue in the introduction to this book, an exclusive attention to the bomb's detonation often serves to occlude the ongoing violence of the nuclear complex. Reading *Almanac* as a nuclear novel not only insists on the centrality of nuclear colonialism and nuclear waste to the nuclear age but also provides a model of nuclear time that stands against the unchanging present of statistical realism that upholds the ongoing practices of nuclear colonialism critiqued in *Infinite Jest* and sustained at the WIPP.

The narrative form of *Almanac of the Dead* is dazzlingly complex, bringing together a number of different temporal structures, including Marxist dialectics, Christian millennialism, capitalist/colonialist/ scientific apocalypticism, Indigenous forms of spiral time, and the prophetic time of the almanac into variously colliding and conflicting combinations that determine the reality of the world at any given moment. In one of the novel's central scenes, for example, Angelita La Escapía (the Meathook), a leader of the Indigenous Mexican revolutionary movement that marches north at the end of the novel, executes Bartolomeo, a white Cuban Marxist who has been providing funds and guns to the tribal insurrection. Bartolomeo, in his white-supremacist timeline, lives out a different version of the chapter than do Angelita and her "people's committee" (525). Silko repeatedly emphasizes Bartolomeo's inability to comprehend what is happening: he "harangued everyone . . . as if he, Bartolomeo, were not on trial but *they* were" (526, emphasis original); he "seemed unable to comprehend who was on trial. What right did they, ignorant Indians, have to put educated Cubans on trial?" (526). When Angelita recites a three-page list of dates and details of Indigenous uprisings, it creates a relationship with the past that affectively charges the present and determines the course of events: "Angelita detected a change. . . . It was as if the recitation of rebellions and rebel leaders had radiated energy to the people gathered in the plaza" (531). Newly energized by an Indigenous historical consciousness, the people now live in a world in which executing Bartolomeo is both plausible and necessary; Bartolomeo, meanwhile, remains unable to enter this world, to accept the concept of an Indigenous history even as his life depends on it. World making here is a function of narrative form: the emplotment of history within which each character resides constructs the world in which each lives.

It is thus easy to see how, in the words of Bridget O'Meara, "the dialectic of historical struggle in Silko's narrative is not simply a backdrop but rather is both its protagonist and driving force, through which gender, class, and race are articulated and rearticulated in specifically counterhegemonic ways."[88] *Almanac*'s narrative form is defined by the multiplicity of forms that it contains and juxtaposes, and this multiplicity is the form of its revolutionary content; as Ann Brigham writes, a wide array of criticism has "repeatedly recognized *Almanac*'s conceptualization of time as its form of critique."[89] By challenging hegemonic constructions of history and time and offering alternative temporal structures from a variety of perspectives, including those of Indigenous peoples, women, and landscapes, Silko creates a world in which reality as it is seen from within a Euro-American colonialist timeline is only one of a number of competing realities—one whose time is running out.

One formal element that has yet to receive critical attention as such, however, is the novel's frame narrative. Containing this spectacular array of temporalities is a very simple story: a giant stone snake emerges from or next to a mound of uranium tailings. No one knows what it means when it appears; after 758 pages of action-packed narrative across five hundred years, its meaning becomes legible. This entire novel, the worlds that it makes and unmakes, serves in the frame a single purpose: it allows Sterling, a Laguna Pueblo Indian who has been banished from the reservation, to return home and understand the meaning of the snake's appearance.

We encounter Sterling in the first chapter working as a gardener for Zeta, a Native woman who runs drugs across the U.S.–Mexican border and is the twin sister of Lecha, a psychic who finds dead people and is the guardian of the intradiegetic Almanac of the Dead. Sterling has found himself in Tucson, we learn, after being banished from Laguna Pueblo for failing to keep a Hollywood film crew away from a giant stone snake that has recently appeared "at the foot of mountains of grayish [uranium] mine tailings" (35). The tailings themselves are the result of an earlier fall from grace due to the arrival of the nuclear complex on tribal land:

> Sterling had already gone away to Barstow to work on the railroad when uranium had been discovered near Paguate Village. He had no part in the long discussions and arguments that had raged over the mining. In the end, Laguna Pueblo had no choice anyway. It had been 1949 and the United States needed uranium for the new weaponry, especially in the face of the Cold War. That was the reason given by the federal government as it overruled the concerns and objections the Laguna Pueblo people had expressed. . . . So the Tribal Council had gone along with the mine because the government gave them no choice, and the mine gave them jobs. They became the first of the Pueblos to realize wealth from something terrible done to the earth. (34)

The colonial practices of the nuclear age seem here to be located in the past: Sterling believes that he has sidestepped the damage because he lived off-reservation at the time of decision and for most of its operation. He "had never dreamed that one day his own life would be changed forever because of that mine" (35). But as we have seen, the threats of radioactive materials are impossible to contain in specific times and places and are not limited to predictable transmission routes. In this regard, the uncanny temporalities of radiation align with the temporal beliefs of the "old ones" of the Laguna: "trouble" will come from the mine, they argue, which "would not necessarily appear right away; it might not arrive for twenty or even a hundred years. Because these old ones paid no attention to white man's time" (35). Sterling realizes too late that the Euro-American temporality of cause and effect that he has assumed to define his relationship to the mine is inadequate: "those old folks had been right all along. The mine had destroyed Sterling's life without Sterling's ever setting foot near the acres of ruined earth at the open pit" (35).

In the novel's final chapter, "Home," which narrates Sterling's return to Laguna Pueblo, Silko underlines the relationship between the emergence of the snake and nuclear waste: what is "remarkable" about the snake, we learn, is not the sudden appearance of a prophetic sign but "how close the giant snake was to the mountains of tailings" (761). This proximity causes the Laguna to interpret the snake's return as a sign of the imminent destruction of the land and the people by the nuclear complex, with "rumors that the snake's message said the mine and all those who had made the mine had won. Rumors claimed the snake's head pointed to the next mesa the mine would devour, and Sterling had believed the mine had won" (762). The vagaries of commodity markets serve in this instance to protect the reservation, however; "the following year uranium prices had plunged, and the mine had closed before it could devour the basalt mesa the stone snake had pointed at" (762). The meaning of the snake remains unclear until the final sentence of the novel, when Sterling, closing the frame that has contained within it the genocide and destruction of five hundred years of colonialism in the Americas, "knew why the giant snake had returned now; he knew what the snake's message was to the people. The snake was looking south, in the direction from which the twin brothers and the people would come" (763). Sterling's epiphany, closing the novel in the great modernist tradition, is the sudden apprehension of a reversal of scale: it is not the nuclear complex that will swallow the people and the land but the people and the land that will swallow the nuclear complex.

If nuclear waste has been pushed to the edges of *Almanac*, then, its marginal position does not make it any less important to the novel's structure. On the contrary, it is out on the margins that nuclear waste becomes the frame: the part of the narrative that establishes the conditions of possibility for the narratives that it contains and whose meaning is in turn reframed by those narratives when we return to it at the novel's close. What does it mean, then, to consider the story of the emergence of the stone snake from a mountain of nuclear waste as a frame narrative for *Almanac of the Dead*? I want to suggest that we think of the frame narrative as operating in a similar fashion to the other narrative forms at work in the novel: as a form that creates a particular world from a particular treatment of time. This definition follows from Ami M. Regier's important argument that objects are at the center of narrative agency in *Almanac of the Dead*. While "the Western novel has long been described in terms of its commitment to deep character development," Regier argues, "Silko's almanac builds a novel structure by eliciting narratives from the otherwise silent artifacts of the anthropological past and from contemporary objects as diverse as kitchen utensils and computers."[90] The stone snake, as a frame object, produces a specific kind of narrative and a specific kind of world in the novel that takes place within its frame.[91]

The world of *Almanac of the Dead*, like those of the Hora report and *Infinite Jest*, can therefore be seen as the world that nuclear waste makes. This world, however, differs significantly from the unchanging presents of both the Gentle administration and the WIPP. If the world of nuclear waste is defined in *Infinite Jest* and Hora et al. as one that has no real relationship to the past, in *Almanac*, it is nuclear waste that kick-starts the deeply embodied and embedded relationship to history that constitutes the novel's political critique of a Euro-American modernity that is resolutely ahistorical: "In the Americas the white man never referred to the past but only to the future. The white man didn't seem to understand he had no future here because he had no past, no spirits of ancestors here" (313). After a brief opening chapter set in the present, the story of the snake's emergence is the first analeptic turn to the past that we encounter in a novel that will spend much of its time telling stories embedded in different points in history. In a 1993 interview with Laura Coltelli, Silko describes her use of flashback as central to the novel's political aim of rewriting the present's relationship to the past: "I used flashbacks because I wanted the moments of the past to be as alive as they really are; I wanted the reader to be there and to see and feel the aliveness of the past. The past does not die. The past is alive, side by side with the present."[92] *Almanac of the Dead* not only tells the story of the past but drags it up onto the page and into the present, creating a particularly embodied form of historical consciousness in the reader, who "feel[s] what the characters felt so the reader cannot distance himself from the history the almanac recounts."[93] As the material embodiment of the past of both the Laguna, for whom the stone snake served as a protector before being drowned by their enemies, and of the colonial nuclear complex, from whose waste the snake reappears, the stone snake simultaneously represents an embodied form of history and initiates the material appearance of the past in the present as a narrative technique, one that will come to define both the politics and the form of the novel. Nuclear waste may be the product of a technoscientific modernity that flourishes by forgetting the past, but it produces here a diegetic world defined by an iterative, increasingly revolutionary historical consciousness.

At the same time, the snake's nuclear components position it as a figure not only of the past but also of the deep future, as its 4.5-billion-year lifespan dwarfs even the 500 years of the novel's epic diegesis. The snake has both analeptic and proleptic qualities, but its two temporal orientations work in significantly different ways. As a material revenant of Native history, it operates as a figure for fixed historical referents even if those referents have been lost to popular awareness. Its proleptic function, however, is to point us toward a future that is not only unknowable but also completely unimaginable. The snake establishes two proleptic horizons at the end of the novel. While the horizon of the novel's characters marching to decolonize the near-future may be conceptually available to us, that of the uranium snake, some four and half thousand million years from now, is not. This is a peculiar use of a proleptic tropism, deploying the form of a flash-forward while holding the content of that forward glimpse empty. The disjuncture between form and content here is the formal incorporation into the novel of nuclear waste's *longue durée* apocalypse: it thrusts us into a distant future, but there is no *there* there, no sense that we know what that future might hold. Our proleptic encounter with the future of nuclear waste reveals only the impossibility of that future within a human perspective.

Almanac's wildly expanded, radically futureless historical consciousness redefines the terms of realism, verisimilitude, and plausibility that we saw in action at the WIPP. As Caren Irr argues, much of the critical blowback against *Almanac* from the white literary establishment (Sven Birkerts's review in the *New Republic* is exemplary) stems from the insult that the novel poses to the critics' sense of the realistic and the plausible, of the "opposition between the plot of 'wish-fulfillment scenarios' and a social reality in which strikes, rebellions, and revolutions are apparently impossible."[94] Such an opposition, Irr suggests, is based on a specific "metaphysics of time" in which "change does not happen, since history is the repetition of self-identical defeats. . . . Any suggestion otherwise—any prophecy or assertion of an alternative futurity, any quoting for instance from *The Communist Manifesto*—violates the initial premise of temporal consistency and must be disallowed."[95] Silko's assertion that a different relationship of the present to the past might lead to a revolutionary future is, within such a temporal metaphysics, laughably unrealistic.

Birkerts's dismissal of a decolonial future for North America as something "so contrary to what we know both of the structures of power and the psychology of the oppressed that the imagination simply balks" is consistent with a much longer history of colonial rhetoric and practice that rejects Native land claims as impossible or unrealistic.[96] The Supreme Court's invocation in their 2005 *City of Sherrill v. Oneida Nation* decision of the "impossibility doctrine" that governs the "impracticability of returning to Indian control land that generations earlier passed into numerous private hands" demonstrates the ongoing power of a white-defined realism to distinguish possible from impossible actions with regard to its own practices of settler colonialism.[97] In this view, for the United States to abide by the terms of its treaties with Native nations is unthinkable; it falls beyond the limits of plausibility that define possible actions. And as Mark Rifkin has argued, the idea of Native sovereignty is not just unrealistic but an epistemological challenge to the real itself, to the construction of reality that maintains life as we know it in the United States.[98] The "sadder realism" called for by Buell must not, therefore, be taken as the neutral generic option in dealing with risk but rather recognized as one that relies on standards of verisimilitude and plausibility that perpetuate the oppression of Indigenous communities whether they are applied directly to nuclear risk or to the legal standards that define the limits of Native self-determination.

Redefining the real, "draw[ing] attention to the possible by showing the contingent dimension of the actual," thus becomes a strategy of decolonization.[99] Realism, in this context, is a self-fulfilling prophecy: the return of Native land is regarded as impossibly implausible by the United States, and so it fails to appear in the imaginable scenarios at key moments of legal and political decision-making and does not come to pass. Consequently, as Ward Churchill writes, all "anti-colonial fighters . . . accepted as their agenda a redefinition of reality in terms deemed quite impossible within the conventional wisdom of their oppressors"; any decolonial movement will require a counterrealist political and aesthetic strategy. *Almanac* suggests that apocalypse remains a potent force in redefining reality against colonial norms even as the novel re-forms our traditional understanding of nuclear apocalypse. No longer sudden and total, *Almanac* gives us the *longue durée* apocalypse of nuclear waste, an apocalypse defined not by the sudden absence of the future but rather by the impossibility of constructing any mechanism by which we might imagine a specific future or futures.

Such an apocalypse is neither a sudden ending nor a revelation of eternal truth but rather a narratological shift that transfigures the present through a radical futurelessness. Apocalypse stands, in *Almanac,* against the futurological equivalent of what Michael Bernstein has critiqued as "backshadowing": the historiographical tendency to construct the past backward from the present, occluding the contingency of the present, limiting the presents-that-could-have-been to one, and including in the historical narrative only those factors that gave rise to this specific outcome.[100] A predetermined future, as Bernstein's subtitle *Against Apocalyptic History* suggests, does exactly the same thing: it binds the present to the future with a single unfrayed rope and makes the present the necessary, unchangeable precursor to a known future. These imagined futures, despite their virtuality, have significant material effects in the present, making certain things possible and rendering others unthinkable, as we saw at the WIPP, where a plausible set of future scenarios allowed the repository to open and foreclosed the possibility of shutting down nuclear manufacturing. In an Indigenous context, meanwhile, the historical determinism instantiated by the imagined futures of the nuclear state has rendered Native nations paradoxically futureless, since Indigenous lands and communities are by far the most damaged by the ongoing mining, processing, testing, and dumping practices of the nuclear–military–industrial complex.

Apocalypse, then, becomes visible in Silko's novel not as a model

of linear historical determinism, as in the Genesis-to-Revelation teleology that has long subtended Christian historiographies, but rather
as a narrative form that explodes such determinism to reveal the contingent nature of the present and allow for other possibilities in both
the present and the future. The epistemological challenges to human
understanding posed by the deep time of nuclear waste are taken up
by Silko to reveal not simply the multiplicity of possible futures (a conceptual leap which, as Annie McClanahan and R. John Williams have
shown, was made within the nuclear–military–industrial complex and
has been profitably taken up by global corporations to deeply conservative ends) but the absolute impossibility of imagining any specific
future at all.[101] Exploding the reservoir of probable futures that traditionally structures the novel form transforms the novel's present in
much the same way that, in radical historiography, telling a different
story about the past does, as the apocalyptic uranium snake creates
new conditions of possibility for both the novel's form and its world.[102]

Silko's alignment of nuclear and Native temporalities in the figure
of the uranium snake is itself a powerful argument about the relationship between the nuclear complex, nuclear materials, and Native nations. From the perspective of the nuclear complex, nuclear materials
and Native Americans are connected through a logic of metonymy;
their material proximity on unironically named "nuclear reservations"
means that one comes to stand in for the other as research "kivas" replace those of the Pueblos, and Zuni, Yuma, and Tewa missiles are detonated in the Pacific while their eponymous nations are decimated in
the Southwest.[103] The linear timeline that undergirds both settler colonialism and Euro-American technomodernity makes this metonymic
slippage possible, as the historical positioning of the "Vanishing Indian"
leaves the present and the future available for the Indian's replacement
by the nuclear complex. This linear temporality also undergirds a woe-
fully common ecocritical approach in which the "ecological Indian,"
inhabiting and representing a premodern time, is used to figure an alternative way of life that white people might imitate in the present as
an alternative to the destructive modernity of the nuclear age.[104] In
both accounts, the valuable quality of the Native American—whether
arcane knowledge, warlike attitude, or kinship with nature—is made
available to whiteness by figuring Native Americans as obsolete, with
no real claim upon the modern present.

Silko's juxtaposition of the Native and the nuclear offers a radically different interpretation of the relationship between the two. Regier contrasts the uranium-coated stone snake to the figures of the "little grandparents" stolen from the Laguna eighty years prior to the emergence of the snake: while the little grandparents are the ancient, "pure" products of an isolated tribe, the snake is an "impure object" that is nonetheless crucial to the novel's politics—"far from being made ineffective by impure contact, and becoming the vehicle of another narrative of loss, the snake becomes the final harbinger of revolution."[105] The nuclear complex, in this figure, does not succeed the Indian on a linear timeline that consigns Native Americans to a vanishing past but rather forms a hybrid of the nuclear and the Native that betokens a radically undetermined future within a "'contaminated' narrative form appropriate to the history of colonial encounter."[106] The stone snake brings together the most toxic products of Western technoscience with one of the most sacred symbols in Laguna and other mythologies, but it does not do so to suggest an opposition between them. Rather, the uranium tailings and the snake fuse together, wrenching the nuclear out of a Western timeline and into an Indigenous one.

The consequences of this temporal shift are, as are all temporal shifts in a novel that aligns temporality with world making, world changing. In contrast to the presentist, linear thinking that defines the nuclear complex at the WIPP and beyond, the Indigenous temporalities that the snake occupies are those of a *longue durée* that spirals and returns, in which "these days and years were all alive, and all these days would return again" (247). The qualitatively different future whose possibility is so vigorously unimagined at the WIPP is here an inescapable, apocalyptic future that is, in a nonlinear time frame, also a part of the present. Actions and objects have a different reality-effect in this light. When macaws speak of revolution, when opals bleed and grant visions, when ghosts weigh down a donkey, none of these things are unrealistic or even magically realistic. Rather, they are manifestations of deep-time temporalities, simultaneously Native and nuclear, producing impossible juxtapositions of space-time (dead riders on a live mule, the future projected on an opal screen) within the Western chronology of the novel form.

By aligning an impossible future of decolonization with nuclear waste, Silko both establishes the shared ground of the Native and nuclear and rewrites that ground as a different kind of prophecy: not of the perpetuation of the nuclear–colonial complex, as at the WIPP, but of its inevitable destruction. In this way, Silko's novel reverses the prophetic form of statistical realism that oils the gears of the nuclear complex at the WIPP. In Hora et al., a totalizing description of the real allows for the projection of a future that will not be qualitatively different from the present. In *Almanac,* the reverse is true. Including the impossible, the implausible, and the incalculable (from a colonial perspective) within her accounting of the real, Silko reveals the apocalyptic overturning of the actual at work within the days of the present, an overturning prophesied by the nuclear materials that are supposed to maintain the present of the United States at the expense of its unimagined communities. Forcing us to inhabit the *longue durée* by their own unthinkable durability, the by-products of the nuclear complex situate us as inhabitants of an impossible world: one in which the United States does not last, one in which apocalypse, or revolution, or decolonization, is not only thinkable but inevitable.

The Map, the Territory, and the Future: Risk and the Real World

Colonial power becomes visible in *Almanac of the Dead* as a function of both space and time, whereby occupations of space are made possible by writing that space into the timeline of Euro-American modernity. In recontextualizing Western chronologies within the apocalyptically deep temporalities of the Native and the nuclear, Silko reinscribes the history of Euro-American colonialists in the Americas as the frantic pop history of *Infinite Jest*'s Gentle administration: gaudy finger puppets playing out their violent stories on a constructed stage as the land waits patiently underneath them for the balsa wood stage and its tissue paper finery to crumble and blow away. The oppositions that we have seen recurring throughout the three core texts of this chapter between risk and danger, statistical model and reality, and colonial and Indigenous operate in an uneasy tension around the figure of nuclear waste, as colonial powers model its reality in order to translate danger into risk. In closing this chapter, I turn now to moments in *Infinite Jest* and the Hora report that extend Silko's reversal of this configuration, as the obstinate, uncontainable reality of nuclear waste works instead

to overturn the models and aesthetic forms that would secure the future as a continuation of the present.

One of the most spectacular sequences in *Infinite Jest* is an account
of the live action role-playing game Eschaton that some of the students at Enfield Tennis Academy play each year on Interdependence
Day. Eschaton is a combination of RAND-style war games, conducted
through written scenarios and immensely complex algorithms, and
tennis: "in the game," we learn, "Combatants' 5-megaton warheads can
only be launched with hand-held tennis rackets. Hence the requirement of actual physical targeting-skill that separates Eschaton from
rotisserie-league holocaust games played with protractors and PCs
around kitchen tables" (324). This reenactment of Cold War culture is
described by Wallace as the closest thing that its players have to a sense
of history, as its players' "weird kind of nostalgia for stuff you never
even knew" is defined in a footnote as "what more abstraction-capable
post-Hegelian adults call 'Historical Consciousness'" (322, 1023). This
may be a deeply compromised form of historical consciousness, as the
descriptor "nostalgia," much maligned by Jameson, would suggest, but
it is the only one available to the young Eschaton players.

The tightly choreographed collapse of this elegant and complex
game into bloody reality forms one of the major set pieces of the novel.
After several pages of detailed and acronym-riddled description ("poor
old SOVWAR is absorbing such serious collateral SUFDDIR that it's
being inexorably impelled by game-theoretic logic to a position where
it's going to pretty much have no choice but to go SACPOP against
AMNAT" [330]), snow starts to fall on the Enfield tennis courts. Eschaton relies on the statistical realism of game theory, which in its Cold
War heyday used scenarios and probability modeling to contain the
risk of uncertain futures in much the same way that we saw in SNL's
approach to the WIPP. By transforming the unknown future into a
probability function (if we fire on Moscow, this leader, under these cir-
cumstances, and believing these things about us, is 98 percent likely
to fire back, with a 70 percent chance of a direct hit, etc.), game theory is used "to make war 'scientific'—that is, less risky, more control-
lable."[107] And, as at the WIPP, the question of the realistic scenario is
central to Eschaton and is also its most fragile point. Just as it starts to
snow, "gamemaster and statistician of record" Otis P. Lord is "number-
crunching so fiendishly at the cart's Yushityu, trying to confirm the

verisimilitude of the peace terms AMNAT and SOVWAR are hashing out" that he misses seeing whether a tennis ball strike on Karachi was a direct or an indirect hit (322, 333). In the ensuing argument, INDPAK representative J. J. Penn causes an ontological crisis by claiming that "now that it's snowing the snow totally affects blast area and fire area and pulse-intensity and maybe also has fallout implications, and he says Lord has to now completely redo everybody's damage parameters before anybody can form realistic strategies from here on out" (333).

The question of realism and its verisimilitude becomes immediately central and disastrous. While Penn sees the snow as internal to the world of the game and thus as part of its reality, Eschaton's inventor Michael Pemulis interprets such a claim as a potential "theater-boundary-puncturing threat" to "the game's whole sense of animating realism": "It's snowing on the goddamn *map*, not the *territory*, you *dick!*" (333, emphasis original). For Pemulis, thoroughly committed to statistical realism, events that are intradiegetic to the world of the novel are only intradiegetic to the world of the game if they have been included in the field of possibility from the outset: "it's only real-world snow if it's already in the scenario!" (334). In the midst of this ontological crisis, a warhead/tennis ball is fired into the back of a player for the first time in the history of Eschaton, further collapsing the distinctions between the map and the territory on which the game depends. With the disintegration of these distinctions, bodies become fair game and represented violence is incarnated in a choreographed, quasi-slapstick fight scene that results in Lord going headfirst through the screen of the computer on which Eschaton runs.[108]

We might, then, read the Eschaton scene as an example of the metafiction that Grausam argues is a critique of the culture of simulation established by a security state hooked on game theory: "maps are not the territories they hope to represent," Grausam writes, "and no matter how rigorously one tries to imagine a war-gaming environment that understands every contingency, the finite number of players in the game has to represent a much larger community of actors, each of whom adds the considerable complexity of the human factor into the equation of simulation."[109] Simulations can never achieve the totality on which they depend because the scenario construction can never cover every possible occurrence. The failures that both Grausam and Steven Belletto imagine as the undoing of game theory are anthropocentric ones: you never know what people are going to do. The collapse of game theory in *Infinite Jest,* however, offers a more complex vision. For it is neither Penn's claim that the snow is part of the game's world nor Ingersoll's attack on Kittenplan that initiates the collapse of the map–territory distinction; rather, it is the snow itself. Wallace establishes the snow in this scene not as a single contradiction in the assumptions governing the game but as an alternative form of world making that ultimately overcomes the logic of the probability-based scenario that has governed the world of Eschaton up until that point. After its first appearance, the snow comes increasingly to define the world within which the players move. When Lord decides that the in-game situation has become bleak enough to warrant his wearing of "the red beanie that signifies Utter Global Crisis," the snow mediates between the landscape of the map and that of the territory as "a real-world chill descends over the grainily white-swirled landscape of the nuclear theater" (336–37). As the situation declines, "the snow is now coming down hard enough to compose an environment" (338). By the time that fists and tennis balls are flying, the snow sets the conditions within which the scene can be viewed and comprehended: "the snow-fall makes everything gauzy and terribly clear at the same time, eliminating all visual background so that the map's action seems stark and surreal" (341). In the final sentence of the Eschaton scene, a Joycean echo that resonates with *Almanac*'s epiphanic ending, the snow has become the foreground to which everything else is background. "The second shift's 1600h. siren down at Sunstrand Power & Light is creepily muffled by the no-sound of falling snow" (342).

It is thus not unpredictable humans that cause the downfall of Eschaton's statistical realism but something entirely nonhuman and, as we can all attest, resistant to our best efforts at forecasting: the weather. Game theory fails rather differently here, when the world beyond the board becomes a player in the game. This man-versus-world scenario is, I suggest, representative of the post–Cold War shift in attitudes to the nuclear that we saw at the WIPP, in which nuclear materials themselves, rather than the men who had their fingers on the button, become the targets of statistical prediction—no longer "how likely is this man to launch the warhead?" but rather "how likely is this uranium slurry to corrode its container?" The ability of the snow to redraw both the map and the territory of Eschaton, its virtual and its actual dimensions, indicates the game-changing potential of this shift, as mathematical technologies that were developed to contain human uncertainties within a supposed totality are revealed to be themselves a part of a much larger system, one that can bury the game board in a second and never even notice.

Speaking of the novel's descriptive strategies in ways that recall Regier's theory of narratological object agency in *Almanac*, Houser writes that "the formal strategies of *Infinite Jest* articulate an ethics of materiality by putting humans and human-like agents on the same narratorial footing as objects described."[110] The Eschaton scene suggests that this redistribution of agency has implications for how we think ourselves not only within an environment, as Houser argues, but also within time. If *Infinite Jest* has a therapeutic approach to time, as both Grausam and Fest argue, then it lies at a larger scale than either critic has approached. Both critics cite the "post-Hegelian" footnote as a straightforward descriptor of what Wallace thinks of historical consciousness, but the collapse of the Eschaton game suggests that this form of historical consciousness is deeply compromised and compromising. Playing Eschaton might be the only form of historical consciousness available in this world, but it is by no means a good one. What we see in the falling snow is rather the confrontation between the limited and limiting constructions of time required by nuclear colonialism—the officially approved "history" of the novel—and the massively distributed deep time of the climate: the *anthropos* versus the Anthropocene, human time versus a *longue durée* that "scoop[s] out the objectified now of the present moment into a shifting uncertainty."[111] Whether we read the snow as a function of climate or as a reference to the nuclear winter that would follow an atomic war, it brings the apocalyptically deep time of the hyperobject into the statistical world of Eschaton, deconstructing the difference between the map and the territory and forcing deep time into the statistical present of the model.

Eschaton, like the WIPP, is the world that the U.S. approach to nuclear waste makes, structured by it in the way that it interprets the present, through probability modeling, and in being constructed out of waste, since its thermonuclear warheads are really "400 tennis balls so dead and bald they can't even be used for service drills anymore" (322). However, *Infinite Jest* indicates that by tying our fortunes to nu-

clear waste, we insert ourselves into a timescale within which our attempts to manage chance through probability modeling necessarily
fail: sooner or later, the snow will come, transforming the carefully
managed distinctions between information and noise upon which
statistical world making depends into a staticky mass of data.[112] In an
Adornian turn, Wallace constructs a world whose breaks and absences
show us the forms of what has been lost or ignored: the unimagined
communities of nuclear colonialism, the deep temporalities of which
we can only catch glimpses in the falling snow, stuck as we are within
a human perspective whose history plays out like a puppet show. At
the same time that we seek to master the world through nuclear technologies and infrastructures, *Infinite Jest* suggests, the material remain-
ders of those technologies and infrastructures form the limits of our
mastery, outlasting us and moving beyond our conceptions of the real
and the possible at every turn. We have no more mastery over nuclear
waste than we do over the weather, but accepting that we live within
its temporality rather than attempting to contain it within ours might
yet allow us to rescale history and reimagine it in other terms, with
other presents, other futures.

Perhaps unexpectedly, the Futures Report itself contains something like a minority report that shares Wallace's and Silko's critique of
statistical realism as a model for deep time. Here, too, an approach to
nuclear waste from an apocalyptically deep-time perspective produces
what we might call, for want of a better term, an aesthetics of the extremely improbable. One of the four teams of experts, the Southwestern Team, have two obvious features that distinguish them from their
peers: they live in the region under discussion and they count a science
fiction author as one of their members. In their report, pleasingly titled
Ten Thousand Years of Solitude?, they characterize themselves as both
more literary and more situated within the territory than the other
three teams. The WIPP site is not, for the Southwestern Team, a collection of lines on a map or a compound cumulative data function but
"an ancient land, and one where the impact of U.S. control is light and,
possibly, transient."[113] This perspective manifests in two ways in *Ten
Thousand Years of Solitude?* The first is a refusal to play the game math-
ematically; the Southwestern Team was the only team to refuse to pre-
emptively assign numerical probabilities to their scenarios (they went
with low, medium, and high). In place of the numerical probability

assignments required by SNL, the Southwestern Team offers apocalyptic science fiction. Pushing the fictional descriptions of the future requested of them to the point of absurdity, they open each section with a short description of the future in a resolutely nonrealistic mode:

> Zzyg lifted his eyes from the visual scanner eyepieces on the survey ship orbiting the blue-green world and said, "It looks like another pre-conscious race didn't make it through their atomic age. That makes three so far this trip, and we have only come seventy-five light years." He sighed and brushed a tear from his center eye with his third-left tendril.[114]

The Futures Panel had already established that such scenarios were to be excluded from their considerations; Martin Pasqualetti, a geographer and member of the Southwestern Team who later published an article discussing his experiences, cites one of the "limiting assumptions" as being that "extraordinary events such as collisions with objects from space, extraterrestrial visits, or negation of gravity do not occur."[115] The expert judgment methodology requires, as we have seen, an adherence to realism in its fictions: the scenarios have to be believable, to extend out from the known and to bring the unknown into our field of control. The Southwestern Team, however, includes pointedly antirealist fictions throughout their report, on the same narrative level as their more plausible accounts of automatic mole miners or the development of the Free State of Chihuahua.

Such a juxtaposition is a form of argument: that in an attempt to imagine future societies over ten thousand years, heuristics such as probability and realism fail to apply. This argument reflects the epistemological challenge that deep time makes to statistical realism, particularly to the claim that statistical realism can be used to manage risk. In his analysis of highly complex systems, Perrow concludes that "multiple and unexpected interactions of failures are inevitable. This is an expression of an integral characteristic of the system, not a statement of frequency."[116] What we consider "accidents," defined by their unforeseeable nature, must rather be considered an inevitable part of the system itself. In van Wyck's terms, "the practice contains the accident, not simply as a *possibility*—as that which may or may not happen—but fully and completely as *virtuality*."[117] The only thing that separates the system from its failure, the possible from the actual, is time; the only reason that there have not been more catastrophic meltdowns, Perrow writes in 1984, is that "we simply have not given the nuclear power system a reasonable amount of time to disclose its potential."[118] The meltdown at the Chernobyl plant two years later, itself experienced, in the words of Barbara Adam, as "the materialization of the impossible," illustrates the accuracy of Perrow's analysis.[119] Probability becomes certainty over a long enough timescale; in the timescale of nuclear waste, "probability models of containment failure converge on certainty."[120] In deep time, the Southwestern Team suggests, the alien that reads the WIPP as a monument to humanity's failure to evolve is no less plausible than the long-term survival of the United States—indeed, the "USA Forever" scenario is discounted quickly in *Ten Thousand Years of Solitude?* because of its absolute implausibility.

By inserting apocalyptic science fiction into the more realistic descriptions of plausible futures in *Ten Thousand Years of Solitude?*, the Southwestern Team write the impossible future into the present as an expression of the existence of the virtual in the actual. In so doing, they establish a nonrealistic form of fiction as a weapon against a state-sponsored realism that insists on the impossibility of radical change, that fails to grasp "the most difficult realization about the future": "that it can be qualitatively different."[121] In this aesthetic approach, they mirror Silko and Wallace, both of whom also bring an apocalyptic future into the present through the discarded materials of the nuclear complex in order to disrupt the claims to realism and totality that keep business going as usual in nuclear as well as other forms of colonialism.

Reading these three texts as analyses of nuclear waste, risk, and colonial power thus produces a different critical heuristic to the paranoid epistemology described by van Wyck and practiced by Hora et al. While paranoid ecocriticism experiences risk as a bad surprise that we could defend against with a totalizing-enough realist understanding of the present, Silko, Wallace, and Benford et al. conceptualize risk within the deep temporality of nuclear waste in which, promising to long outlive the human, radioactive materials push the probabilistic epistemology that subtends our thinking about risk beyond the limits of its reach. As risk approaches a 100 percent probability, it ceases to be shuntable into the future as a possible occurrence and becomes a part of the present as an active danger, a threat in urgent need of redress. By bringing an apocalyptic future into a present defined by the state as unchangeable, Silko, Wallace, and Benford et al. reveal the imbrication of risk theory with colonial logics and suggest that a full inhabitation of risk and its impossible futures is required to overturn the actual and move beyond those logics in a nuclear age that, environmentally, if not infrastructurally, we can never and will never escape.

Nuclear waste is bigger than us, more dangerous than us, and will outlive us. It is our own self-created predator. At the same time, however, it challenges the terms of the reality that produced it: a capitalist/colonialist present that can imagine the future only in the terms of its own continuation. At the end of *Minima Moralia,* Adorno calls for perspectives to be fashioned "that displace and estrange the world, reveal it to be, with its rifts and crevices, as indigent and distorted as it will appear one day in the messianic light."[122] Nuclear waste inhabits the future that Adorno evokes here, appearing in our world like a time traveler from 240,000 years from now, its form only temporarily concealed within that of a glove, or a hair net, or a barrel. Lives lived at risk are not undamaged lives, flowing smoothly until they are disrupted by catastrophic events. Lives lived at risk are already damaged, and discourses of "acceptable risk" mandate that some lives are worth damaging in this way. For those whose lives are sacrificed to the real, nuclear waste offers a perspective within which that reality is revealed in all of its indigence and distortion as a crumbling diorama, a mutated, nonviable cell: contingent, futureless, and open to change beyond all imagining.

Coda
Nuclear Entanglements

All time is unredeemable.

—T. S. Eliot, "Burnt Norton"

Where matter fails, care makes do.

—N. K. Jemisin, *The Stone Sky*

At 4:46 p.m. JST on Friday, March 11, 2011, a seismic slip-rupture event occurred between two tectonic plates off of the coast of Japan. The slow subduction of the Pacific Plate underneath the plate that underlies northern Honshu builds up elastic energy over time that was released, that day, in the form of a 9.1 magnitude earthquake, the fourth largest in recorded history. The Tōhoku earthquake triggered a massive tsunami that struck the coast of Japan less than an hour later. At the Fukushima Daiichi nuclear power plant, the earthquake caused the reactors to automatically shut down their sustained fission reactions. When the tsunami hit, however, it destroyed the emergency generators that provided energy to the cooling systems responsible for keeping the reactors subcritical. Three of the plant's six reactors melted down over the next three days, leading to an ongoing nuclear catastrophe that released plumes of radioactive particles into the air at the time of the meltdowns and that continues to pour millions of gallons of radioactive water into both the groundwater and the Pacific Ocean.

The brutal historical resonance between the violent inauguration of the atomic age at Hiroshima and Nagasaki and its uncanny return to Japan at Fukushima Daiichi has been widely noted. Yet to think of this resonance as a coincidence obscures the causal link between the two events, contributing to the regime of imperceptibility that surrounds the American nuclear complex. The atomic bombing of Japan by the United States was the means to a specific end: the unconditional surrender of the Emperor (as compared to the conditional surrender that had already been offered). The acquisition of this unconditional surrender led to the U.S. occupation of Japan and gave America long-term control (continuing into the present) over Japan's industrial and military trajectories. In the 1950s, American politicians decided that Japan should have nuclear power plants. After a long public relations/PSYOP campaign run by American agencies from the State Department to the CIA, public opposition to nuclear power in Japan was overcome, and the first nuclear power plant was built in 1966 by the British company GEC.[1] The Fukushima Daiichi reactors were built in 1970 by the American company General Electric using a design that had already been marked in the United States as potentially unsafe, on a bluff that was originally tall enough to survive a major tsunami but that was reduced in height by twenty-five meters to decrease the cost of pumping seawater into the reactors, in territory that belonged to the indigenous Emishi people before being colonized by the Japanese empire in the eighth century and that remains a racialized space to this day.[2] Formed, like the rest of the global nuclear complex, at the confluence of capitalism, colonialism, and militarized violence, the 3/11 meltdown was not a historical echo of the earlier atomic trauma but rather a direct consequence of American militarism and neocolonialism at Hiroshima and Nagasaki, during the Cold War, and into our present moment.

The Fukushima Daiichi disaster thus encapsulates the infrastructuring of apocalypse that this book has argued is central to the nuclear age, in which power; capital; technology; environmental despoliation; and the social technologies of race, class, gender, sexuality, indigeneity, and nation come together to produce the ends of some worlds as the mechanism for the continuation of others. In this conclusion, I turn to Fukushima Daiichi as a space to reflect on some of *Infrastructures of Apocalypse*'s key themes and ask what it would mean to think about the world as apocalyptically infrastructured. Infrastructure is relational, entangling us with the world and with the other beings who share it. At the same time, nuclear materials, unbounded and unbindable, constantly escape the infrastructures that seek to contain them and forge their own entanglements with us at the cellular and subcellular levels. In the nuclear age, we are brought into relation with nuclear materials knowingly or not, willingly or not. Vulnerability is a feature here, not a bug. In closing, then, let us consider how apocalypse brought us into this entangled, vulnerable reality and how apocalypse might yet be a means to think productively about how to live in the age of nuclear entanglement.

THE PATH TO THE FUKUSHIMA meltdown originates in a distinctly apocalyptic desire for redemption on the part of the United States. In the early 1950s, President Eisenhower was engaged in massively expanding the nuclear arsenal to reduce the overhead of the conventional armed forces, including developing the hydrogen bomb, whose destructive power would be many hundreds of times that of the first atomic bombs.[3] The problem was that developing the capacity for apocalyptic overkill made the United States look bad to both the American public and the international audience. In a 1952 report to the Psychological Strategy Board, Defense Department official Stefan Possony laid out both the problem facing the United States and the proposed psychological solution:

> Our enemies contend that reliance on this "weapon of mass destruction" reveals the "barbarous" character of American "imperialism." Moreover, our preoccupation with the atomic bomb rather than with atomic energy allegedly is indicative of the warlike character of present American policies. . . . It must indeed be realized that the atom as a peace and prosperity maker will be more acceptable to the world than the atom as a war maker. . . . Even the atomic bomb will be accepted far more readily if at the same time atomic energy is being used for constructive ends.[4]

For Eisenhower and his growing military–industrial complex, in the words of historian Kenneth Osgood, "the development of atoms for war required the cultivation of atoms for peace."[5]

In December 1953, Eisenhower launched the Atoms for Peace program into the world. At a speech given to the UN, Eisenhower proposed the development of an international atomic energy agency whose task would be to mobilize experts to "apply atomic energy to the needs of agriculture, medicine, and other peaceful activities. A special purpose," he emphasized, "would be to provide abundant electrical energy in the power-starved areas of the world."[6] Against the apocalyptic potential of America's nuclear arsenal, especially that of the hydrogen bomb, Atoms for Peace promised to "[find] the way by which the miraculous inventiveness of man shall not be dedicated to his death, but consecrated to his life."[7]

A closer look at the language used to describe Atoms for Peace, and especially Atoms for Peace in the Japanese context, however, reveals the apocalyptic temporal structures that underlie even the supposedly counterapocalyptic infrastructures of the nuclear age. In his speech, Eisenhower moves through a series of familiar descriptors of the apocalyptic threat of nuclear weapons in the world as it currently is. In the world without Atoms for Peace, we are doomed to "confirm the hopeless finality of a belief that two atomic colossi are doomed malevolently to eye each other indefinitely across a trembling world" and "to accept helplessly the probability of civilization destroyed, the annihilation of the irreplaceable heritage of mankind handed down to us from generation to generation, and the condemnation of mankind to begin all over again the age-old struggle upward from savagery towards decency, and right, and justice." The promise of Atoms for Peace is that it will move the world from the apocalyptic present into a millennial future of guaranteed peace and prosperity: "my country's purpose," Eisenhower announces, "is to help us to move out of the dark chamber of horrors into the light, to find a way by which the minds of men, the hopes of men, the souls of men everywhere, can move forward towards peace and happiness and well-being." The benefit of Atoms for Peace, in Eisenhower's account, can be summed up in a single word: in the face of the apocalyptic destruction threatened by nuclear weapons, Atoms for Peace will bring "salvation."[8]

The irony of the Atoms for Peace speech is that the narrative that Eisenhower lays out is no less apocalyptic than the images of total annihilation that he posits as Atoms for Peace's bad other. Nuclear power emerges here as a Christ-like figure, a redeeming agent who can lead men's "souls" from the "dark chamber of horrors" into the "light" of "salvation"; appearing as the redemptive antitype of nuclear weapons, Atoms for Peace is the second coming of the nuclear age. Indeed, the redemptive-apocalyptic logic is the only framework in which the Atoms for Peace program makes any sense. The destructive-apocalyptic threat of massive, growing nuclear arsenals is impacted not at all by the fact that there will now also be nuclear power plants; this logic is akin to addressing the danger of a rattlesnake by putting it next to a tiger. The problem that Eisenhower describes, that of an ever-expanding stockpile of ever-more-destructive nuclear weapons, can only be addressed—then as now—by robust programs of demilitarization and denuclearization. What Atoms for Peace really offers, then, is a framework within which putting more resources into nuclear technology (which has never been separate from the military use of the atom) and exposing more people to the catastrophic dangers of that technology can be interpreted as redemptive-apocalyptic rather than as destructive-apocalyptic: nuclear power will bring a millennial future to pass and save our souls from nuclear bombs.

The American desire for nuclear redemption only intensified when Atoms for Peace was translated into a Japanese context. The program was particularly urgent in Japan because Eisenhower's speech to the UN was followed after only three months by the disastrous detonation of America's first hydrogen bomb at the Bravo test, which showered Japanese fishermen aboard the *Daigo Fukuryu Maru* (Lucky Dragon no. 5)—located eighty-five miles from the test site and outside the official danger zone—with radiation, killing one, and led to a national panic in Japan after radioactive tuna was found being sold in fish markets across the country. These incidents led to a powerful uprising in Japan against the hydrogen bomb in particular and U.S. nuclear weapons more generally; by 1955, thirty-two million people, one-third of Japan's population, had signed a petition launched by women in Tokyo to ban hydrogen bombs. As the only country to have been bombed with nuclear weapons in wartime, Japan had a moral claim in the struggle against nuclear weapons that no other country could match. The United States thus launched one of the biggest psychological operations of the Cold War, using CIA-trained journalists and politicians to promote Atoms for Peace in Japan as an appropriate response to, rather than a continuation of, the nuclear violence that the country

had experienced at Hiroshima and Nagasaki. Because Japan had experienced the violence of nuclear weapons, this operation argued, it
only made sense that Japan should be among the first to benefit from
"nonviolent" uses of the atom.[9]

For Americans, however, bringing nuclear power to Japan was less
about restitution than it was about redemption.[10] In September 1954,
the *Washington Post* reported the proposal of Atomic Energy Council
commissioner Thomas C. Murray that Japan should be the first foreign recipient of a nuclear power plant. The reasons given in the article
were partially to do with Cold War geopolitics ("already the Russians,
sensing the urgent [power] needs of the Japanese and therefore the political opportunities in Japan, are making overtures"), but more space
was given to the idea that America had sinned against Japan and that
redemption was now required:

> Many Americans are now aware, thanks primarily to the United
> States bombing survey, that the dropping of the atomic bomb on
> Japan was not necessary. In retrospect, the war seemed to have
> been virtually over when we obliterated Hiroshima and Nagasaki.
> How better to make a contribution to amends than by offering
> Japan the means for the peaceful use of atomic energy.[11]

The biblical framework within which these amends were to be understood is most apparent in the quotation from Murray around which
the article is structured: building a nuclear reactor in Japan under the
aegis of Atoms for Peace, Murray says, "would be a dramatic and Christian gesture which could lift all of us far above the recollection of the
carnage of those cities."[12] Characterizing Atoms for Peace as operating
within a Christian framework, Murray makes explicit what the rest of
the article implies: that Hiroshima and Nagasaki are the original sin of
the American nuclear age, needing to be redeemed by Atoms for Peace
for America to regain the moral righteousness that, as we saw in chapter 2, was so urgent to its Cold War mission.

Murray's language indicates that Atoms for Peace will operate
within a particularly apocalyptic model of redemption. Whereas the
newspaper describes a Japanese reactor as partial amends for the original sin of bombing Hiroshima and Nagasaki, Murray describes a salvation that comes not through earthly justice or restitution but from a
divine perspective after the end of time. Redemption here "lift[s] all of

us" up on a vertical axis to get us away from sin, recalling the verticality that is, for Erich Auerbach, definitive of the divine or postapocalyptic perspective that can see time whole: in the figural or typological system of interpreting history, "the interpretation is always sought from above"; the historical event is "viewed primarily in immediate vertical connection with a divine order which encompasses it."[13] The stakes of this difference become clear when we consider the end to which Murray puts the redemptive act; he does not seek to provide justice to the Japanese victims of American atom bombs or to alleviate their suffering in the present but rather to "lift all of us far above the recollection of the carnage of those cities." Deploying the "checkbook" model of apocalyptic typological history, in which a later redemptive act annuls the earlier sinful one as if it had never been, Atoms for Peace will cancel out Hiroshima and Nagasaki as if they had never happened, wiping out even "the recollection of the carnage" that is America's moral debt.

THE SALVATIONAL LOGIC OF Atoms for Peace is the worst kind of apocalyptic temporality: one that produces redemption for the inflictor of injury without any kind of justice for the injured; one that uses a later act to wipe the earlier act from history and to annul any claim for redress that the earlier act might make upon the present. James Baldwin argued that the desire for a such a dehistoricizing ideology of redemption was the defining feature of the American "innocence" that precludes the possibility of reparation for slavery and genocide, and the postmillennial future of plenty that allows for no claims from the injured past that Eisenhower evokes is also familiar from other moments that this book has analyzed, from the evacuation of social and personal history in the radical autopoiesis that Rand imagines to the closed temporal circuit of retrocontainment in the Reaganite imaginary to the endless present claimed by the nuclear state at the Waste Isolation Pilot Plant. These visions of postmillennial stasis have devastating impacts on the present, perpetuating harm in the name of its undoing, evacuating the past of its capacity to call upon the present for justice and the future of its capacity for radical difference. Taking upon themselves the vertical standpoint that is supposed to be reserved for the divine or postapocalyptic perspective, Atoms for Peace and other millennial nuclear campaigns also seize the power to fix the meaning of past and present events that is the privilege of that perspective. In so doing, they seek to fix into a static form the mutability of the event's meaning that is central to both Auerbach's definition of what it means to live in the profane world and the capacity for radical thinkers and artists to transfigure the present that this book has discussed.

The Fukushima Daiichi disaster, however, wrenches the veil of redemption from the "peaceful" use of the atom and reveals it to have been what it has always been: a technology whose corporate uses are fully entangled with its military uses; an infrastructure that can redeem nothing, whose only disposition is to produce futurelessness for beings, ecosystems, and planets. In his powerful reflections on the catastrophe at Fukushima, Muto Ichiyo describes the apocalypticism inherent in the nuclear regime:

> Because radioactive contamination is at the heart of this destruction, the disaster lingers on, and it will take dozens—no, hundreds—of years to run its course, poisoning and harming natural and human beings all the while. While society can rehabilitate from natural disasters, restoration in the sense of going back to the pre-disaster status is not possible in this case. This is the true meaning of nuclear disaster. As radioactive contamination continues to affect human bodies and the environment over an extremely long time span, this destruction is irreversible.[14]

This is the true meaning of nuclear disaster. Nuclear apocalypse in the present forces upon us the realization that even dismantling the infrastructures of planetary destruction cannot take us back to an unspoiled time or forward into a nonnuclear future; while the infrastructures of nuclear apocalypse may be temporary, the environmental alterations that they produce are effectively permanent. Fantasies of a condition of nonnuclear purity will get us nowhere, which is not to say that disassembling the world's nuclear stockpiles and their attendant infrastructures is not among the most urgent ethical demands of the present. Rather, we must set any nuclear politics *against purity* in the way that Alexis Shotwell calls for in her book of that name, understanding that "to be against purity is to start from an understanding of our implication in this compromised world, to recognize the quite vast injustices informing our everyday lives, and from that understanding to act on our *wish that it were not so.*"[15] We must ask what it means to accept that we live now, apocalyptically, within the foreclosed futurity of a nuclear age that can be redeemed by no millennial future that might cancel out the past or cleanse what is to come. Ruth Ozeki's 2013 novel *A Tale for the Time Being* is an extraordinary reckoning with precisely these questions. The text both interrogates the postmillennial desire to abrogate the moral claim of histories of injury that defines Atoms for Peace and takes up the imposed futurelessness of military violence and the Fukushima disaster to transfigure the present and open it up to different kinds of ethical demands. The novel tells the entangled stories of Ruth, a Japanese American filmmaker and writer living on a small island off of the coast of British Columbia, and Nao, a Japanese teenager who has recently returned to living in Japan after growing up in California. Ruth encounters Nao's story when Nao's diary washes up on the island in a plastic lunchbox, along with other debris from Japan that has crossed the Pacific in the wake of the 3/11 tsunami. Nao's diary is a fully nuclear text, a survivor of the present-day apocalypse of Fukushima and itself potentially radioactive. What happens when Nao's text entangles itself with Ruth as its reader is thus a model for thinking what it means to read, write, live, and care in the nuclear age.

When Ruth first finds Nao's diary, she approaches it as a Kermodian reader, operating on the same typological premises as Atoms for Peace, who expects to find meaning through the consonance of beginning and end. Checking the end of the diary to see if Nao's writing continues all the way through, "Ruth snapped the book shut and closed her eyes for good measure to keep herself from cheating and reading the final sentence, but the question lingered, floating like a retinal burn in the darkness of her mind: *What happens in the end?*"[16] Even here at the novel's most end-directed moment, however, Ozeki troubles the delineation of beginning and ending, the idea that the past will stay where it's put without making demands of the present and that the future will provide both closure and revelation. Immediately before checking on the end of Nao's book, Ruth contemplates her own work in progress, a disorganized pile of papers and files that refuses to be organized into an account of the time that Ruth spent caring for her mother, who suffered from Alzheimer's. Far from providing a meaningful end that reveals the shape of a life, Ruth's mother's slow death leaves her in a perpetual present, asking over and over again which war they are watching on TV (273). The text that comes from it is "a tall messy stack of notes and manuscript pages, bristling with Post-its and wound with cramped marginalia," a "confused mess" that resists all of Ruth's efforts to "sort it all out" (30–31). The sense of an ending remains nonsensical, here, with the book sprawling outward in an accumulation of mundane detail rather than moving horizontally toward closure.

The militarized violence of the past, too, seeps insistently into the present in this sequence, shaping lives and making it impossible to tell where the past ends and the present begins. In the scene immediately following Ruth's check on the diary's end, we learn that she insists on using the old name for one of the properties on the island, "Jap Ranch," which had been taken from its original Japanese owners when they were interned during World War II. Ruth refuses to let that violent history be forgotten: "Once Ruth heard the nickname, she stubbornly persisted in using it. As a person of Japanese ancestry, she said, she had the right, and it was important not to let New Age correctness erase the history of the island" (32). Ruth wants Nao's diary to move coherently from beginning to end, but the novel frames that desire as emerging from a real world where beginnings, as well as ends, cannot be so clearly demarcated, telling us at this moment that the lives of Ruth and her husband, Oliver, are the product of the Second World War. "Their marriage was like this, an axial alliance—her people interned, his firebombed in Stuttgart—a small accidental consequence of a war fought before either of them was born. 'We're by-products of the mid-twentieth century,' Oliver said. 'Who isn't?'" (32). Whereas Atoms for Peace seeks to annul the atrocities of World War II and leave them in the past, prior to the beginning of the present, Ozeki emphasizes that its consequences are everywhere, woven into the fabric of everyday life at every scale from the intimacy of marriage to the new international conflicts of the wars in Iraq and Afghanistan.

The desire for an ending to bestow meaning on the whole appears in the novel not only at the textual level but also at the scale of the individual life. Suicide is a major theme: Nao writes the diary to record her life in advance of killing herself; Nao's father attempts suicide several times; and the World War II–era letters that accompany Nao's diary to the United States tell the story of Nao's great uncle Haruki as he faces the demands placed upon him as a drafted kamikaze pilot. For the would-be suicides, as Nao's father Harry writes, "making a suicide is finding the edge of life. It stops life in time, so we can grasp what shape it is and feel it is real, at least for just a moment. It is trying to make some real solid thing from the flow of life that is always changing" (87). The desire for Kermodian closure here is the desire for static figuration that Atoms for Peace also shares, the desire to transform the shifting, mutable form of the event into "something graspable." Against life, which is "always changing, like a puff of wind in the air, or a wave in the sea, or even a thought in the mind," closure—whether at the end of life that Harry considers, the end of a book that Ruth needs to know is there, or the end of history that Atoms for Peace attempts to instantiate—offers hermeneutic stasis and certainty (87).

This closure is, however, both unethical and impossible within Ozeki's novel. At the scale of the individual life, we learn from Nao's diary how much her father's desire to end his life in order to give it a fixed form has devastated her, even as she shares it. As a kamikaze pilot, Haruki is also called on, this time by the militarized state, to end his life in a way that will both devastate others and reduce the complexities of his life and death to the single meaning of that devastation. Written into an inevitable, static end by his structural position within the world, Haruki nonetheless manages to defy the apocalyptic logic of closure when he decides to fly into the ocean rather than complete his mission as instructed by crashing into an American ship. In so doing, he follows a different kind of ethical demand and wrenches the story of his death from the military narrative that it is meant to complete into one of his own making, rendering the meaning of the event mutable at the moment that it is meant to be most static.

It is at the scale of the text, however, that Ozeki most dazzlingly undoes the novel's supposed drive toward its own ending, an ending consonant with a beginning that will give meaning to the whole. *A Tale for the Time Being* stages the entanglement of different temporalities throughout; Nao's diary is written in a hollowed-out copy of *In Search of Lost Time,* and the novel's opening address speaks to the entangled time of reader and writer: "A time being is someone who lives in time, and that means you, and me, and every one of us who is, or was, or ever will be. As for me, right now I am sitting in a French maid café in Akiba Electricity Town, listening to a sad chanson that is playing sometime in your past, which is also my present, writing this and wondering about you, somewhere in my future. And if you're reading this, then maybe by now you're wondering about me, too" (3). When deciding how to read the diary, Ruth decides to let her own temporal rhythms be organized by those of the diary. Asking herself how to read "this improbable text," Ruth considers that "perhaps a clue lay in the pacing. Nao had written her diary in real time, living her days, moment by moment. Perhaps if Ruth paced herself by slowing down and not reading faster than the girl had written, she could more closely replicate Nao's experience." "If she sensed the girl was on a roll," Ruth theorizes, "she could allow herself to read further and more quickly, but if it felt like the pace of the writing was slowing down, then she would slow her reading down, too, or stop altogether. This way she wouldn't end up with an overly compressed or accelerated sense of the girl's life and its unfolding, nor would she run the risk of wasting too much time" (38). As a reader, Ruth is deliberately engaging here in the process that Ricoeur called mimesis$_3$, allowing the encounter between the textual world and her own world to reorganize her rhythms and sense of emplotted time.

As the novel progresses, Ruth's world is more and more transfigured by her encounter with Nao's diary, as the shared time of the present that is produced between the writer, the reader, and the text in mimesis$_3$ changes her phenomenological experience of the world. She obsesses over finding Nao and her father, watching footage from the tsunami over and over again and researching the Fukushima meltdown. When Oliver points out that the time of Ruth's world is not in fact lined up with the narrated time of the diary—that in fact, the diary must have been written almost ten years earlier—Ruth can only account for her confusion by thinking about her experiences in the real world as novelistic: "It wasn't that she'd forgotten, exactly. The problem was more a kind of slippage. When she was writing a novel, living deep inside a fictional world, the days got jumbled together, and entire weeks or months or even years would yield to the ebb and flow of the dream. . . . Fiction had its own time and logic. That was its power" (313–14). In the time of reading, of mimesis$_3$, fictional time, historical time, and personal time are "jumbled together."

The transfiguration of Ruth's world through the act of reading the nuclear text shifts the novel itself out of the realist mode and into a more speculative relationship to reality. What might seem like a relatively simple metafictional acknowledgment of the peculiar temporalities of reading, writing, and narration becomes more complex when the end of Nao's diary, whose promise to reveal "what happened" to Nao has been so important to Ruth as she reads it, disappears. In the diary, Nao experiences futurelessness as time shrinks down around her: "I don't believe I exist," she writes, "and soon I won't. I am a time being about to expire" (340). Nao's quest to experience the single moment is attained here, as her horizon of futurity shrinks to nothing: "I guess this is it. This is what now feels like" (341). When Ruth reads these words aloud, Oliver comments on the collapse of time to a single point within Nao's world, saying that "she caught up with herself" (342). Ruth and Oliver pause in their reading, sitting within the temporal suspension of futurity that Nao has experienced, written, and caused her readers to experience. When the readers attempt to get time moving again, however, they find that the book itself has become, impossibly, futureless:

> Oliver finally spoke. "Go on," he said. "Don't stop."
> Ruth turned the page, felt her heart miss a beat.
> The page was blank.
> She turned another. Blank.
> And the page after that. Blank.
> She skipped ahead further. There were perhaps twenty pages still remaining in the book, and all of them were blank. . . .
> It made no sense. She knew the pages had once been filled because on at least two occasions she had checked, riffling through to see if the girl's handwriting had persisted to the end of the book, and indeed it had. The words had once been there, she was sure of it, and now they weren't. (342–43)

Ruth and Oliver attempt to reckon with a kind of causality that seems impossible, whereby a phenomenon (words on a page) can be altered by a later decision: "'Words can't just disappear.' 'Well, they did. I can't explain it. Maybe she changed her mind or something.' 'That's a bit of a stretch, don't you think? She can't just reach in and take them back.' 'But I think she did,' Ruth said. She switched off the headlamp. 'It's like her life just got shorter. Time is slipping away from her, page by page'" (343). Meanwhile, the diegetic world of Ruth and Oliver, too, shrinks its temporal horizons down into the now at this moment, as the lantern-lit, battery-lit dark of a multiday power cut brings together "oil lamps and LEDs. The old technologies and the new, collapsing time into a paradoxical present" (344). Narrative is defined by its forward drive, by its ability to give shape to time. But at this moment in this narrative, where entangled time itself shrinks to a single point, the forward drive of narrative is suspended in the paradoxical present where the future is nowhere and the past is close enough to touch.

The time of the futureless present, shared between the reader and the writer through the mediation of the text, creates a world of radically different possibilities to the will they/won't they story lines that have been in place to this point. Within the diary, Harry has gone to the forest to kill himself, and Nao, finding out, intends to do the same. Will they, won't they? When Ruth falls asleep at this moment of textual futurelessness, however, she finds herself impossibly able to reverse the one-way flow of information from text to world. From within the collapsed moment of the futureless present, she dreams her way into the past world about which she has been reading: "What does separation look like? A wall? A wave? A body of water? A ripple of light or a shimmer of subatomic particles, parting? What does it feel like to push through?" (346). Finding her way to Harry, she convinces him not to commit suicide. And so, when she awakes, the diary has resumed telling the story that it will now, after Ruth's impossible intervention, tell. Nao's diary does not initially contain the possibility that an intervention by a Japanese American women dreaming nearly a decade after the event would impact how her story would play out. And yet futurelessness produces here, as it does for Toni Cade Bambara in *The Salt Eaters*, a world whose possibilities are radically otherwise.

Ozeki's reference to "a shimmer of subatomic particles, parting" speaks backward through time to the nuclear fission events that forever marked Japan at Hiroshima, Nagasaki, and Fukushima. But it also looks sideways at the framework that Ozeki will posit as a counter-modeling of the world that emerges from a very different splitting of the atom, that of quantum entanglement (even as this difference depends on the inseparability of the two, since "quantum physics and the atom bomb are deeply and directly entangled").[17] The futurelessness that comes from the violent consequences of nuclear fission at Fukushima here produces (by bringing the diary to Ruth) the conditions of possibility for a quantum world in which the act of reading entangles Ruth and Nao such that a change to one of them will produce a change in the other. In Ruth's second appendix to the novel, "Quantum Mechanics," Ozeki posits the novel itself as a measuring apparatus within a quantum universe: an agential observer whose modeling of the universe will also cause that universe to *be* a specific way—for the time being. The three key elements of quantum mechanics are, according to the appendix, "superposition: by which a particle can be in two or more places or states at once (i.e., Zen Master Dōgen is both alive and dead?)"; "entanglement: by which two particles can coordinate their properties across space and time and behave like a single system (i.e., a Zen master and his disciple; a character and her narrator; old Jiko and Nao and Oliver and me?)"; and "the measurement problem: by which the act of measuring or observation alters what is being observed (i.e., the collapse of a wave function; the telling of a dream?)" (409). Ozeki suggests here that the novel is an apparatus of observation equivalent to the laboratory equipment used by scientists in a quantum world in which "apparatuses are specific material configurations (dynamic reconfigurings) of the world that play a role in the production of phenomena."[18] In the quantum universe, the novel is the apparatus or infrastructure by which an observer alters what is being observed, in this case bringing the character and the narrator (who is here also a metafictional version of the author) out of superposition into one reality through the act of observation. The function of futurelessness here is to suspend that collapse into one reality and put the entangled particles *back* into superposition, into a world in which an impossibly large array of possibilities might still happen and indeed are all happening at once, a world where not knowing "what happens at the end" "keeps all the possibilities open. It keeps all the worlds alive" (402).

What's remarkable about this entanglement-under-futurelessness is that, unlike our traditional models of textual agency, it goes both ways. It is not simply that Nao, the writer, experiences her world as emplotted (mimesis$_1$), reconfigures it in her diary (mimesis$_2$), and transfigures the experience of her reader when the reconfigured world of the diary opens out onto the world of the reader (mimesis$_3$). Here the futurelessness of Ruth's experience of time that has been produced by the diary (mimesis$_3$) changes the emplotment of the text itself, disrupting its capacity to reach its end in a form of reverse-mimesis$_3$; as Ruth's friend Muriel argues, "it's not about Nao's now. It's about yours.

You haven't caught up with yourself yet, the now of your story, and you can't reach her ending until you do" (377). Ruth's dream, able within the futureless present to reopen the quantum superpositions of the entangled system, reconfigures both the diary (reverse-mimesis$_2$) and Nao's actual world (reverse-mimesis$_1$), allowing Harry and Nao to live. The act of reading, in the quantum universe, does not so much complete the meaning of the text—as it does in more Newtonian narrative theories—as it changes the text itself.

The stakes of a quantum approach to narrative are not, however, limited to thinking about fiction. When Ruth first realizes that her time is in fact out of joint with Nao's, she is devastated by the fact that her ethical relation to the past appears to have been foreclosed: "it's too late," she says, "to help her. . . . So what's the point? The diary's just a distraction. What difference does it make if I read it or not?" (314). This question is central to those of us who study the past, even the recent past, even the past that continues to structure the present in devastating and unlivable ways. The question that this "what's the point" poses is one of the meaning of the event, one that Atoms for Peace, perversely, understands quite well: how can a later action alter an earlier one? Within Newtonian physics and history, the answer is simply that it can't. Within the typological history of Atoms for Peace, the hope is that a later action will cancel out an earlier one and fix its meaning as being a necessary precursor to a later salvific action.

What quantum mechanics teaches us, however, is that the event is not yet over as long as we remain entangled with it and attentive to it. As quantum physicist and feminist philosopher Karen Barad demonstrates in *Meeting the Universe Halfway: The Entanglement of Matter and Meaning,* it is incorrect to think of the phenomenon or event as something that the observer observes from the outside, thereby collapsing the event's superpositions into a single object, because the observer is a part of the phenomenon itself. No matter how far apart observer and observed are in space and time, as soon as the observer starts observing, the phenomenon now includes the observer and observation as a fundamental part of the phenomenon itself. Indeed, space and time are *only produced within such observations*; "the past was never simply there to begin with and the future is not simply what will unfold; the 'past' and the 'future' are iteratively reworked and enfolded through the iterative practices of spacetime mattering. . . . All are *one phenom-*

enon."[19] As long as we are paying attention, in other words, the event has not ceased. Ruth can still help Nao. There is no "too late." And the urgency of the call does not diminish, entangled as we are with objects and events and times that, co-constituting the world with us, can never be completely lost, might yet always be regained.

IN THE END, the three models of being in time examined by *A Tale for the Time Being*—quantum mechanics, Zen Buddhism, and the novel form itself—have the entanglements produced by afuturity as both their precondition and their consequence. Zen meditation aims to reduce the experience of being in time to the single futureless moment, with the effect of entangling the self both with the world and the radical openness of the quantum universe: "Maybe if you sat enough zazen, your sense of being a solid, singular self would dissolve and you could forget about it. What a relief. You could just hang out happily as part of an open-ended quantum array. To forget the self is to be enlightened by all myriad things. Mountains and rivers, grasses and trees, crows and cats and wolves and jellyfishes" (398). Futurelessness produces a set of new relations here: to the world's myriad beings, to one's own quantum being, to possibility in formation and to the capacity for right action. Haruki, facing his imminent death the night before his final flight, finally understands what it means to be in the present: "in even a fraction of a second, we have the opportunity to choose, and to turn the course of our action either toward the attainment of truth or away from it. Each instant is utterly critical to the whole world" (324). The futureless instant offers an uncertain yet crucial capacity for ethical action. "In the end, then," Haruki writes, "what volition will arise in me?"

Ozeki thus proposes a world in which nuclear entanglements, a forced encounter with our own impossible futures, lead to other kinds of entanglements within the radically open present of a quantum array. In this, *A Tale for the Time Being* offers a very different way of thinking about time within an entangled world than those that have emerged over the past two decades in other theories of entanglement. Stacy Alaimo writes of the new materialisms that have emerged within ecocriticism, feminist science and technology studies, literary studies, and philosophy that "they stress encounters, inter-action, intra-action, co-constitution, and the pervasive material agencies that cut across and reconfigure ostensibly separate objects and beings."[20] In this way, the new materialisms are relatively well equipped to deal with the nuclear materials that refuse to keep themselves separate from us. However, the temporal orientation of the new materialisms is crucially different from the futureless horizon with which nuclear objects force us to reckon. Alaimo's work, like that of scholars including Karen Barad, Jane Bennett, Donna Haraway, Catherine Keller, and Alexis Shotwell, takes up Deleuze and Guattari's notion of "becoming" as almost synonymous with entanglement to get at the flexibility of matter and the contingency of assemblages, to replace the ontological claims of being that fix the world into an overly knowable object with a becoming that captures something of the ways in which the universe is constantly coming-into-mattering.[21] In the face of an apocalyptic closure of futurity that any ecological thinker must consistently encounter, becoming offers the consolation of a future built into the very nature of matter itself.

Nuclear entanglements, however, challenge the framework of becoming. Becoming relies on the Newtonian, linear spacetime that, as Michelle M. Wright has argued, "dominates how all disciplines and laypersons organize knowledge as *progressive*," orienting reactive and progressive movements alike along an axis from past to future.[22] Threatening the future itself, profoundly apocalyptic, nuclear entanglements make impossible the futural horizon upon which becoming relies; being co-constituted with or by nuclear things might force us to acknowledge our deep vulnerability, our porous bodies, our fragile DNA, but such entanglements are difficult to imagine as opening us up to any kind of future. In the nuclear age, as Barad writes, "time is/ had been crossed out."[23] Instead, nuclear entanglements bring us face-to-face with what Rebekah Sheldon has called our "a-volitional restriction to the present tense" in the Anthropocene—or, as Sheldon correctly renames it, "the anthro-no-more-cene."[24] Rather than present this as a mournful limit to a philosophical approach that offers comfort to vulnerable beings, however, I want to consider here the limits of becoming as a model for being in the world and what apocalypse, were we to take it seriously, might offer in its place.

Claire Colebrook critiques becoming from a philosophical standpoint, arguing that far from being "*the* notion that would free us at once from moralizing normativity and rigid identity politics . . . the contemporary valorization of becoming over being *repeats* rather than destabilizes a highly traditional and humanist sentiment of privileging act over inertia, life and creativity over death and stasis, and pure existence or coming-into-being over determination."[25] Shaped by the humanism that it aims to overcome, the world as it is imagined through the lens of becoming has a present disarticulated from its past that opens out onto a welcoming future. Such a world is closer to that imagined by Atoms for Peace, which also seeks to jettison its past as the price of futurity, than it is to the lived experience of the Black, queer, and Indigenous writers operating under the shadow of the nuclear complex who have been forced to reckon with the ways in which the past impacts the present and the future is foreclosed, and who have responded to this reality not by developing theoretical models within which this is not the case but by learning how to operate in a futureless present while salvaging the injured past that they do not wish to leave behind.

Turning to the lived realities of the nuclear complex as a manifestation of settler-colonial, racial, and antiqueer violence in the present also reveals the political normativity of becoming. In *The Transit of Empire: Indigenous Critiques of Colonialism,* Jodi Byrd reveals the ways in which the figure of the Indian stands as both the bad other of Deleuze-and-Guattarian rhizomatics and becoming and as the featureless ground across which those rhizomatic becomings make their way. "Drawing on the paradigmatic Indian wilderness to encapsulate an America in which arboresence becomes rhizomatic," she argues, "*A Thousand Plateaus* performs a global, nomadic reframing in which the frontier becomes, again, Frederick Jackson Turner's site of transformation, possibility, and mapping."[26] The result of this is that any politics that requires acknowledging the importance of a grounded relationship to land, whether that be an indigenous, decolonial political movement or a movement to shut down nuclear power plants in the name of protecting local bodies, will be seen by Deleuzian theory as either falling on the wrong side of or standing in the way of the free flows, proliferations, and becoming-entanglements that have become synonymous with the right way of doing politics. Becoming here is the consolation prize that contemporary cultural studies gets for looking at the devastating, devastated present before turning away from it into "a call for transformational new worlds of relation and relationship that move us toward a joyously cacophonic multiplicity and away from the lived colonial conditions of indigeneity within the postcolonizing settler society."[27]

Infrastructures of Apocalypse is committed to the devastated present. It does not seek to console, nor does it seek to move away from the lived conditions of the nuclear complex that both perpetuate and intensify conditions of imposed futurelessness for Indigenous, ethnic, Black, queer, disabled, poor, and female peoples. If it contains comfort, that comfort comes from the ways in which writers and activists have taken up the apocalyptic narratives that produce nuclear infrastructures and repurposed them to form differently apocalyptic narratives of resistance. Becoming, with its futural orientation and its tendency to turn away from lived colonial conditions, is inadequate to this purpose. A more adequate framework to a world infrastructured by apocalypse, perhaps, would be the one posed by Ozeki as she reckons with the aftermath of the Fukushima Daiichi disaster: that we think of the world as it is—real, now, grounded, there—as being "for the time being." In place of the salvational teleology of Atoms for Peace—a teleology that is more upheld than challenged by new materialism's focus on becoming—Ozeki offers to the apocalyptically entangled world the contingent now of for the time being.

A theory for the time being would be one that can analyze the conditions of the real, a real shaped by the past, without staking a claim to the future. Nuclear criticism from below might be one example of such a theory, showing the world as it has been infrastructured by apocalypse for the time being—but only for the time being. We are locked into a militarized reality that threatens to produce a planet-destroying nuclear catastrophe at any second—for the time being. We are in the middle of the Indian Wars, combatants or noncombatants of a genocidal campaign to take the land from its Indigenous inhabitants—for the time being. We live in the wake of the slave trade, a wake that devastates African American life in the present—for the time being. Resources that might be used for reparations, for justice, for life, are poured endlessly into technologies of death—for the time being. Grappling with the implications of the Fukushima Daiichi disaster in *After Fukushima: The Equivalence of Catastrophes,* Jean-Luc Nancy writes that "no option will make us emerge from the endless equivalence of ends and means if we do not emerge from finality itself—from aiming, from planning, and projecting a future in general."[28] Apocalypse as radical afuturity casts us into a present without ends—"not an immobile present but a present within historical mobility, a living sense of each moment, each life, each *hic et nunc* [here and now]."[29] In a world infrastructured by and toward apocalypse, the writers in this book have taught us, each moment has the capacity for radical action, for the transfiguration of the present. In the end, then, what volition will arise in us?

Acknowledgments

THIS BOOK BEGAN AS A DISSERTATION at the University of Pennsylvania, where I was fortunate enough to experience not only the intellectual community and generosity that made the project possible but also the mentorship and material support that enabled a first-generation college student and recent immigrant to survive in academia. Jed Esty, Amy Kaplan, Nancy Bentley, Suvir Kaul, and Margreta de Grazia were teachers and mentors, and this book was shaped significantly by Tsitsi Jaji's suggestion to include James Baldwin and Samuel R. Delany. Ann Marie Pitts and Tim Weal handled my frequent bureaucratic panics with grace, keeping me in paychecks and the correct visa status. My English department cohort was unusually large and produced something of a resource crisis but resisted the logic of competition to become—and remain—a model of supportive and collaborative endeavor. *Infrastructures of Apocalypse* would not exist without the support and guidance of Paul Saint-Amour, whose unfailing enthusiasm, wisdom, and intellectual generosity have been a beacon of light across many years of researching topics that are invariably dark. Heather Love and Jim English kept me accountable and showed me the way. All three members of my committee have also written countless reference letters for me over many years, and their time and effort spent keeping me in the profession should not go unmentioned here. Thanks are due to each of them and must remain inadequate.

At the University of Chicago, the dissertation transformed into a book in conversation with the other members of the Society of Fellows, the Environmental Studies workshop, the ring-taught class The Nuclear Age, and the nuclear film club of 2018 (especially Norma Field, Paola Iovene, Maria Anna Mariani, Susan Su, and Helina Mazza-Hilway). Thanks go to each of these stimulating intellectual communities.

Deb Neibel's administrative work gave me access to the resources I needed, while her friendship kept me afloat in challenging times. Debbie Nelson was a redoubtable faculty mentor, reading chapters and book proposal drafts and writing recommendation letters with never-flagging attention. I am also profoundly grateful to Priscilla Wald and Sean Goudie for inviting me to participate in the First Book Institute at Penn State; this was a transformative experience for both me and the book, and the collective dedication of Priscilla, Sean, and the other participants to developing the best possible version of the project is a debt that I will spend a lifetime trying to pay forward. My writing and accountability groups, stemming from the FBI, have kept me on track with writing and inspired by an ongoing engagement with the every-day brilliance of other scholars: thank you to Sunny Yang, Joo Ok Kim, Meina Yates-Richard, and Abby Goode for the support and solidarity. I completed the manuscript during my first days as a faculty member in the English department at George Mason University; I am grateful for the department's support in securing the time and resources that were necessary to see the project to its close.

Invitations from the Starr Center for the Study of the American Experience at Washington College, the English department at the College of Wooster, and the Department of Social and Cultural Analysis at New York University allowed me to experiment with the manuscript in different forms, and conversations with students, graduate students, and faculty at these locations kept alive the idea that apocalypse might have something to offer us even as the times became increasingly apocalyptic. Audiences and copanelists at the Association for the Study of the Arts of the Present, Association for the Study of Literature and the Environment, American Comparative Literature Association, American Studies Association, Modern Language Association, and Society for Novel Studies conferences, as well as at the Futures of American Studies Institute and the Penn Program in Environmental Humanities, have given generous and incisive feedback on many sections of the manuscript. This book was completed alongside a special issue of *ASAP/Journal* on the topic of "Apocalypse" (2018); thanks are due to my coeditor, Dan Sinykin, for the intellectual companionship and solidarity; the journal editor, Jonathan Eburne, for the support and for pushing the project far beyond where we had imagined it could go; and to all of the contributors for their inspiring work.

This project received financial support from the Wolf Humanities Center, GAPSA, and the Provost's Office at the University of Pennsylvania; the book subvention fund at the University of Chicago Society of Fellows (secured by our union, SEIU); and the American Council of Learned Societies through the Mellon/ACLS Dissertation Completion Fellowship. I am grateful for the opportunities that they have provided. Thanks go to the journal editors, peer reviewers, and copy editors of *American Literature* and *Comparative Literature Studies* whose work on articles from this project fed back into and improved the book manuscript; I am grateful too, in the end, to the peer reviewers who rejected various versions of articles drawn from the book, whose critiques were nonetheless valuable labor from which the book has benefited. I was immensely fortunate to receive rigorous and insightful critiques of the manuscript from the two reviewers for the University of Minnesota Press, whose responses saw the book as it wanted to be and pushed me to bring it closer to the best version of itself. Many improvements here are due to them; all errors and flaws remain my own. Thanks go to Danielle Kasprzak for bringing the book to Minnesota, to Leah Pennywark for taking it up with such enthusiasm, and to Anne Carter for shepherding it through the publication process.

This project has developed alongside and become entangled with a number of performance projects, and I am endlessly grateful for my Applied Mechanics collaborators: Rebecca Wright, Maria Shaplin, Mary Tuomanen, and Thomas Choinacky. Writing with John Jarboe has always been a true gift and has fed my work here in myriad ways. Nava EtShalom taught me the radicalism of kindness and has shaped both my research and my pedagogy with her unshakeable commitment to a better world. My students have kept me in touch with the joy of learning; thank you for letting me learn with you and from you. Laura Finch has read every page of this book in multiple versions, and her mind and friendship are as inextricable from this project as they are from my life. My mother and sister, Patricia and Sarah Hurley, redeem the concept of the nuclear family with their love and support. And George Urgo is my partner in all things, an exceptional human whose lived gender politics, in particular, have allowed me to take the time away from domestic labor that writing this book required. *Infrastructures of Apocalypse* could not exist, in a very literal way, without that gift of time and focus. These thanks will have to be lived over a lifetime and will always be a work in progress.

Infrastructures of Apocalypse was written on Lenape, Nanticoke Lenni-Lenape, and Ramapough Lunnape land in what is currently Pennsylvania; Miami and Potawatomi land in what is currently Illinois; and Manahoac land in what is currently Virginia. Decolonization, like apocalypse, is not a metaphor (with final thanks to Eve Tuck and K. Wayne Yang). This book is for all those whose futures are impossible and who go on fighting anyway.

Notes

Introduction

1. Lydia Millet, *Oh Pure and Radiant Heart* (Brooklyn, N.Y.: Soft Skull Press, 2005), 19. Further page references will be to this edition and will be given in the body of the text.

2. Gabrielle Hecht, *Being Nuclear: Africans and the Global Uranium Trade* (Cambridge, Mass.: MIT Press, 2014); Langston Hughes (1945), quoted in Ken Cooper, "The Whiteness of the Bomb," in *Postmodern Apocalypse: Theory and Cultural Practice at the End,* ed. Richard Dellamora (Philadelphia: University of Pennsylvania Press, 1995), 79.

3. Don DeLillo, *Underworld* (New York: Scribner, 1997), 122.

4. See, e.g., David Dowling, *Fictions of Nuclear Disaster* (Iowa City: University of Iowa Press, 1987); Tony Jackson, "Postmodernism, Narrative, and the Cold War Sense of an Ending," *Narrative* 8, no. 3 (2000): 324–38; Peter Schwenger, *Letter Bomb: Nuclear Holocaust and the Exploding Word* (Baltimore: Johns Hopkins University Press, 1992); Albert E. Stone, *Literary Aftershocks: American Writers, Readers, and the Bomb* (New York: Macmillan, 1994); Roland Végső, *The Naked Communist: Cold War Modernism and the Politics of Popular Culture* (New York: Fordham University Press, 2013). This is still a dominant paradigm in the field, as in Matthew Grant and Benjamin Ziemann, eds., *Understanding the Imaginary War: Culture, Thought and Nuclear Conflict, 1945–90* (Manchester, U.K.: Manchester University Press, 2017).

5. Daniel Cordle, *States of Suspense: The Nuclear Age, Postmodernism, and United States Fiction and Prose* (Manchester, U.K.: Manchester University Press, 2008); Daniel Grausam, *On Endings: American Postmodern Fiction and the Cold War* (Charlottesville: University of Virginia Press, 2011), 5.

6. Rebecca Solnit, *Savage Dreams: A Journey into the Hidden Wars of the American West* (Berkeley: University of California Press, 2014), 5.

7. Keith Myers, "Some Unintended Fallout from Defense Policy: Measuring the Effect of Atmospheric Nuclear Testing on American Mortality Patterns," March 7, 2019, https://static1.squarespace.com/static/59262540b

3db2b0d0d6d7d2b/t/5c81809a419202f922f0cfa4/1551990940274/Fallout MortDraft_3-5-2019.pdf. Note that this analysis has not yet been through peer review.

8. Barbara Rose Johnston, "Half-Lives, Half-Truths, and Other Radioactive Legacies of the Cold War," in *Half-Lives and Half-Truths: Confronting the Radioactive Legacies of the Cold War*, ed. Barbara Rose Johnston (Santa Fe, N.M.: School for Advanced Research Press, 2007), 3.

9. Michelle Murphy, *Sick Building Syndrome and the Problem of Uncertainty: Environmental Politics, Technoscience, and Women Workers* (Durham, N.C.: Duke University Press, 2006), 10. In their introduction to a recent special issue of *Modern Fiction Studies* titled "Infrastructuralisms," Michael Rubenstein, Bruce Robbins, and Sophia Beal describe how "infrastructure tends to go unnoticed when it's in fine working order," going on to suggest that this is a user-located phenomenon caused either by a personal response to the technological sublime that infrastructures provoke or by the fact that infrastructures, as a common good, lack the fetishized aura that defines commodities. In such accounts, infrastructures are naturalized as preexisting environmental conditions, with imperceptibility coming to seem like an inherent trait that defines infrastructure itself, that makes infrastructure what it is. See Sophia Beal, Bruce Robbins, and Michael Rubenstein, "Infrastructuralism: An Introduction," *Modern Fiction Studies* 61, no. 4 (2015): 576. Brian Larkin provides a strong counterargument in his account of infrastructure's aesthetics in "The Politics and Poetics of Infrastructure," *Annual Review of Anthropology* 42 (2013): 327–43.

10. For more on how emissions and exposures at the Hanford plant went resolutely unmonitored, see Kate Brown, *Plutopia: Nuclear Families, Atomic Cities, and the Great Soviet and American Plutonium Disasters* (Oxford: Oxford University Press, 2013).

11. Robert Jungk, *Brighter than a Thousand Suns: A Personal History of the Atomic Scientists* (Middlesex, U.K.: Penguin Books, 1960), 279; for more on the politics of visualization with regard to the nuclear complex, see Elizabeth M. DeLoughrey, "Radiation Ecologies and the Wars of Light," *Modern Fiction Studies* 55, no. 3 (2009): 468–98.

12. I take the opposition between indirect and direct violence from Johan Galtung, "Violence, Peace, and Peace Research," *Journal of Peace Research* 6, no. 3 (1969): 167–91. This essay coined the term *structural violence,* which I will use frequently here.

13. The term charismatic mega-concept comes from Heather Davis and Etienne Turpin's analysis of the term *Anthropocene,* where it describes a critical heuristic that catches on so quickly and totally that it comes to organize whole fields of knowledge. See "Art and Death: Lives between the Fifth Assess-

ment and the Sixth Extinction," in *Art in the Anthropocene: Encounters among Aesthetics, Politics, Environments, and Epistemologies,* ed. Heather Davis and Etienne Turpin, 3–30 (London: Open Humanities Press, 2015).

14. Jacques Derrida, "No Apocalypse, Not Now (Full Speed Ahead, Seven Missiles, Seven Missives)," *diacritics: A Review of Contemporary Criticism* 14, no. 2 (1984): 23.

15. Derrida.

16. I do agree, however, with Drew Milne and John Kinsella when they argue that even in his turn to nuclear fact, Derrida is overly focused on the bomb and nuclear war such that "Derrida's essay deflects nuclear criticism not just away from weapons testing, accidents and waste, but from non-military uses and from pressing scientific, technological, military and political questions. The acceleration of the argument skips beyond the whole mycelium of uranium extraction, enrichment, nuclear testing, weapons delivery systems, power stations and the rest." Milne and Kinsella, "Nuclear Theory Degree Zero, with Two Cheers for Derrida," *Angelaki* 22, no. 3 (2017): 5. Barbara Adam offers a powerful analysis of the dialectical inseparability of language and radiation in the context of the Chernobyl disaster in *Timescapes of Modernity: The Environment and Invisible Hazards* (London: Routledge, 1998), 200.

17. Frances Ferguson, "The Nuclear Sublime," *diacritics* 14, no. 2 (1984): 7.

18. See Herman Kahn, *Thinking about the Unthinkable* (New York: Horizon Press, 1962); David E. Nye, *American Technological Sublime* (Cambridge, Mass.: MIT Press, 1995). The idea of the atom bomb as devastating in its unthinkability is also behind another influential theory of how we encounter the nuclear, Robert Jay Lifton and Greg Mitchell's theory of "psychic numbing." Lifton and Mitchell explain the surprising lack of engagement with the threat of nuclear war in Cold War America by arguing that American psyches are overwhelmed and consequently numbed by an (imaginary) encounter with what we are here calling the nuclear sublime. See Robert Jay Lifton and Greg Mitchell, *Hiroshima in America: Fifty Years of Denial* (New York: Putnam's Sons, 1995).

19. For two scathing critiques of how an exclusive focus on the mushroom cloud has occluded the devastating material consequences of atomic detonations, see Lane Fenrich, "Mass Death in Miniature: How Americans Became Victims of the Bomb," in *Living with the Bomb: American and Japanese Cultural Conflicts of the Nuclear Age,* ed. Laura Elizabeth Hein and Mark Selden, 122–33 (Armonk, N.Y.: M. E. Sharpe, 1997), and Peter B. Hales, "The Atomic Sublime," *American Studies* 32, no. 1 (1991): 5–31.

20. See DeLoughrey, "Radiation Ecologies and the Wars of Light," and Molly Wallace, *Risk Criticism: Precautionary Reading in an Age of Environmental Uncertainty* (Ann Arbor: University of Michigan Press, 2016); see also Fabienne Collingon's literary analysis of nuclear artifacts and spaces in *Rocket States:*

Atomic Weaponry and the Cultural Imagination (London: Bloomsbury, 2014). Both Grausam and Cordle have also recently taken a more materialist turn in their approach to nuclear criticism; see Daniel Cordle, "Sciences/Humans/ Humanities: Dexter Masters' *The Accident* and Being in the Nuclear Age," *Journal of Literature and Science* 10, no. 2 (2017): 74–87; and Daniel Grausam, "Imagining Postnuclear Times," *Common Knowledge* 21, no. 3 (2015): 451–63.

21. I take the concepts of nuclearity and nuclear things from Hecht, *Being Nuclear.*

22. This is not meant to dismiss this as a project; for a compelling account of how the anticipation of future wars impacted the literary imagination both before and after World War II, see Paul K. Saint-Amour, *Tense Future: Modernism, Total War, Encyclopedic Form* (Oxford: Oxford University Press, 2015).

23. Dwight D. Eisenhower, "Farewell Radio and Television Address to the American People," January 17, 1961, Dwight D. Eisenhower Presidential Library, https://www.eisenhower.archives.gov/all_about_ike/speeches/farewell _address.pdf.

24. Michael Geyer, "The Militarization of Europe, 1941–1945," in *The Militarization of the Western World,* ed. John R. Gillis (New Brunswick, N.J.: Rutgers University Press, 1989), 79.

25. See Cynthia H. Enloe, *Maneuvers: The International Politics of Militarizing Women's Lives* (Berkeley: University of California Press, 2000).

26. C. Wright Mills, *The Power Elite* (1956; repr., New York: Oxford University Press, 2000), 202.

27. Catherine Lutz, "Militarization," in *A Companion to the Anthropology of Politics,* ed. David Nugent (Oxford: Blackwell, 2008), 320.

28. Lutz, 324–26.

29. Caroline Levine, "'The Strange Familiar': Structure, Infrastructure, and Adichie's *Americanah,*" *Modern Fiction Studies* 61, no. 4 (2015): 599.

30. Lauren Berlant, "The Commons: Infrastructures for Troubling Times," *Environment and Planning D* 34, no. 3 (2016): 394.

31. Brown describes these trade-offs at length in *Plutopia.* For the ways that these communities organized for justice when the bodily damage began to outweigh the social benefits, see Natasha Zaretsky, "Radiation Suffering and Patriotic Body Politics in the 1970s and 1980s," *Journal of Social History* 48, no. 3 (2015): 487–510.

32. Gregory Bateson, *Steps to an Ecology of Mind: Collected Essays in Anthropology, Psychiatry, Evolution, and Epistemology* (Northvale, N.J.: Jason Aronson, 1987), 182.

33. Matthew Eatough, "Planning the Future: Scenario Planning, Infrastructural Time, and South African Fiction," *Modern Fiction Studies* 61, no. 4 (2015): 690–714.

34. Joseph Masco, *The Nuclear Borderlands: The Manhattan Project in Post-Cold War New Mexico* (Princeton, N.J.: Princeton University Press, 2006), 12.

35. See Peter Galison, "War against the Center," *Grey Room* 1, no. 4 (2001): 6–33, and David S. Meyer, *A Winter of Discontent: The Nuclear Freeze and American Politics* (New York: Praeger, 1990).

36. Keller Easterling, *Extrastatecraft: The Power of Infrastructure Space* (London: Verso, 2016), 72. For more on the political agency of objects in nuclear-apocalyptic scenarios, see Jessica Hurley, "Still Writing Backwards: Literature after the End of the World," *Frame* 26, no. 1 (2013): 61–76.

37. Obviously I'm invoking here Rob Nixon, *Slow Violence and the Environmentalism of the Poor* (Cambridge, Mass.: Harvard University Press, 2011).

38. See Ward Churchill and Winona LaDuke, "Native North America: The Political Economy of Radioactive Colonialism," in *The State of Native America: Genocide, Colonization, and Resistance,* ed. M. Annette Jaimes, 241–66 (Boston: South End Press, 1992); Manning Marable, "Nuclear War and Black America," in *Speaking Truth to Power: Essays on Race, Resistance, and Radicalism,* 165–72 (Boulder, Colo.: Westview Press, 1996); Shannon Cram, "Becoming Jane: The Making and Unmaking of Hanford's Nuclear Body," *Environment and Planning D* 33, no. 5 (2015): 796–812; and David K. Johnson, *The Lavender Scare: The Cold War Persecution of Gays and Lesbians in the Federal Government* (Chicago: University of Chicago Press, 2004).

39. Toni Cade Bambara, *The Salt Eaters* (New York: Vintage Books, 1992), 242–43. Further page references will be to this edition and will be given in the body of the text.

40. Peter Coviello, "Apocalypse from Now On," in *Queer Frontiers: Millennial Geographies, Genders, and Generations,* ed. Joseph Allen Boone, Martin Dupuis, Martin Meeker, Karin Quimby, Cindy Sarver, Debra Silverman, and Rosemary Weatherston (Madison: University of Wisconsin Press, 2000), 61.

41. Foucault sees atomic weapons as a paradoxical limit case for biopolitics, as when the state gains the ability to destroy *all* life, it loses the power to save it. This is only true of a universal apocalypse, however; at a smaller scale, biopolitical logics flourish in the nuclear age. See Michel Foucault, *Society Must Be Defended: Lectures at the Collège de France, 1975–76* (New York: Picador, 2003), 263–64. William Chaloupka discusses the biopolitics of survival in the nuclear age in *Knowing Nukes: The Politics and Culture of the Atom* (Minneapolis: University of Minnesota Press, 1992), 1–7. For more on national sacrifice zones, see chapter 4.

42. Lisa Yoneyama, *Hiroshima Traces: Time, Space, and the Dialectics of Memory* (Berkeley: University of California Press, 1999), 15.

43. Andrew Hammond, "From Rhetoric to Rollback: Introductory Thoughts on Cold War Writing," in *Cold War Literature: Writing the Global*

Conflict, ed. Andrew Hammond (London: Routledge, 2006), 3. This is certainly true of literary studies; Grausam, for example, acknowledges only in his afterword that "the archive-and-witness-erasing power of thermonuclear weapons may look somewhat different from those communities struggling to enter those archives in the first place, and to testify to the unrecorded facts of American history." Grausam, *On Endings,* 155. Joseph Dewey describes James Baldwin as the ultimate representative of the "apocalyptic temper" that Dewey is theorizing before spending the rest of the book discussing that temper exclusively in the works of white men. See Joseph Dewey, *In a Dark Time: The Apocalyptic Temper in the American Novel of the Nuclear Age* (West Lafayette, Ind.: Purdue University Press, 1990). Welcome attention is paid to race by Paul Williams, *Race, Ethnicity, and Nuclear War: Representations of Nuclear Weapons and Post-Apocalyptic Worlds* (Liverpool, U.K.: Liverpool University Press, 2011); Patrick B. Sharp, *Savage Perils: Racial Frontiers and Nuclear Apocalypse in American Culture* (Norman: University of Oklahoma Press, 2007); Alan Nadel, *Containment Culture: American Narrative, Postmodernism, and the Atomic Age* (Durham, N.C.: Duke University Press, 1995), although Sharp analyses the treatment of race in white-authored texts.

44. Some of the best work undertaking this project includes Heonik Kwon, *The Other Cold War* (New York: Columbia University Press, 2010); Vincent Intondi, *African Americans against the Bomb: Nuclear Weapons, Colonialism, and the Black Freedom Movement* (Stanford, Calif.: Stanford University Press, 2015); Emily K. Hobson, *Lavender and Red: Liberation and Solidarity in the Gay and Lesbian Left* (Oakland: University of California Press, 2017); Valerie Kuletz, *The Tainted Desert: Environmental Ruin in the American West* (New York: Routledge, 1998); Andrew Hammond, ed., *Cold War Literature: Writing the Global Conflict* (London: Routledge, Taylor and Francis, 2008); Andrew Hammond, ed., *Global Cold War Literature: Western, Eastern and Postcolonial Perspectives* (New York: Routledge, 2012); Adriana Petryna, *Life Exposed: Biological Citizens after Chernobyl* (Princeton, N.J.: Princeton University Press, 2013); Gabrielle Hecht, ed., *Entangled Geographies: Empire and Technopolitics in the Global Cold War* (Cambridge, Mass.: MIT Press, 2011); Naomi Oreskes and John Krige, eds., *Science and Technology in the Global Cold War* (Cambridge, Mass.: MIT Press, 2015).

45. Shiloh R. Krupar, *Hot Spotter's Report: Military Fables of Toxic Waste* (Minneapolis: University of Minnesota Press, 2013), 281.

46. Youngman might well share the questions raised by Andrew McMurry at the end of his 1996 essay "The Slow Apocalypse": "is this apocalypse I have described really an apocalypse, or just the motion of history itself? For the multitudes who have died, are dying, and will die under modern history's

heavy feet there is no significant difference. Perhaps it is time to ask ourselves the questions we have foolishly assumed this same history has already settled. Who says the human presence on this earth was ever sustainable? Why do we continue to believe so strongly in our competency to manage the risks we compound daily? Where is this secret heart of history we trust has been beating? What precisely leads us to believe our world is not perishing? Why isn't this the Apocalypse?" See Andrew McMurry, "The Slow Apocalypse: A Gradualistic Theory of the World's Demise," *Postmodern Culture* 6, no. 3 (1996).

47. Readers will doubtless note that David Foster Wallace is not an Indigenous writer; I include *Infinite Jest* because of its astute diagnosis of a particularly nuclear settler-colonial literary form, while *Almanac of the Dead* serves as the hot spotter text in this chapter.

48. Joshua Bennett, "We Who Can Die Tomorrow: Black Optimism and the Atomic Bomb," *Syndicate,* May 2019, https://syndicate.network/symposia/literature/cultivation-and-catastrophe/.

49. Catherine Keller, *Cloud of the Impossible: Negative Theology and Planetary Entanglement* (New York: Columbia University Press, 2015), 313.

50. Kath Weston, *Animate Planet: Making Visceral Sense of Living in a High-Tech, Ecologically Damaged World* (Durham, N.C.: Duke University Press, 2017), 3.

51. Frank Kermode, *The Sense of an Ending: Studies in the Theory of Fiction—with a New Epilogue,* New ed. (Oxford: Oxford University Press, 2000), 8.

52. Kermode, 46.

53. Robyn Wiegman, "Feminism's Apocalyptic Futures," *New Literary History* 31, no. 4 (2000): 807.

54. Claire Colebrook, *Sex after Life: Essays on Extinction* (Ann Arbor, Mich.: Open Humanities Press, 2014), 2:13. Matthew A. Taylor makes a similar argument about the latent anthropocentrism of posthumanist theory in *Universes without Us: Posthuman Cosmologies in American Literature* (Minneapolis: University of Minnesota Press, 2013).

55. Darieck Scott, *Extravagant Abjection: Blackness, Power, and Sexuality in the African American Literary Imagination* (New York: New York University Press, 2010), 55.

56. Kermode, *Sense of an Ending,* 8. Berger's book is one of several post–Cold War studies of post-1945 apocalypticism that defines it as a posttraumatic response to the horrors of World War II that manifests as a postpolitical postapocalypticism: the sense of imminent crisis that defined modernism, he writes, "has not disappeared, but in the late twentieth century it exists together with another sense, that the conclusive catastrophe has already occurred, the crisis is over (perhaps we were not aware exactly of when it transpired), and

the ceaseless activity of our time—the news with its procession of almost indistinguishable disasters—is only a complex form of stasis." Such an elision of historical specificity into a realm of theoretical trauma has been powerfully critiqued by Dominick LaCapra in "Trauma, Absence, Loss," *Critical Inquiry* 25, no. 4 (1999): 696–727. See James Berger, *After the End: Representations of Post-Apocalypse* (Minneapolis: University of Minnesota Press, 1999), xiii. Berger's triangulation of posttrauma, postapocalyptic, and postpolitical is shared by Teresa Heffernan, *Post-Apocalyptic Culture: Modernism, Postmodernism, and the Twentieth-Century Novel* (Toronto: University of Toronto Press, 2008); and Elizabeth K. Rosen, *Apocalyptic Transformation: Apocalypse and the Postmodern Imagination* (Lanham, Md.: Lexington Books, 2008). Mary Manjikian offers a more nuanced reading of how apocalypse works in contemporary politics, reading fiction alongside documents from her own discipline of political science to show how the idea of apocalypse as postpolitical is used for a variety of political ends. See Mary Manjikian, *Apocalypse and Post-Politics: The Romance of the End* (Lanham, Md.: Lexington Books, 2012).

57. Rebekah Sheldon, *The Child to Come: Life after the Human Catastrophe* (Minneapolis: University of Minnesota Press, 2016), 47.

58. For the millennia-long history of apocalypse's dual affordances as both conservative and revolutionary depending on its emplotment and relationship to the status quo, see Catherine Keller, *Apocalypse Now and Then: A Feminist Guide to the End of the World* (Boston: Beacon Press, 1996), and Stephen D. O'Leary, *Arguing the Apocalypse: A Theory of Millennial Rhetoric* (New York: Oxford University Press, 1998).

59. Johannes Fabian, *Time and the Other: How Anthropology Makes Its Object* (New York: Columbia University Press, 1983), xxxvii.

60. Paul Gilroy, *Against Race: Imagining Political Culture beyond the Color Line* (Cambridge, Mass.: Belknap Press of Harvard University Press, 2000), 56.

61. Valerie Rohy, *Anachronism and Its Others: Sexuality, Race, Temporality* (Albany: SUNY Press, 2009), x; Lee Edelman, *No Future: Queer Theory and the Death Drive*, Series Q (Durham, N.C.: Duke University Press, 2004); Mark Rifkin, *Beyond Settler Time: Temporal Sovereignty and Indigenous Self-Determination* (Durham, N.C.: Duke University Press, 2017), 5.

62. See Cooper, "Whiteness of the Bomb."

63. See David Monteyne, *Fallout Shelter: Designing for Civil Defense in the Cold War* (Minneapolis: University of Minnesota Press, 2013), and chapter 2.

64. For Cold War–era critiques from African American politicians and activists of how funding the nuclear complex led to the devastation of the inner city, see Intondi, *African Americans against the Bomb.*

65. John A. Williams, *Captain Blackman* (New York: Doubleday, 1972), 330, italics original.

66. Williams, 331, italics original. Comparing *Captain Blackman* to historical reality provides an instructive lesson in the difference between radical disruption and diversity when it comes to the infrastructures of power. The election of Barack Obama as the forty-fourth president of the United States fulfilled Eldridge Cleaver's imaginary campaign slogan "PUT A BLACK FINGER ON THE NUCLEAR TRIGGER," but the Obama administration did not change the disposition of nuclear infrastructures (indeed, it intensified them by committing to a trillion-dollar nuclear buildup over the next thirty years). Eldridge Cleaver, *Soul on Ice* (New York: Laurel/Dell, 1992), 144; for Obama's transition from a commitment to disarmament to a commitment to buildup, see the concluding chapter of Intondi, *African Americans against the Bomb.*

67. See Theodor W. Adorno, *Negative Dialectics,* trans. E. B. Ashton (New York: Seabury Press, 1973).

68. This project shares a concern with how different emplotments of time create different possibilities in the present with, among others, Lauren Berlant, *Cruel Optimism* (Durham, N.C.: Duke University Press, 2011); Saidiya Hartman, *Lose Your Mother: A Journey along the Atlantic Slave Route* (New York: Farrar, Straus, and Giroux, 2007); José Esteban Muñoz, *Cruising Utopia: The Then and There of Queer Futurity* (New York: New York University Press, 2009); Dorothy Roberts, *Killing the Black Body: Race, Reproduction, and the Meaning of Liberty* (New York: Pantheon Books, 1997); and David Scott, *Conscripts of Modernity: The Tragedy of Colonial Enlightenment* (Durham, N.C.: Duke University Press, 2004).

69. Paul Ricoeur, *Time and Narrative,* vol. 1, trans. Kathleen McLaughlin and David Pellauer (Chicago: University of Chicago Press, 2009), xi.

70. Ricoeur, 1:10.

71. Augustine 20:26, quoted in Ricoeur, 1:11.

72. Ricoeur, 1:11. For contemporary analyses of how the future acts virtually within the present in a variety of contexts, see Brian Massumi, *Parables for the Virtual: Movement, Affect, Sensation* (Durham, N.C.: Duke University Press, 2002); Richard A. Grusin, *Premediation: Affect and Mediality after 9/11* (Basingstoke, U.K.: Palgrave Macmillan, 2010); Andrew Baldwin, "Whiteness and Futurity: Towards a Research Agenda," *Progress in Human Geography* 36, no. 2 (2012): 172–87.

73. Ricoeur, *Time and Narrative,* 1:52.

74. Ricoeur, 1:xi.

75. George H. Taylor, "Prospective Political Identity," in *Paul Ricoeur in the Age of Hermeneutical Reason: Poetics, Praxis, and Critique,* ed. Roger W. H. Savage (Lanham, Md.: Lexington Books, 2016), 133.

76. Paul Ricoeur, *Time and Narrative,* vol. 3, trans. Kathleen Blamey and David Pellauer (Chicago: University of Chicago Press, 2008), 176.

77. Erich Auerbach, *Scenes from the Drama of European Literature* (Minneapolis: University of Minnesota Press, 1984), 12.

78. Auerbach.

79. Auerbach, 68.

80. Walter Benjamin, "Theses on the Philosophy of History," in *Illuminations*, ed. Hannah Arendt, trans. Harry Zohn (New York: Schocken Books, 2007), 261.

81. Janelle Collins discusses the nuclear power elements of the novel at length, although she mainly focuses on the metaphors of fusion and fission as models for selfhood. See Janelle Collins, "Generating Power: Fission, Fusion, and Postmodern Politics in Bambara's *The Salt Eaters*," *MELUS* 21, no. 2 (1996): 35–47.

82. Carter Mathes describes how "Bambara's balancing of the unknown qualities of the upheaval marked by sonic disruption against the healing renewal of Velma resists a vision of political futurity as linear progression" and connects it to Achille Mbembe's theory of temporal contingency in *Necropolitics*. See Carter Mathes, "Scratching the Threshold: Textual Sound and Political Form in Toni Cade Bambara's *The Salt Eaters*," *Contemporary Literature* 50, no. 2 (2009): 3393.

83. Margot Anne Kelley discusses the multiple-realities structure of the novel in "'Damballah Is the First Law of Thermodynamics': Modes of Access to Toni Cade Bambara's *The Salt Eaters*," *African American Review* 27, no. 3 (1993): 489.

84. Taylor, "Prospective Political Identity," 133.

85. I'm drawing on my own experiences of these remarkable texts here, but their Amazon reviews suggest that is widely shared (although such disorientation is evidently not to everyone's taste). I should also note that this is not always a pleasurable experience; the experience of having one's world reshaped by *Atlas Shrugged* is deeply unpleasant. Nonetheless, the effect is real, as is its cause, and the book thinks of itself as using apocalypse for liberatory purposes even though its political project is very different to the other texts that I discuss here. It is for this reason that I have included this politically and aesthetically terrible book: apocalypse itself is not distributed along ideological lines; there are just as many right-wing apocalypses as there are left-wing ones, and no robust theory of apocalypse can address only one side or the other. *Atlas Shrugged* has sold more than sixty million copies, so any account of what apocalypse does for people cannot afford to ignore it or its readers. How the difference between Rand's apocalypticism and that of the other texts plays out in practice will become clear over the course of the book.

86. Seyla Benhabib, *Critique, Norm, and Utopia: A Study of the Foundations of Critical Theory* (New York: Columbia University Press, 1986), 13.

87. Benhabib, 41–42.

88. Christina Sharpe, *In the Wake: On Blackness and Being* (Durham, N.C.: Duke University Press, 2016), 9.

89. See Elizabeth Freeman, *Time Binds: Queer Temporalities, Queer Histories* (Durham, N.C.: Duke University Press, 2010); Heather Love, *Feeling Backward: Loss and the Politics of Queer History* (Cambridge, Mass.: Harvard University Press, 2007).

90. Benjamin, "Theses," 254, 262.

91. I discuss Benjamin further (including the Angel of History, in case you were wondering where they had gotten to) in chapter 3.

92. Arjun Appadurai, *The Future as Cultural Fact: Essays on the Global Condition* (London: Verso Books, 2013), 295. I discuss probability and risk as futural models at great length in chapter 4.

93. Bambara, quoted in Collins, "Generating Power," 46.

94. Anna Lowenhaupt Tsing, *The Mushroom at the End of the World: On the Possibility of Life in Capitalist Ruins* (Princeton, N.J.: Princeton University Press, 2015), 24–25.

95. Tsing, 21.

96. Scott, *Conscripts of Modernity*, 1; Raymond Williams, quoted in Scott, 2.

97. Donna J. Haraway, *Staying with the Trouble: Making Kin in the Chthulucene* (Durham, N.C.: Duke University Press, 2016), 35.

98. Rebecca Solnit, *Hope in the Dark: Untold Histories, Wild Possibilities* (Chicago: Haymarket Books, 2016), 21; Timothy Morton, *Hyperobjects: Philosophy and Ecology after the End of the World* (Minneapolis: University of Minnesota Press, 2013), 6–7.

99. Weston, *Animate Planet*, 181.

100. Tsing, *Mushroom at the End of the World*, 61.

101. Tsing, 27.

102. My thinking about radical redefinitions of temporality and being at the end of the world has been profoundly shaped by Indigenous knowledge practices. A nonexhaustive list would include Zoe Todd, "Relationships," in *Theorizing the Contemporary*, January 21, 2016, https://culanth.org/fieldsights/relationships; Kyle Powys Whyte, "Our Ancestors' Dystopia Now: Indigenous Conservation and the Anthropocene," in *Routledge Companion to the Environmental Humanities*, ed. Ursula Heise, Jon Christensen, and Michelle Niemann, 206–15 (New York: Routledge, Taylor and Francis, 2017); and Gerald Vizenor, "Aesthetics of Survivance: Literary Theory and Practice," in *Survivance: Narratives of Native Presence*, 1–23 (Lincoln: University of Nebraska Press, 2008).

1. White Sovereignty and the Nuclear State

1. David E. Lilienthal, "Democracy and the Atom," *Phi Delta Kappan* 29 (January 1948): 215.

2. Végső, *Naked Communist,* 70. In his survey of the cultural mood in America regarding the atom bomb between 1945 and 1950, Paul S. Boyer notes that one of the biggest concerns about the emergence of atomic technology in the immediate postwar period was the "ominous scenario of centralized government power." Boyer, *By the Bomb's Early Light: American Thought and Culture at the Dawn of the Atomic Age* (New York: Pantheon, 1985), 143.

3. Elaine Scarry, *Thermonuclear Monarchy: Choosing between Democracy and Doom* (New York: W. W. Norton, 2014), 14–15.

4. Scarry, 4, 5, 27.

5. Scarry, 261.

6. Scarry's commitment to an idealized version of the settler state comes out most clearly in her unfortunate nostalgia for the good old days of U.S. warmongering that produced a more Enlightenment-based moral/rational discourse: "Once Congress regains its authority over war, however, there is every reason to believe that it will travel back along the reverse path, reacquiring the stature, intelligence, eloquence, and commitment to the population it once had. In the chapter ahead, we look at the nature of congressional debate in the country's five constitutionally declared wars—the War of 1812, the Mexican–American War of 1846, the Spanish–American War of 1898, World War I, World War II—deliberations in which the full stature of the assembly comes clearly into view. The high quality of congressional analysis contrasts sharply with the low quality of debate carried out in secret presidential deliberations about whether to drop the atomic bomb in the Taiwan straits in 1954 and on East Germany in 1959." Scarry, 33.

7. William Pietz, "The 'Post-Colonialism' of Cold War Discourse," *Social Text,* no. 19/20 (1988): 58.

8. *Atlas Shrugged* was voted the second most influential book of all time in a poll by the Library of Congress in 1991, beaten out only by the Bible. It continues to sell hundreds of thousands of copies a year more than fifty years after its first publication.

9. Jennifer Burns, *Goddess of the Market: Ayn Rand and the American Right* (Oxford: Oxford University Press, 2009), 2.

10. Burns, 279. The *New York Times* obviously never saw Paul Ryan coming or it would have held this appellation in reserve.

11. Gene H. Bell-Villada's "Who Was Ayn Rand?" was the first work to read Rand's work in the context of her early life in Russia, and is excellent. Cynthia Burack and Susan Love Brown trace the impact of her novels in Ameri-

can public life. Stacy Olster contextualizes Objectivism in the broader moves toward withdrawal that appeared in 1950s literature. Judith Wilt's "The Romances of Ayn Rand" offers a critical yet sensitive reading that draws out the dangerous appeal of the novel while resisting Rand's self-mythologizing. See Bell-Villada, "Who Was Ayn Rand?," *Salmagundi* 141–42 (Winter–Spring 2004): 227–42; Burack, "Just Deserts: Ayn Rand and the Christian Right," *Journal of Religion and Popular Culture* 19 (2008): 3; Brown, "Ayn Rand as Public Intellectual: Notes from the Margin," *Studies in the Humanities* 35, no. 2 (2008): 180–97; Olster, "Something Old, Something New, Something Borrowed, Something (Red, White, and) Blue: Ayn Rand's *Atlas Shrugged* and Objectivist Ideology," in *The Other Fifties: Interrogating Midcentury American Icons*, ed. Joel Foreman, 288–306 (Urbana: University of Illinois Press, 1997); and Wilt, "The Romances of Ayn Rand," in *Feminist Interpretations of Ayn Rand*, ed. Mimi Reisel Gladstein, Chris Matthew Sciabarra, and Nancy Tuana, 173–98 (University Park: Pennsylvania State University Press, 1999).

12. See Myka Tucker-Abramson, *Novel Shocks: Urban Renewal and the Origins of Neoliberalism* (New York: Fordham University Press, 2019); Andrew Hoberek, *The Twilight of the Middle Class: Post–World War II American Fiction and White-Collar Work* (Princeton, N.J.: Princeton University Press, 2005).

13. See Ayn Rand, *Journals of Ayn Rand* (New York: Dutton, 1997), 345–70.

14. See Rand, 371–81.

15. Rand's pugilistic relationship to both the Left and the Right during the Cold War reminds us that, as Richard Gid Powers has shown, even the universalist ideology of anticommunism was conceived and practiced differently across a wide range of political positions. See Powers, *Not without Honor: The History of American Anticommunism* (New York: Free Press, 1995), 192.

16. Rand only sold four screenplays during her time in Hollywood, but the fourth, for the screen adaptation of *The Fountainhead* (1949), went for what was at the time a stunning $50,000, and Rand was given the also almost unheard-of promise by Warner Bros. that her script would not be altered by anyone but her.

17. The script itself has never been unearthed; an outline of the screenplay appears in Rand, *Journals*, 335–44.

18. Rand, 312.

19. Rand, 344.

20. See Jackie Orr, *Panic Diaries: A Genealogy of Panic Disorder* (Durham, N.C.: Duke University Press, 2006); Brian Massumi, ed., *The Politics of Everyday Fear* (Minneapolis: University of Minnesota Press, 1993); and Tracy C. Davis, *Stages of Emergency: Cold War Nuclear Civil Defense* (Durham, N.C.: Duke University Press, 2007). For continuities between the Cold War and the War on Terror in terms of state-structured fear meant to produce affective and

material investments in "security" at any cost, see Joseph Masco, *The Theater of Operations: National Security Affect from the Cold War to the War on Terror* (Durham, N.C.: Duke University Press, 2014). Ken Alder accurately describes the mechanisms of Cold War foreign policy when he writes that "the audience for the theater of deterrence was largely at home." Alder, "America's Two Gadgets: Of Bombs and Polygraphs," *Isis* 98 (2007): 134.

21. See George E. Webb, "The Manhattan Project Revealed: Local Press Response to the Atomic Bomb Announcements, August–September 1945," in *The Atomic Bomb and American Society: New Perspectives,* ed. Rosemary Mariner and G. Kurt Piehler, 43–64 (Knoxville: University of Tennessee Press, 2009).

22. Dwight Macdonald, "Editorial," *Politics* (1945), quoted in Boyer, *By the Bomb's Early Light,* 234–5.

23. Robert DeVore, "Passport to the Golden Age," *Collier's* (1947), quoted in Boyer, 144.

24. Oscar M. Ruebhausen and Robert B. von Mehren, "The Atomic Energy Act and the Private Production of Atomic Power," *Harvard Law Review* 66, no. 8 (1953): 145.

25. The routine state scrutiny of the individual established by the AEA would only intensify in the coming years, especially during the Red Scare, "until at least 13.5 million Americans underwent investigation in the course of applying for jobs. One agent working out of Chicago calculated that the only place big enough to put all the local suspects the FBI planned to arrest in a crisis was the football stadium, Soldiers' Field. People were investigated as security risks for inter-racial friendships and homosexuality as well as more overtly political stances, such as a history of support for republican Spain or protest against nuclear testing." See Laura Elizabeth Hein and Mark Selden, "Commemoration and Silence: Fifty Years of Remembering the Bomb in America and Japan," in Hein and Selden, *Living with the Bomb,* 15.

26. Timothy Melley, *The Covert Sphere: Secrecy, Fiction, and the National Security State* (Ithaca, N.Y.: Cornell University Press, 2012), 4.

27. National Security Council, *NSC 68: United States Objectives and Programs for National Security: A Report to the President Pursuant to the President's Directive of January 31, 1950* (Washington, D.C.: National Security Council, 1950), 3. Further page references to this document will be given in the body of the text.

28. Melley, *Covert Sphere,* 27.

29. Pietz, "'Post-Colonialism' of Cold War Discourse," 58, 59. Russia's racial instability, alternating between European and Asiatic at different times and for different purposes, predates the Cold War but was mobilized in different ways during it—both by Western speakers activating a yellow peril response

by insisting on the USSR's Oriental nature and by the Soviets themselves as they attempted to claim "natural" connections with the decolonizing world as an Asian power to rival China. See Michael Freeberne, "Racial Issues and the Sino-Soviet Dispute," *Asian Survey* 5, no. 8 (1965): 408–9.

30. Jodi Kim, *Ends of Empire: Asian American Critique and the Cold War* (Minneapolis: University of Minnesota Press, 2010), 21.

31. For the long history of the yellow peril imaginary in the West, see John Kuo Wei Tchen and Dylan Yeats, *Yellow Peril! An Archive of Anti-Asian Fear* (New York: Verso, 2014).

32. The Chinese Exclusion Act of 1882 was the first limitation that had ever been set on America's open immigration policy; senators debating the act referred in the Senate to Chinese immigrants as "packs of dogs," "mildew," and "a cancer." See Andrew Gyory, *Closing the Gate: Race, Politics, and the Chinese Exclusion Act* (Chapel Hill: University of California Press, 1998), 5. In 1924, the Asian Exclusion Act prohibited any immigration of Arabs, East Asians, and Indians and rendered those of Chinese origin ineligible for citizenship.

33. See Wendy L. Ng, *Japanese American Internment during World War II: A History and Reference Guide* (Westport, Conn.: Greenwood Press, 2002).

34. Colleen Lye, *America's Asia: Racial Form and American Literature, 1882–1945* (Princeton, N.J.: Princeton University Press, 2004), 8.

35. Unlike citizens of Japan and Japanese American U.S. citizens, citizens of enemy states coded as white (Germany and Italy, for instance) resident in America during World War II were never interned as a racial bloc; white saboteurs were tried individually.

36. In an important essay that works, as does this chapter, to underscore the necessity of thinking about the racialized aspects of the Western construction of communism/totalitarianism, Leerom Medovoi describes the Cold War as a "race war without race," arguing that ideology supplants biological race in the Cold War as a way of making racialized distinctions between the inside and outside of the nation-state, those who must be protected and those who must be killed. While I agree with Medovoi's readings of specific texts, I think that the evacuation of racial content from the form of "race war" gains a larger theoretical reach by sacrificing attention to historical specificity. It's important, in other words, that totalitarianism is racialized *as oriental*; it positions it within a certain genealogy that has consequences and contingencies and allows for different orientations toward the world than would, say, totalitarianism as Black or as Jewish. The Orientalization of totalitarianism, in particular, is what allows it to be perceived as a yellow peril and thus not only as an external threat but also as a spur to the kind of internal racial degeneration of whiteness that Rand depicts. Leerom Medovoi, "The Race War Within: The

Biopolitics of the Long Cold War," in *American Literature and Culture in an Age of Cold War: A Critical Reassessment*, ed. Steven Belletto and Daniel Grausam, 163–86 (Iowa City: University of Iowa Press, 2012).

37. Rand's use of the language of savagery to describe an "Oriental" scene is typical of the way that "in colonial discourse, the great companion of Orientalism is primitivism," whereby primitivism acts as a kind of booster for Orientalist logics. See Pietz, "'Post-Colonialism' of Cold War Discourse," 73.

38. Rand considered Galt's speech to be the ultimate statement of her own philosophy; for this reason, I use "Galt" and "Rand" somewhat interchangeably when describing the source of these thoughts.

39. In a 1971 letter to a fan who had written to ask what he should do about being deindividuated by the racism of American society, Rand doubled down on a race-neutral individualism: "Do not allow anyone ever to make you feel ashamed of being black. That would be an acceptance of the vicious racist premises of other people. The best way to fight racists of any color, black or white, is never to allow their ideas into your own mind." Ayn Rand, *Letters of Ayn Rand* (New York: Dutton, 1995), 654; see also Burns, *Goddess of the Market*, 206–8.

40. Burns notes that the published versions of Rand's *Journals* have cut much of her writing on race, and particularly her "Spenglerian" attitude toward the degeneration of the white race. Burns, *Goddess of the Market*, 44.

41. Wilt, "Romances of Ayn Rand," 177–78.

42. Sara Ahmed, "A Phenomenology of Whiteness," *Feminist Theory* 8, no. 2 (2007): 154.

43. Ahmed, 150.

44. William J. Grace, "The Social Impact of Current Tensions," *American Journal of Economics and Sociology* 9, no. 4 (1950): 463.

45. Frederick M. Dolan, *Allegories of America: Narratives, Metaphysics, Politics* (Ithaca, N.Y.: Cornell University Press, 1994), 75.

46. Fred J. Cook, *The Warfare State* (New York: Macmillan, 1962), 106; Leander Boykin, "Where Do We Go from Here? A Social and Educational Prospectus," *Journal of Educational Sociology* 23, no. 2 (1949): 98.

47. This also sets Rand apart from the majority of other examples of the nuclear apocalypse genre, in which the end of civilization allows for a fantasy of life outside the social contract generally represented as a glorious return to patriarchal, heteronormative, and white supremacist values. See Claire P. Curtis, *Postapocalyptic Fiction and the Social Contract: "We'll Not Go Home Again"* (Lanham, Md.: Lexington Books, 2010).

48. Rand captures here what Johan Galtung would later call the "indirect violence" of the nuclear complex: "When a person, a group, a nation is displaying the means of physical violence, whether throwing stones around or testing

nuclear arms, there may not be violence in the sense that anyone is hit or hurt, but there is nevertheless the *threat of physical violence* and indirect threat of mental violence that may even be characterized as some type of psychological violence since it constrains human action. Indeed, this is also the intention: the famous balance of power doctrine is based on efforts to obtain precisely this effect." However, her analysis of structural violence is limited to a critique of the state and never extended to other forms of indirect violence, that is, capitalism, which she defines as a uniquely nonviolent way for men to relate to each other. Galtung, "Violence, Peace, and Peace Research," 170.

49. Rey Chow, *The Age of the World Target* (Durham, N.C.: Duke University Press, 2006), 32. See also Deak Nabers, "Hiroshima and the Nuclear Event," *Post45*, December 2011, http://post45.research.yale.edu/2011/09/hiroshima-and-the-nuclear-event/.

50. The town upon which Atlantis was modeled, Ouray, Colorado, has a population of 813.

51. It seems likely that Rand is alluding to Executive Order 9066 (which ordered the internment of Japanese Americans in 1942) with her fictional Directive 10-289. Both involve the forced removal of individual property by the state, forced relocation, and forced immobility; Rand is likely to have been conscious of the internment while writing *Atlas Shrugged* because the secretary and typist who worked with her while she was writing the novel had been interned during the war.

52. Grausam, *On Endings*, 76; Végső, *Naked Communist*, 42.

53. Scarry, *Thermonuclear Monarchy*, 264. The fear that changes in the structure of the public sphere will cause a kind of social atavism is not limited to nuclear infrastructures; Jurgen Habermas, for example, expressed a fear that strategic mass communications would lead to the "refeudalization" of society. Timothy Melley notes that this argument—that mass culture has swung the rational Enlightenment back toward the irrationality of the premodern or feudal—is a version of what Horkheimer and Adorno called "the dialectic of Enlightenment"; what I want to emphasize here is that "irrational" and "feudal" have racial, and specifically Orientalist, overtones that we would do well not to overlook in our analysis of any anxiety that expresses itself through a fear of social reversion. Melley, *Covert Sphere*, 32.

54. Tchen and Yeats, *Yellow Peril!*, 280.

55. This allows Rand to set her dystopia in a much closer time period than other American miscegenation-based horror stories; Ignatius Donnelly's 1889 novel *Caesar's Column*, for example, has to be set more than a hundred years in the future to allow for the genetic degeneration of the white race after the end of Chinese exclusion.

56. Lye, *America's Asia*; David Palumbo-Liu, *Asian/American: Historical*

Crossings of a Racial Frontier (Stanford, Calif.: Stanford University Press, 1999),
2. See also Alexander Saxton, *The Indispensable Enemy: Labor and the Anti-Chinese Movement in California* (Berkeley: University of California Press, 1971); John Kuo Wei Tchen, "Notes for a History of Paranoia: 'Yellow Peril' and the Long Twentieth Century," *The Psychoanalytic Review* 97, no. 2 (2010): 263–83; Stanford M. Lyman, "The 'Yellow Peril' Mystique: Origins and Vicissitudes of a Racist Discourse," *International Journal of Politics, Culture, and Society* 13, no. 4 (2000): 683–747.

57. Christina Klein, *Cold War Orientalism: Asia in the Middlebrow Imagination, 1945–1961* (Los Angeles: University of California Press, 2003), 9.

58. Klein, 41.

59. Klein.

60. Klein, 16.

61. Klein, 48–49. See also Burton I. Kaufman, *Trade and Aid: Eisenhower's Foreign Economic Policy, 1953–1961* (Baltimore: Johns Hopkins University Press, 1982).

62. Klein, *Cold War Orientalism*, 49.

63. Barbara Grizzuti Harrison, "Psyching Out Ayn Rand," in Gladstein et al., *Feminist Interpretations of Ayn Rand*, 71.

64. For analyses of America's neocolonial aid tactics, see George M. Guess, *The Politics of United States Foreign Aid* (London: Croom, Helm, 1987); Steven W. Hook, *National Interest and Foreign Aid* (Boulder, Colo.: Lynne Rienner, 1995); Margaret Huff-Rousselle, *Foreign Aid and Neocolonialism: The Policies, Procedures, and Politics Influencing Foreign Aid Dependent Organizations in Haiti and the Commonwealth Caribbean* (Cave Hill, Barbados: University of the West Indies, 2000).

65. Former Oak Ridge scientists Cuthbert Daniel and Arthur M. Squires, for example, wrote in the *Bulletin of Atomic Scientists* that "the atomic bomb makes world government inevitable in our time." Daniel and Squires, "Scientists' Responsibilities on the Way to Peace, and After," *Bulletin of the Atomic Scientists* 5, no. 1 (1949): 27. The leading nuclear scientists of the age captured the stakes of world cooperation in the nuclear age in the title of their coauthored volume *One World or None* (1946). In society at large, the years between 1945 and 1949 saw the biggest movement toward world government at any time in history; see Boyer, *By the Bomb's Early Light*, 27–46.

66. See Walter Benn Michaels, *Our America: Nativism, Modernism, and Pluralism* (Durham, N.C.: Duke University Press, 1995), 29–40.

67. Lye, *America's Asia*, 54.

68. Lye, 52.

69. Iyko Day, *Alien Capital: Asian Racialization and the Logic of Settler Colonial Capitalism* (Durham, N.C.: Duke University Press, 2016), 32.

70. Klein, *Cold War Orientalism*, 53.

71. For a reading of the sentimental negotiations between *Uncle Tom's Cabin* and *The King and I*, see Lauren Berlant, *The Female Complaint: The Unfinished Business of Sentimentality in American Culture* (Durham, N.C.: Duke University Press, 2008), 33–68.

72. Kathleen M. Woodward, *Statistical Panic* (Durham, N.C.: Duke University Press, 2009), 112.

73. Melissa Jane Hardie, "Fluff and Granite: Rereading Ayn Rand's Camp Feminist Aesthetics," in Gladstein et al., *Feminist Interpretations of Ayn Rand*, 358.

74. Rand, *Journals*, 633.

75. Palumbo-Liu, *Asian/American*, 133.

76. Timothy Melley, *Empire of Conspiracy: The Culture of Paranoia in Postwar America* (Ithaca, N.Y.: Cornell University Press, 2000), 49.

77. Quoted in Burns, *Goddess of the Market*, 199–200.

78. Ayn Rand, *The Romantic Manifesto* (New York: Signet Books, 1971), 167.

79. Relatedly, Myka Tucker-Abramson analyzes the mechanisms by which Rand trains her white readers to identify with capital instead of with their own class position in *Novel Shocks*, 91.

80. Philip Fisher, *The Vehement Passions* (Princeton, N.J.: Princeton University Press, 2002), 144, emphasis original.

81. Matthew Frye Jacobson describes the revival of white ethnicities as a strategy of maintaining white supremacy after the end of state-sanctioned racism. See Jacobson, *Roots Too: White Ethnic Revival in Post–Civil Rights America* (Cambridge, Mass.: Harvard University Press, 2006).

82. Lye, *America's Asia*, 9. See also Edlie Wong, "In a Future Tense: Immigration Law, Counterfactual Histories, and Chinese Invasion Fiction," *American Literary History* 26, no. 3 (2014): 511–35.

83. Tchen and Yeats, *Yellow Peril!*, 4–6.

84. See Rand, *Journals*, 342.

2. Civil Defense and Black Apocalypse

1. James Baldwin, *Go Tell It on the Mountain* (New York: Dial Press Trade Paperbacks, 2005), 27.

2. James Baldwin, *Tell Me How Long the Train's Been Gone* (New York: Vintage International, 1998), 478. Further page references will be to this edition and will be given parenthetically in the body of the text.

3. Samuel R. Delany, *Dhalgren* (New York: Vintage Books, 2001), 249. Further page references will be to this edition and will be given parenthetically in the body of the text.

4. Ralph Ellison, "Going to the Territory," in *The Collected Essays of Ralph Ellison,* ed. John F. Callahan (New York: The Modern Library, 2003), 604.

5. Erich Auerbach, *Scenes from the Drama of European Literature* (Minneapolis: University of Minnesota Press, 1984), 30.

6. Christopher Columbus, *Journals and Other Documents on the Life and Voyages of Christopher Columbus,* trans. Samuel Eliot Morison (New York: Heritage Press, 1963), 291. For the full range of Columbus's prophetic and eschatological beliefs, see Christopher Columbus, *The Libro de Las Profecías of Christopher Columbus,* trans. D. C. West and A. Kling (Gainesville: University of Florida Press, 1991). Apocalypticism was at the center of early modern encounters with the Americas; for particularly compelling arguments, see Djelal Kadir, *Columbus and the Ends of the Earth: Europe's Prophetic Rhetoric as Conquering Ideology* (Berkeley: University of California Press, 1992), and Keller, *Apocalypse Now and Then,* 140–67.

7. Cotton Mather, quoted in Sacvan Bercovitch, "Typology in Puritan New England: The Williams-Cotton Controversy Reassessed," *American Quarterly* 19, no. 2 (1967): 184–85.

8. Bercovitch, 185–86.

9. For the argument that Spanish and English colonization projects in the Americas were spurred by the perceived nature of the New World as "a worldly space for other-worldly ends," see Kadir, *Columbus and the Ends of the Earth,* 51.

10. See Gilroy, *Against Race,* and Rohy, *Anachronism and Its Others.*

11. Cotton Mather, quoted in Bercovitch, "Typology in Puritan New England," 184. Werner Sollors describes the process of community identification through typological identification as "typological ethnogenesis," a useful concept for thinking about how typology has functioned in both white and Black communities in America, although my focus will be more on the historiographic implications of typology than on Sollors's more identitarian analysis. See Werner Sollers, *Beyond Ethnicity: Consent and Descent in American Culture* (New York: Oxford University Press, 1986), 40–65.

12. Houston A. Baker, *Long Black Song: Essays in Black American Literature and Culture* (Charlottesville: University Press of Virginia, 1972), 44.

13. Eric J. Sundquist gives a comprehensive overview of African American uses of typology in *Strangers in the Land: Blacks, Jews, Post-Holocaust America* (Cambridge, Mass.: Belknap Press of Harvard University Press, 2008).

14. Jane Jacobs, *The Death and Life of Great American Cities* (New York: Random House, 1961), 6; Marable, "Nuclear War and Black America," 166–67.

15. Kathryn Bond Stockton, *Beautiful Bottom, Beautiful Shame: Where "Black" Meets "Queer"* (Durham, N.C.: Duke University Press, 2006), 76.

16. Stockton, 75.

17. Malcolm X, *Malcolm X Speaks: Selected Speeches and Statements*, ed. George Breitman (New York: Grove Weidenfeld, 1990), 175.

18. Scott, *Conscripts of Modernity*, 41.

19. "Welcome Film by President Truman to Students at CD Staff College and CD Technical Training Centers" (1951), Truman Papers, Truman Library, OF, Box 1843, Folder 1591, pp. 1–2.

20. Ernest Lee Tuveson, *Redeemer Nation: The Idea of America's Millennial Role* (Chicago: University of Chicago Press, 1968), 214.

21. William V. Spanos, *Shock and Awe: American Exceptionalism and the Imperatives of the Spectacle in Mark Twain's "A Connecticut Yankee in King Arthur's Court"* (Hanover, N.H.: Dartmouth College Press, 2013), 58.

22. John Winthrop, *A Modell of Christian Charity* (1630), Collections of the Massachusetts Historical Society (Boston, 1838), 3rd series, Hanover College History Department, https://history.hanover.edu/texts/winthmod.html.

23. Matthew Brophy, "Burlesquing America's Errand: Savage Satire in Irving's *History of New York* and Melville's *The Confidence-Man*," in *American Exceptionalisms: From Winthrop to Winfrey*, ed. Sylvia Söderlind and James Taylor Carson (Albany: SUNY Press, 2011), 71.

24. In Richard M. Gamble's account, the phrase itself occurs repeatedly throughout the seventeenth, eighteenth, and nineteenth centuries but is used almost exclusively to refer to the original context in the book of Matthew. When "A Modell of Christian Charity" was published in the nineteenth century, it began to be quoted in histories of America, but "city on a hill" not only failed to be used as shorthand for the American national mission; it failed to appear at all. See Gamble, *In Search of the City on a Hill: The Making and Unmaking of an American Myth* (London: Continuum, 2012).

25. Perry Miller, *Errand into the Wilderness* (Cambridge, Mass.: Harvard University Press, 1984), 11.

26. See Amy Kaplan, "'Left Alone with America': The Absence of Empire in the Study of American Culture," in *Cultures of United States Imperialism*, ed. Donald E. Pease and Amy Kaplan, 3–21 (Durham, N.C.: Duke University Press, 1993).

27. Nicholas Guyatt, "'An Instrument of National Policy': Perry Miller and the Cold War," *Journal of American Studies* 36, no. 1 (2002): 107–49. Miller may have been in the Congo in the early 1920s, but he was in England working for the Office of Strategic Services (later relaunched as the CIA) from 1942 to 1945 and traveled on "quasi-governmental cultural missions" to Europe and Japan after the war (108).

28. For a strong analysis and critique of this slippage between exemplar

and redeemer nation, see T. Jeremy Gunn, *Spiritual Weapons: The Cold War and the Forging of an American National Religion* (Westport, Conn.: Praeger, 2009), 44.

29. United States and John F. Kennedy, *John F. Kennedy: Containing the Public Messages, Speeches, and Statements of the President* (Washington, D.C.: Office of the Federal Register, National Archives and Records Service, General Services Administration: Supt. of Docs., U.S. GPO, 1962), 234.

30. The line from Miller to Kennedy is not direct; the city on a hill trope exploded in popularity in the late 1950s and early 1960s, featuring in, among others, Daniel Boorstin's massive *The Americans* (1964), Richard Schlatter's "The Puritan Strain" (1962), and Reinhold Niehbuhr and Alan Heimert's *A Nation So Conceived: Reflections on the History of America from Its Early Visions to Its Present Power* (1964). Miller's aim was distinctly not to provide a rationale for aggressive national chauvinism under cover of democratic redemption; as he wrote in *Errand into the Wilderness*, "the Puritans were not rugged individualists . . . they abhorred freedom of conscience; and they did not believe at all in democracy" (160). How his phrase was taken up was, as ever, beyond his control.

31. As the work of Guy Oakes, Tracy C. Davis, Andrew D. Grossman, and Laura McEnaney has shown, while civil defense was presented to the public as a path to victory through making a nuclear war survivable, in fact the relationship between civil defense and military strategies for winning the Cold War was rather more occult. Throughout the Cold War, the only acceptable strategies for nuclear age warfare were deterrence and mutually assured destruction, which required that an ever-increasing amount of national capital and resources be channeled into the nuclear complex. To support this strategy, the voting public had to be finessed into a particular structure of feeling: they needed to be alarmed enough by the prospect of nuclear war that they would support hyperinvestment in the nuclear complex to prevent war through deterrence, but they could not be so terrified of the prospect of a nuclear war actually happening that they would demand more drastic measures to prevent it from happening—a weapons freeze, say, or unilateral disarmament. Consequently, the function of civil defense as it was understood by its architects was not actually to make nuclear war survivable but rather to convince the public that nuclear war, while terrible, was winnable; by this means, it would produce a scared but not terrified electorate and thus enable the strategy of deterrence to continue, winning the Cold War. See Oakes, *The Imaginary War: Civil Defense and American Cold War Culture* (New York: Oxford University Press, 1994); Davis, *Stages of Emergency: Cold War Nuclear Civil Defense* (Durham, N.C.: Duke University Press, 2007); Grossman, *Neither Dead nor Red: Civilian Defense and American Political Development during the*

Early Cold War (New York: Routledge, 2001); McEnaney, *Civil Defense Begins at Home: Militarization Meets Everyday Life in the Fifties* (Princeton, N.J.: Princeton University Press, 2000).

32. Quoted in Kenneth D. Rose, *One Nation Underground: The Fallout Shelter in American Culture* (New York: New York University Press, 2004), 34.

33. Quoted in Oakes, *Imaginary War*, 143; Oakes's analysis of Cold War throwbacks to early America as a specific "Cold War ethic" focuses more on character than on temporality but is very useful for any consideration of how civil defense participated in and influenced American nation building.

34. Frederick Jackson Turner, *The Frontier in American History* (New York: Holt, Rinehart, and Winston, 1962), 4. Another classic work of Cold War American studies, Richard Slotkin's 1973 *Regeneration through Violence: The Mythology of the American Frontier, 1600–1860* (Middletown, Conn.: Wesleyan University Press, 1973), analyses the role of the frontier in America's formation at length.

35. George F. Kennan, *Sketches from a Life* (New York: Pantheon Books, 1989), 211, 131. Oakes discusses the antiurbanism of John Foster Dulles and Kennan at length in *Imaginary War*, 23–30.

36. Secretary of defense Robert McNamara's "no cities" doctrine would be launched in 1962, but it did little to disconnect the by that point extremely tightly yoked connection between cities and nuclear strikes in the public imaginary. Besides, the "no cities" doctrine suggested only that the United States not strike Soviet cities with the first round of nukes; it also called for (and produced) the capacity for second-round strikes that would indeed be aimed at cities. The ultimate outcome of the new counterforce doctrine would be a buildup of both conventional military forces and a diversified set of nuclear weapons, strengthening the nuclear complex overall.

37. Gunnar Myrdal, *An American Dilemma,* quoted in Mary L. Dudziak, *Cold War Civil Rights: Race and the Image of American Democracy* (Princeton, N.J.: Princeton University Press, 2000), 8.

38. Dudziak, *Cold War Civil Rights,* 90.

39. Bernard Brodie, "Military Policy and the Atomic Bomb," *Infantry Journal* 59 (1946): 33.

40. Norbert Wiener, quoted in Jacobs, *Death and Life,* 124. Jacobs also gives an important history of the ideology of decentralization, which predates the Cold War and is only intensified after 1945 under the policy of dispersal.

41. Quoted in William H. Whyte Jr., "Urban Sprawl," in *The Exploding Metropolis,* ed. Editors of Fortune (Garden City, N.Y.: Doubleday, 1958), 144. For more on how the envisioning of nuclear strikes was operationalized to reshape America's cities around a commitment to dispersal, see Peter Galison, "War against the Center," *Grey Room* 1, no. 4 (2001): 6–33.

42. See David Monteyne, *Fallout Shelter: Designing for Civil Defense in the Cold War* (Minneapolis: University of Minnesota Press, 2013), 65–66. Monteyne, an architectural historian, provides a detailed description of how civil defense expense, architects, and urban planners worked together to remake the urban environment for the Cold War as well as an excellent analysis of how racial logics undergirded such projects.

43. Ann Petry's *The Street* (1946) and Richard Wright's *Native Son* (1940) offer exemplary formal representations of how race and space come together to determine the emplotment of a life.

44. Kenneth T. Jackson, *Crabgrass Frontier: The Suburbanization of America* (New York: Oxford University Press, 1985), 209.

45. Gilroy, *Against Race,* 14.

46. Jacobs, *Death and Life,* 301.

47. The essays collected in Adrienne Brown and Valerie Smith, eds., *Race and Real Estate* (New York: Oxford University Press, 2015), offer an excellent overview of recent critical approaches to race and the built environment.

48. Dean MacCannell, "Baltimore in the Morning . . . After: On the Forms of Post-nuclear Leadership," *diacritics* 14, no. 2 (1984): 40.

49. Foertsch writes that "the massive exodus to the suburbs conducted by white middle-class Americans during this period constitutes its own defensive, precautionary response to imminent nuclear disaster. Their very homes were multi-room, beautifully decorated 'bomb shelters' whose comfortable kitchens stocked with the latest in long-lived canned and packaged foods provided a vital sense of security, however false that sense may have been." Jacqueline Foertsch, *Reckoning Day: Race, Place, and the Atom Bomb in Postwar America* (Nashville, Tenn.: Vanderbilt University Press, 2012), 7.

50. James Orange and Frank Brown, quoted in Intondi, *African Americans against the Bomb,* 85, 102. Intondi documents the direct links between increased defense spending and reduced spending on cities, especially under Reagan.

51. For other accounts of the apocalyptic politics of ghettoization in the nuclear age, see Matthew Farish, "Disaster and Decentralization: American Cities and the Cold War," *Cultural Geographies* 10, no. 2 (2003): 125–48; MacCannell, "Baltimore in the Morning"; Sharp, *Savage Perils*; and Williams, *Race, Ethnicity, and Nuclear War.*

52. The inherent violence of this move can be seen in the language that Morrison uses to describe it: "the act of enforcing racelessness in literary discourse is itself a racial act. Pouring rhetorical acid on the fingers of a black hand may indeed destroy the prints, but not the hand." Toni Morrison, *Playing in the Dark: Whiteness and the Literary Imagination* (Cambridge, Mass.: Harvard University Press, 1992), 46.

53. Nikhil Pal Singh, *Black Is a Country: Race and the Unfinished Struggle for Democracy* (Cambridge, Mass.: Harvard University Press, 2004), 39.

54. Pat Frank, *Alas, Babylon* (New York: Perennial, 2005), 190–91.

55. Jacqueline Foertsch, "'Extraordinarily Convenient Neighbors': African-American Characters in White-Authored Post-atomic Novels," *Journal of Modern Literature* 30, no. 4 (2007): 122–38.

56. Philip Wylie, *Tomorrow!* (Lincoln: University of Nebraska Press, 2009), 295.

57. S. J. Collier and A. Lakoff, "Distributed Preparedness: The Spatial Logic of Domestic Security in the United States," *Environment and Planning D* 26, no. 1 (2008): 8.

58. Farish, "Disaster and Decentralization," 126.

59. Hypothetical Test Narrative, "General Outline: Civil Defense Plan for the City and County of Philadelphia," City of Philadelphia Archives, Box A5311, 1951. For more on the Hypothetical Test Exercise and race in Philadelphia, including the bombs that were in fact dropped close to the West Philadelphia Ground Zero on May 13, 1985, by the city's government, see Jessica Hurley, "Philadelphia," https://fromthebombtothecrash.squarespace.com/content-2.

60. Kenneth Clark, 1965, quoted in Steven H. Jaffe, *New York at War: Four Centuries of Combat, Fear, and Intrigue* (New York: Basic Books, 2012), 298; Jennifer Light, "Urban Planning and Defense Planning, Past and Future," *Journal of the American Planning Association* 70, no. 4 (2004): 401–4.

61. Wylie, *Tomorrow!*, 367.

62. Martha A. Bartter, "Nuclear Holocaust as Urban Renewal," *Science Fiction Studies* 13, no. 2 (1986): 148.

63. Farish, "Disaster and Decentralization," 126; Eugene Gordon, "The Fallout Shelter," quoted in Foerstch, *Reckoning Day,* 20.

64. Baldwin, *Go Tell It on the Mountain,* 27.

65. Baldwin, 40, emphasis original.

66. Hortense Spillers, afterword to *James Baldwin: America and Beyond,* ed. Cora Kaplan and Bill Schwarz (Ann Arbor: University of Michigan Press, 2011), 244–45.

67. James Baldwin, *The Evidence of Things Not Seen* (1985; repr., New York: Henry Holt, 1995), 56.

68. James Baldwin, *No Name in the Street* (1972; repr., New York: Vintage Books, 2007), 196.

69. James Baldwin, *The Fire Next Time* (1963; repr., New York: Vintage International, 1993), 105. Perry Miller's account of early American rejections of the jeremiad indicate another angle from which Baldwin might have viewed the dangers of the form: "whatever they may signify in the realm of theology, in that of psychology they are purgations of soul; they do not discourage

but actually encourage the community to persist in its heinous conduct. The exhortation to a reformation which never materializes serves as a token payment upon the obligation, and so liberates the debtors." Miller, *Errand into the Wilderness*, 9.

70. Cora Kaplan and Bill Schwarz, "Introduction: America and Beyond," in Kaplan and Schwarz, *James Baldwin*, 1. For other examples of the Baldwin declension narrative, see Hilton Als, "The Enemy Within: The Making and Unmaking of James Baldwin," *New Yorker*, February 16, 1998, https://www.newyorker.com/magazine/1998/02/16/the-enemy-within-hilton-als, and Henry Louis Gates Jr., "The Fire Last Time: What James Baldwin Can and Can't Teach America," *New Republic*, June 1992, 37–43.

71. Irving Howe, "James Baldwin: At Ease in Apocalypse," *Harper's* 237 (1968): 94.

72. "'Milk Run,' Review of *Tell Me How Long the Train's Been Gone* by James Baldwin," *Time*, June 7, 1968, 104; Calvin C. Hernton, "A Fiery Baptism," in *James Baldwin: A Collection of Critical Essays*, ed. Keneth Kinnamon (Englewood Cliffs, N.J.: Prentice Hall, 1974), 119. Lynn Orilla Scott discusses this aspect of *Tell Me*'s reception in *Witness to the Journey: James Baldwin's Later Fiction* (East Lansing: Michigan State University Press, 2002).

73. The closest thing to a conception of Baldwin's disappointment as productive can be found in an analysis of *No Name* by Mel Watkins, who describes not Baldwin's aesthetic use of disappointment but rather disappointment as Baldwin's social function: "Baldwin and King, while demonstrating that blacks were 'the conscience of the nation,' exposed the depth of American intransigence regarding the racial issue. They were instrumental in exhausting the dream of an effective moral appeal to Americans, and, in effect, set the stage for Malcolm X, and the emergence of Stokely Carmichael, 'Rap' Brown, Huey Newton, Eldridge Cleaver and George Jackson—figures who reacted in a purely pragmatic (and therefore quintessentially American) manner to the blighted expectations of the sixties' failed idealism." "The Fire Next Time This Time," in *James Baldwin*, ed. Harold Bloom (New York: Chelsea House, 2007), 178.

74. See the essays collected in Dwight A. McBride, ed., *James Baldwin Now* (New York: New York University Press, 1999), and Kaplan and Schwarz, *James Baldwin*. Of the sixteen essays collected in E. Patrick Johnson and Mae Henderson, *Black Queer Studies: A Critical Anthology* (Durham, N.C.: Duke University Press, 2005), three are analyses of Baldwin's work: 18.75 percent.

75. Michelle M. Wright, *Physics of Blackness: Beyond the Middle Passage Epistemology* (Minneapolis: University of Minnesota Press, 2015), 109.

76. George Shulman, *American Prophecy: Race and Redemption in American Political Culture* (Minneapolis: University of Minnesota Press, 2008), 164–65.

77. David Leeming, *James Baldwin: A Biography* (New York: Knopf, 1994), 282, and Scott, *Witness to the Journey*, 50–55.

78. Martin Luther King Jr., April 3, 1968, quoted in David Fleer and Dave Bland, *Reclaiming the Imagination: The Exodus as Paradigmatic Narrative for Preaching* (St. Louis, Mo.: Chalice Press, 2009), 120–21; Eldridge Cleaver, *Soul on Ice* (New York: Laurel/Dell, 1992), 240.

79. Frederick Douglass, *Frederick Douglass: Selected Speeches and Writings*, ed. Philip Sheldon Foner and Yuval Taylor (Chicago: Lawrence Hill Books, 1999), 189, 194.

80. James Baldwin, "The Price of the Ticket" (1985), in *Collected Essays* (New York: Library of America, 1998), 841.

81. Disingenuously claiming that he is not talking about Baldwin in the midst of a long critique of Baldwin, Cleaver writes that "the case of James Baldwin aside for a moment, it seems that many Negro homosexuals, acquiescing in this racial death-wish, are outraged and frustrated because in their sickness they are unable to have a baby by a white man. The cross they have to bear is that, already bending over and touching their toes for the white man, the fruit of their miscegenation is not the little half-white offspring of their dreams but an increase in the unwinding of their nerves—though they redouble their efforts and intake of the white man's sperm." *Soul on Ice*, 102. Kevin Birmingham describes the wide range of constituencies who attempted to delegitimize Baldwin's work through his sexuality: "when the FBI was no longer around to document Baldwin's sex life, Eldridge Cleaver and Amiri Baraka were more than happy to follow Edgar's lead. Although Baldwin was already 'out,' he was constantly being outed." Birmingham, "'History's Ass Pocket': The Sources of Baldwinian Diaspora," in Kaplan and Schwarz, *James Baldwin*, 154. For powerful analyses of the centrality of homophobia to the Black Arts and Black Power movements, see Lee Edelman, "The Part for the (W)hole: Baldwin, Homophobia, and the Fantasmics of 'Race,'" in *Homographesis: Essays in Gay Literary and Cultural Theory*, 42–78 (New York: Routledge, 1994); Roderick A. Ferguson, *Aberrations in Black: Toward a Queer of Color Critique* (Minneapolis: University of Minnesota Press, 2004); Robert Reid-Pharr, "Tearing the Goat's Flesh: Homosexuality, Abjection, and the Production of Late Twentieth-Century Black Masculinity," *Studies in the Novel* 28, no. 3 (1996): 372–94; and Darieck Scott, *Extravagant Abjection: Blackness, Power, and Sexuality in the African American Literary Imagination* (New York: New York University Press, 2010).

82. "I'm just a poor wayfarin' stranger / While travelin' through this world below / Yet there's no sickness, no toil, nor danger / In that bright land to which I go. / I'm goin' there to see my Father / And all my loved ones who've gone on / I'm just goin' over Jordan / I'm just goin' over home."

83. Robert F. Kennedy, *RFK: Collected Speeches,* ed. Edwin O. Guthman (New York: Viking, 1993), 158.

84. See David Bobbitt and Harold Mixon, "Prophecy and Apocalypse in the Rhetoric of Martin Luther King, Jr.," *Journal of Communication and Religion* 17, no. 1 (1994): 27–38; Chandan Reddy, *Freedom with Violence: Race, Sexuality, and the U.S. State* (Durham, N.C.: Duke University Press, 2011); Shulman, *American Prophecy*; Singh, *Black Is a Country.*

85. Martin Luther King Jr., "I Have a Dream . . . ," 1963, http://www .archives.gov/press/exhibits/dream-speech.pdf.

86. Baldwin references here through the young Leo a strong tradition in African American thought. Abby J. Kinchy collects similar observations from Malcolm X, Langston Hughes, and the opinion page of the *Chicago Defender.* "As a *Washington Afro American* editorial, published less than two weeks after the bombing of Hiroshima, noted, 'use of the atomic bomb for the first time against Japan, although it was reportedly possible to have it ready for use against the Germans, has revived the feeling in some quarters that maybe the Allies are fighting a racial war after all.'" "African Americans in the Atomic Age: Postwar Perspectives on Race and the Bomb, 1945–1967," *Technology and Culture* 50, no. 2 (2009): 296.

87. Wallace Terry, "Novelist Baldwin Links Civil Rights and Peace," *Washington Post,* April 1, 1961, A1. Baldwin's involvement with nuclear activism stands against Jacqueline Foertsch's description of his "striking a-nuclearism"; while Foertsch makes many excellent arguments, my argument in this chapter also seeks to complicate her positioning of Baldwin as an integrationist rather than a racially conscious peace activist whereby "Baldwin's decision to join his white friends for drinks—and to join them if necessary in whatever cataclysm Muhammad envisioned befalling them—instead of a session of anti-nuclear organizing is the ideal response to the atomic threat hanging over his age." Baldwin's work with SANE would suggest that he was, in fact, a habitué of antinuclear organizing sessions. Foertsch, *Reckoning Day,* 163, 169.

88. The quote is from Langston Hughes's alter ego Simple in a story called "The Atomic Age" published in *Simple Stakes a Claim* in 1957. Quoted in Cooper, "Whiteness of the Bomb," 79; Cooper's essay offers a fuller overview of African American critiques of the whiteness of the bomb.

89. Barbara Omolade, "Women of Color and the Nuclear Holocaust," *Women's Studies Quarterly* 12, no. 2 (1984): 12.

90. James Baldwin, "Notes on the House of Bondage" (1980), in *Collected Essays,* 804.

91. George Shulman, "Baldwin, Prophecy, and Politics," in Kaplan and Schwarz, *James Baldwin,* 121.

92. Samuel R. Delany, "The Necessity of Tomorrows," in *Starboard Wine:*

More Notes on the Language of Science Fiction (Middletown, Conn.: Wesleyan University Press, 2012), 26.

93. Fred Moten, "The Case of Blackness," *Criticism* 50, no. 2 (2008): 215.

94. The question of to what degree *Dhalgren* can be called science fiction or speculative fiction has been hotly debated by readers, reviewers, and critics. Jeffrey Allen Tucker surveys this debate, which has on one side Theodore Sturgeon describing *Dhalgren* as "the very best to come out of the science fiction field" and on the other Harlan Ellison's definition of the book as "a tragic failure" and Algis Burgis's dismissal of it as "not science fiction, or science fantasy, but allegorical quasi-fantasy." See Burgis, *A Sense of Wonder: Samuel R. Delany, Race, Identity, and Difference* (Middletown, Conn.: Wesleyan University Press, 2004), 56–57.

95. W. Gilbert Adair, *The American Epic Novel in the Late Twentieth Century: The Super-genre of the Imperial State* (Lewiston: E. Mellen Press, 2008), 180.

96. Scott Edelman, "Samuel R. Delany Exposes the Heart of *Dhalgren* over a Naked Lunch," *Sci Fi Weekly,* June 18, 2001, ftp://asavage.dyndns.org/Literature/scifi.com/www.scifi.com/sfw/interviews/sfw7131.html. Jason Haslam and Mary Kay Bray both have strong analyses of the relationship between mid-century urban space and myths of American exceptionalism in Delany's novel. See Jason Haslam, "Memory's Guilted Cage: Delany's *Dhalgren* and Gibson's *Pattern Recognition,*" *English Studies in Canada* 32, no. 1 (2006): 77–104, and Mary Kay Bray, "Rites of Reversal: Double Consciousness in Delany's *Dhalgren,*" *Black American Literature Forum* 18, no. 2 (1984): 57–61.

97. Delany describes Lacan's essay "Of Structure as an Inmixing" as a major influence on *Dhalgren* in *The Straits of Messina.*

98. Jacques Lacan, "Of Structure as an Inmixing of an Otherness Prerequisite to Any Subject Whatever," in *The Structuralist Controversy: The Languages of Criticism and the Sciences of Man,* ed. Richard Macksey and Eugenio Donato (Baltimore: Johns Hopkins University Press, 1972), 189.

99. Delany, "Of Sex, Objects, Signs, Systems, Sales, SF, and Other Things." Delany's theory recalls Malcolm X's question "How are you going to incite people who are living in slums and ghettos? It's the city structure that incites." X, *Malcolm X Speaks,* 191.

100. Delany, "Of Sex, Objects, Signs."

101. See Samuel R. Delany, *Times Square Red, Times Square Blue* (New York: New York University Press, 1999), 153–54.

102. Robert Beauregard describes race as precisely the myth that brought these incoherent semes together into a coherent whole: "what made the years between roughly 1960 and the recession of 1973 unique in the discourse on urban decline was the emergence of a single theme that unified its various

fragments and turned urban decline into a society-wide problem. The theme was race, the problem was the concentration, misery, and rebellion of Negroes in central cities, and the reaction was one of fear and eventually panic." Carlo Rotella demonstrates how literature participated in the relationship between "cities of fact" and "cities of feeling" in the twentieth century. See Beauregard, *Voices of Decline: The Postwar Fate of U.S. Cities* (Oxford: Blackwell, 1993), 169; and Rotella, *October Cities: The Redevelopment of Urban Literature* (Berkeley: University of California Press, 1998), 3.

103. Emily Apter, *Continental Drift: From National Characters to Virtual Subjects* (Chicago: University of Chicago Press, 1999), 232.

104. Mark Chia-Yon Jerng, "A World of Difference: Samuel R. Delany's *Dhalgren* and the Protocols of Racial Reading," *American Literature* 83, no. 2 (2011): 271.

105. Delany, quoted in Tucker, *A Sense of Wonder*, 18.

106. In 1921, the state ordered the bombing of the Black neighborhood of Tulsa in a decision that bears an uncertain logical relationship to the fact that it was being destroyed by white rioters—it can hardly have been to protect Black lives or property. See James S. Hirsch, *Riot and Remembrance: The Tulsa Race War and Its Legacy* (Boston: Houghton Mifflin, 2002). The Philadelphia Police Department firebombed the residence of the MOVE organization in 1985.

107. Sandra Y. Govan, "The Insistent Presence of Black Folk in the Novels of Samuel R. Delany," *Black American Literature Forum* 18, no. 2 (1984): 47.

108. Moten, "Case of Blackness," 180.

109. Baldwin, *Fire Next Time*, 9.

110. Samuel R. Delany, *The Motion of Light in Water: Sex and Science Fiction Writing in the East Village, 1957–1965* (New York: Arbor House/William Morrow, 1988), 144, 146.

111. McEnaney, *Civil Defense Begins at Home*, 150.

112. Quoted in Oakes, *Imaginary War*, 39.

113. Quoted in McEnaney, *Civil Defense Begins at Home*, 149.

114. The quality of having been here all along is one of Kid's most uncanny features; even though the novel narrates his arrival in Bellona and his acclimation to being there, evidence such as the notebook that already contains his writing suggests that somehow he has also been there before, has always been there.

115. Jared Sexton and Huey Copeland, "Raw Life: An Introduction," *Qui Parle* 13, no. 2 (2003): 53.

116. See Hortense J. Spillers, "Mama's Baby, Papa's Maybe: An American Grammar Book," *diacritics* 17, no. 2 (1987): 65–81.

117. Darko Suvin defines science or speculative fiction as fiction that pro-

duces cognitive estrangement, that makes you speculate, in *Metamorphoses of Science Fiction: On the Poetics and History of a Literary Genre* (New Haven, Conn.: Yale University Press, 1979).

118. Moten, "Case of Blackness," 178.

119. Moten, 179.

120. Moten, 215.

121. See Peter Brooks, *Reading for the Plot: Design and Intention in Narrative* (Cambridge, Mass.: Harvard University Press, 1984); and Kermode, *Sense of an Ending.*

122. Kermode, *Sense of an Ending,* 46.

123. Delany, "Of Sex, Objects, Signs."

124. Kermode, *Sense of an Ending,* 8.

125. James Baldwin, *The Devil Finds Work: An Essay* (New York: Vintage International, 2011), 46.

126. Delany, "Of Sex, Objects, Signs."

127. The influential nuclear strategist Bernard Brodie, for instance, insisted on the impossibility of mechanisms other than an ever-expanding nuclear complex (including both weapons and civil infrastructures such as civil defense) at two key points in the Cold War, arguing against the possibility of an international ban on nuclear weapons and for a nuclear deterrent in 1946, and for the development of second strike capacities rather than disarmament treaties in 1959. See Bernard Brodie, ed., *The Absolute Weapon: Atomic Power and World Order* (New York: Harcourt, Brace, 1946), and Bernard Brodie, *Strategy in the Missile Age* (Princeton, N.J.: Princeton University Press, 1959).

128. Delany, *Motion of Light in Water,* 148; Baldwin, "Price of the Ticket," 842.

129. Hartman, *Lose Your Mother,* 103.

130. Paul Gilroy, *The Black Atlantic: Modernity and Double Consciousness* (Cambridge, Mass.: Harvard University Press, 1993), 37.

131. Gilroy, 38.

132. Gilroy.

133. Kermode, *Sense of an Ending,* 48.

134. It is crucial to distinguish this presentism as fully as possible from the exceedingly white presentism of the contemporaneous Beats; Norman Mailer, for example, wrote that "whether the life is criminal or not, the decision is to encourage the psychopath in oneself, to explore that domain of experience where security is boredom and therefore sickness, and one exists in the present, in that enormous present which is without past or future, memory or planned intention, the life where a man must go until he is beat, where he must gamble with his energies through all those small or large crises of courage and unforeseen situations which beset his day, where he must be with it or

doomed not to swing." This attitude is clearly not shared by Baldwin or Delany even at their most countercultural. Mailer, "The White Negro," in *White Riot: Punk Rock and the Politics of Race,* ed. Stephen Duncombe and Maxwell Tremblay (London: Verso, 2011), 21. I am also thinking here of Madhu Dubey's excellent critique of the racial assumptions of white postmodern theory (namely, that a loss of faith in Western metanarratives is a recent invention, as if the West's constitutive others have not long held such a critique) in *Signs and Cities: Black Literary Postmodernism* (Chicago: University of Chicago Press, 2003).

135. X, *Malcolm X Speaks,* 31.

136. Robert Cushman, "Reasons and Considerations Touching the Lawfulness of Removing out of England into the Parts of America" (1622), quoted in Gamble, *In Search of the City on a Hill,* 63–64. Cushman is representative of a longer theological countertradition stemming from Augustine's distinction between the City of Man, which is situated within earthly space and historical time, and the City of God, "which is heavenly, and is a pilgrim on the earth." For Augustine, as for Cushman, biblical types refer forward only to the New Testament or to the Second Coming or are to be read allegorically as instructions for individual salvation. Cushman's claim to eternal pilgrim status is thus a rejection of the practical typology that has defined American settler colonialism in favor of a commitment to perpetual wandering until either a postmortem arrival in the City of God or the postapocalyptic arrival of the City of God after the end of historical time. See Augustine, *The City of God,* trans. Marcus Dods (New York: Modern Library, 1950), 18.54.

137. Ellison, "Going to the Territory," 604; Ralph Ellison, "Harlem Is Nowhere," in Callahan, *Collected Essays,* 20.

3. Star Wars, AIDS, and Queer Endings

1. Tony Kushner, *Millennium Approaches,* 1st ed., *Angels in America* pt. 1 (New York: Theatre Communications Group, 1993), 112. Further page references to this text are from this edition and will be given parenthetically in the main body of the text, preceded by *MA.*

2. Tony Kushner, *Perestroika,* 1st ed., *Angels in America* pt. 2 (New York: Theatre Communications Group, 1994). Further page references to this text are from this edition and will be given parenthetically in the main body of the text, preceded by *P.*

3. See Nadel, *Containment Culture.*

4. I date the start of the Reagan era not necessarily at his election in 1980, although that would be neater, but from the beginning of his rise to national prominence and the first public expressions of what would become

known as Reaganism. When I refer to the eighties, this should be taken as convenient periodizing shorthand that includes the late 1970s; Reagan's primary run against Gerald Ford in 1976 put him on the national stage and also coincided with the early days of the right-wing nuclear hysteria movement, later to become the hawkish lobby group High Frontier, who were responsible for the upswing in nuclear fear in the late 1970s/early 1980s. This resurgence led to the nuclear freeze movement, which was countered by Reagan with the SDI. See Frances FitzGerald, *Way Out There in the Blue: Reagan, Star Wars, and the End of the Cold War* (New York: Simon and Schuster, 2000). The late 1970s also saw the first fifties nostalgia films; *Grease*, for example, was released in 1977.

5. Michael Dwyer, "'Fixing' the Fifties: Alex P. Keaton and Marty McFly," in *The 1980s: A Critical and Transitional Decade*, ed. Kimberly Moffitt and Duncan Campbell (Lanham, Md.: Lexington Books, 2011), 202.

6. Tom Shales, "The Re Decade," *Esquire*, March 1986, 67, quoted in Michael D. Dwyer, *Back to the Fifties: Nostalgia, Hollywood Film, and Popular Music of the Seventies and Eighties* (New York: Oxford University Press, 2015), 1.

7. Mary Caputi, *A Kinder, Gentler America: Melancholia and the Mythical 1950s* (Minneapolis: University of Minnesota Press, 2005), 1.

8. This is closer to today's Randian neoconservatism, with Fox's incessant hawking of gold and the obsession at the far ends of both the left and right wings for living "off the grid."

9. Quoted in Jessie Swigger, "New Right, New History, Common Ground: Populism and the Past," in Moffitt and Campbell, *The 1980s*, 165.

10. Michael Rogin discusses the connections between Reagan's Hollywood career and his presidency that enabled him to perform this metonymic function in *Ronald Reagan, the Movie, and Other Episodes in Political Demonology* (Berkeley: University of California Press, 1988), 1–43.

11. Dwyer, "'Fixing' the Fifties," 204–5; Stephanie Coontz, *The Way We Never Were: American Families and the Nostalgia Trap* (New York: Basic Books, 1992), 9.

12. Fredric Jameson, *Postmodernism; or, The Cultural Logic of Late Capitalism* (Durham, N.C.: Duke University Press, 1991), 19, 25.

13. Jameson, 21.

14. Dwyer surveys the field in *Back to the Fifties*, 8–9.

15. Caputi, *A Kinder, Gentler America*, 17. As indicated, the question of whether the 1945–60 period really was one of American world domination and blissful life on the home front is more or less irrelevant to the desire to have it back again. As Patricia White suggests in her coinage of the term retrospectatorship, the original version of an object is inaccessible to a subject who has had his consciousness constructed around the legacy of that object;

in this case, years of talk about post–World War II American superiority create the belief that it was indeed so, and the 1940s and 1950s thus become available as the object of a desire whose real aim is the sense of dominance with which they have become saturated. See White, *Uninvited: Classical Hollywood Cinema and Lesbian Representability* (Bloomington: Indiana University Press, 1999), 196.

16. Alan Nadel, "The Empire Strikes Out: *Star Wars* (IV, V, and VI) and the Advent of Reaganism," in *American Literature and Culture in an Age of Cold War: A Critical Reassessment,* ed. Steven Belletto and Daniel Grausam (Iowa City: University of Iowa Press, 2012), 187.

17. Susan Jeffords, *Hard Bodies: Hollywood Masculinity in the Reagan Era* (New Brunswick, N.J.: Rutgers University Press, 1994), 27.

18. George Kennan, "The Sources of Soviet Conduct," *Foreign Affairs,* 1947, http://www.historyguide.org/europe/kennan.html.

19. Phyllis Schafly, "Apostle of Hopelessness," *Reading Eagle,* August 21, 1985, 9.

20. William Rusher, "The End of Horror," *Rome News-Tribune,* May 11, 1984, 3. For an overview of neoconservative rejections of containment as a national security policy, see Edward Tabor Linenthal, *Symbolic Defense: The Cultural Significance of the Strategic Defense Initiative* (Urbana: University of Illinois Press, 1989), 47.

21. Caspar Weinberger, interviewed by Paul Kengor, *The Crusader: Ronald Reagan and the Fall of Communism* (New York: Regan Books, 2006), 42.

22. Ronald Reagan, "Address to the Nation on National Security, March 23, 1983," http://www.fas.org/spp/starwars/offdocs/rrspch.htm.

23. Reagan.

24. While missile defense technology had been developed on and off since the 1960s, these ground-based antimissile infrastructures never promised (and indeed had, since the signing of the Anti-Ballistic Missile Treaty in 1972, been prevented from promising) the kind of impenetrable national shield pledged by SDI. For a full overview of missile defense systems in the United States from 1945 to the present, see Union of Concerned Scientists, "US Ballistic Missile Defense Timeline: 1945–Today," https://www.ucsusa.org/nuclear-weapons/us-missile-defense/missile-defense-timeline.

25. The wing of the Defense Department that grew out of the Strategic Defense Initiative Organization is now called the Missile Defense Organization; its budget in 2019 was $10.491 billion, and it has received $215.721 billion of federal funding to date (1985–2020). See federal data at http://www.mda.mil/global/documents/pdf/histfunds.pdf and https://www.mda.mil/news/budget_information.html. The most successful of its products have shot down

ten out of nineteen incoming targets, which is not that great if you think of the targets as nuclear ICBMs heading toward the United States.

26. Dick Locher, "Modern Warfare," *Chicago Tribune*, December 4, 1984, sec. 1, 18.

27. Reagan, "Address to the Nation on National Security."

28. Citizens Advisory Council on National Space Policy, *Space: The Crucial Frontier: Report of the Spring, 1981 Council Meeting* (Tucson, Ariz.: L-5 Society, 1981), title page. The council included the science fiction authors Poul Anderson, Robert Heinlein, Larry Niven, and Jerry Pournelle; for more on the background of this document and its centrality to the SDI, see John Wenz, "How Two Sci-Fi Writers Fueled a U.S. President's Wild Quest to Weaponize Space," *Thrillist*, November 10, 2017, https://www.thrillist.com/entertainment/nation/strategic-defense-initiative-reagan-star-wars-jerry-pournelle-larry-niven.

29. See Larkin, "Politics and Poetics of Infrastructure."

30. Nadel, *Containment Culture*, 3.

31. Alan Nadel, *Flatlining on the Field of Dreams: Cultural Narratives in the Films of President Reagan's America* (New Brunswick, N.J.: Rutgers University Press, 1997), 77. Nadel reads *Back to the Future* as the paradigmatic film of the Reagan presidency; just as Marty McFly defends himself against being bullied at school by going back in time to empower his father against Biff Tannen, so Reagan proposed going back to the beginning of the Cold War to save America from the Soviet threat.

32. Jeffery B. Cook, "Ronald W. Reagan: Redefining the Presidency," in Moffitt and Campbell, *The 1980s*, 21.

33. Reagan, "Address to the Nation on National Security."

34. Quoted in Union of Concerned Scientists, *The Fallacy of Star Wars* (New York: Vintage Books, 1984), 28.

35. E. P. Thompson, "Folly's Comet," in *Star Wars*, ed. Rip Bulkeley and E. P. Thompson (Harmondsworth, U.K.: Penguin Books, 1985), 137–38.

36. Donna Haraway, "The Biopolitics of Postmodern Bodies: Constitutions of Self in Immune System Discourse," in *Simians, Cyborgs, and Women: The Reinvention of Nature* (New York: Routledge, 1991), 224. For other analyses of military metaphors in the discourse of AIDS, see Susan Sontag, *AIDS and Its Metaphors* (New York: Farrar, Straus, and Giroux, 1989); Paula A. Treichler, *How to Have Theory in an Epidemic: Cultural Chronicles of AIDS* (Durham, N.C.: Duke University Press, 1999); Cathy Waldby, *AIDS and the Body Politic: Biomedicine and Sexual Difference* (London: Routledge, 1996); and Michael S. Sherry, "The Language of War in AIDS Discourse," in *Writing AIDS: Gay Literature, Language, and Analysis*, ed. Timothy F. Murphy and Suzanne Poirier, 39–53 (New York: Columbia University Press, 1993).

37. Paul Conrad, "Speaking of the Need for Condoms," *Los Angeles Times*, February 22, 1987, part 5 (E), 5, ellipses original.

38. FitzGerald, *Way Out There in the Blue*, 247.

39. Steven F. Kruger, *AIDS Narratives: Gender and Sexuality, Fiction and Science* (New York: Garland, 1996), 22.

40. Senator Joseph Biden described SDI as a "Maginot Line that is ravaging our economic capital, nuclearizing the heavens and yielding the fate of our children's world to the malfunction of a computer"; Steven Chapple and David Talbot wrote of the "only-gays-get-AIDS" prevention strategy that "[Surgeon General] Koop would not put his faith in this Maginot Line between the infected and uninfected." Biden quoted in *Executive Intelligence Review* 14, no. 25 (1987): 36; Chapple and Talbot, "Burning Desires" (1988), in *While the World Sleeps: Writing from the First Twenty Tears of the Global AIDS Plague*, ed. Chris Bull (New York: Thunder Mouth Press, 2003), 149.

41. Jacqueline Foertsch, *Enemies Within: The Cold War and the AIDS Crisis in Literature, Film, and Culture* (Urbana: University of Illinois Press, 2001), 28.

42. Sarah Schulman, *People in Trouble* (New York: Dutton, 1990), 1. For more on the apocalypticism of queer literary responses to the AIDS epidemic, see Richard Dellamora, *Apocalyptic Overtures: Sexual Politics and the Sense of an Ending* (New Brunswick, N.J.: Rutgers University Press, 1994).

43. Arthur Kroker and Marilouise Kroker, "Panic Sex in America," in *Body Invaders: Panic Sex in America,* ed. Arthur Kroker and Marilouise Kroker (New York: St. Martin's Press, 1987), 15, 12–13, emphasis original.

44. Kroker and Kroker, 11, emphasis original.

45. Richard Meyer, "Rock Hudson's Body," in *Inside/Out: Lesbian Theories, Gay Theories,* ed. Diana Fuss (New York: Routledge, 1991), 283. Hudson thus serves as a dark mirror to Reagan, whose body was imagined as so invulnerable that even his cancer was not really cancer: Reagan himself did not have cancer; rather, "I had something inside of me that had cancer in it and it was removed." Quoted in Nadel, *Flatlining on the Field of Dreams*, 64.

46. Daryl Ogden, "Cold War Science and the Body Politic: An Immuno/Virological Approach to *Angels in America*," *Literature and Medicine* 19, no. 2 (2000): 241–61.

47. Marlon Riggs, "Ruminations of a Snap Queen: What Time Is It?," *Out/Look* 12 (1991): 18.

48. Eve Kosofsky Sedgwick, *Epistemology of the Closet* (Berkeley: University of California Press, 1990); Leo Bersani, *Is the Rectum a Grave? and Other Essays* (Chicago: University of Chicago Press, 2010); Edelman, *No Future*.

49. Kosofsky Sedgwick, *Epistemology of the Closet*, 127.

50. Johnson, *Lavender Scare*, 6.

51. I do not mean to suggest here that visions of apocalypse and genocide

are not absolutely integral to representations of AIDS; that they have been foundational to its discursive life has been extensively documented and analyzed by, for example, Susan J. Palmer, *AIDS as an Apocalyptic Metaphor in North America* (Toronto: University of Toronto Press, 1997); Lee Edelman, "The Mirror and the Tank: 'AIDS,' Subjectivity, and the Rhetoric of Activism," in Murphy and Poirier, *Writing AIDS*, 9–38; Susan Sontag, *AIDS and Its Metaphors*; Cindy Patton, *Sex and Germs: The Politics of AIDS* (Boston: South End Press, 1985); Coviello, "Apocalypse from Now On"; and Simon Watney, *Policing Desire: Pornography, AIDS, and the Media* (Minneapolis: University of Minnesota Press, 1987). I argue, rather, that situating AIDS discourse within a more general retrocontainment discourse makes it possible to see that an apocalypse narrative doesn't only work forward.

52. Edelman, "The Mirror and the Tank," 22.

53. See Gayle Rubin, "The Leather Menace: Comments on Politics and S/M," in *Deviations: A Gayle Rubin Reader*, 109–36 (Durham, N.C.: Duke University Press, 2011).

54. There was, discursively, no such thing as a straight person with AIDS in the early years of the epidemic: "the strong belief in superficial markers for deeply hidden traits which characterizes contemporary Western notions of personhood works out in strange ways in AIDS discourse: the unconscious wish for a physical marker or test for homosexuality collapses in the insistent linkage between homosexuality and AIDS to construct the HIV antibody test as a mechanism for revealing hidden homosexuality." A diagnosis of AIDS was equivalent to a diagnosis of homosexuality. Patton, *Inventing AIDS*, 113.

55. Tim Dean, "Bareback Time," in Fuss, *Inside/Out*, 81, 84.

56. See the opening shot of David Lynch's masterpiece of failed retrocontainment, *Blue Velvet* (1986). For a best-selling example of the connection between nuclear annihilation and a return to nuclear family values specifically defined by nonqueerness, see Jonathan Schell's 1982 book *The Fate of the Earth*, reprinted as *"The Fate of the Earth," and, "The Abolition"* (Stanford, Calif.: Stanford University Press, 2000).

57. I am thinking particularly here of Toni Morrison's 1987 novel *Beloved*, which speaks so powerfully to the material effects of being excluded from history. The rise of identity politics and efforts to gain institutional recognition for women's, gay and lesbian, and African American histories also took place on this historiographic battleground.

58. Francis Fukuyama, "The End of Man?," *National Interest*, 1989, http://www.kropfpolisci.com/exceptionalism.fukuyama.pdf.

59. John M. Clum, *Acting Gay: Male Homosexuality in Modern Drama* (New York: Columbia University Press, 1992), 324, quoted in David Savran,

"Ambivalence, Utopia, and a Queer Sort of Materialism: How *Angels in America* Reconstructs the Nation," *Theatre Journal* 47, no. 2 (1995): 207–8.

60. Savran, "Ambivalence, Utopia, and a Queer Sort of Materialism," 212.

61. Savran, 223.

62. Charles McNulty, "*Angels in America*: Tony Kushner's Theses on the Philosophy of History," *Modern Drama* 39, no. 1 (1996): 91, 94; Martin Harries, "Flying the Angel of History," in *Approaching the Millennium: Essays on Angels in America*, ed. Deborah R. Geis and Steven F. Kruger (Ann Arbor: University of Michigan Press, 1997), 194.

63. Roger Bechtel stands up for Kushner's dialectical thinking in "'A Kind of Painful Progress': The Benjaminian Dialectics of *Angels in America*," *Journal of Dramatic Theory and Criticism* 16, no. 1 (2001): 99–121; dialectical accounts of hope are offered in James Corby, "The Audacity of Hope: Locating Kushner's Political Vision in *Angels in America*," *Forum for Modern Language Studies* 47, no. 1 (2011): 16–35; and Susan Knabe, "History and AIDS in *Was* and *Angels in America*," *Extrapolation* 49, no. 2 (2008): 214–39.

64. The epilogue is officially set in 1990, but the breaking of the fourth wall for the first time in the play when Prior addresses the audience directly serves to establish a shared present between the play's final moments and its audience. See Bechtel, "A Kind of Painful Progress," 112.

65. Fran Lebowitz, "The Impact of AIDS on the Artistic Community," in Bull, *While the World Sleeps*, 74.

66. Stephen J. Bottoms, "Re-staging Roy: Citizen Cohn and the Search for Xanadu," *Theatre Journal* 48, no. 2 (1996): 157.

67. Ogden, "Cold War Science and the Body Politic," 242.

68. Roy's first fictional appearance is in the 1977 McCarthy biopic *Tail Gunner Joe*. For the cultural history of Ethel Rosenberg, see Adam Liptak, "Truth, Fiction and the Rosenbergs," *New York Times*, January 21, 2006, sec. Books, http://www.nytimes.com/2006/01/21/books/21rose.html. Ethel's two main appearances are in Sylvia Plath's *The Bell Jar* and E. L. Doctorow's *The Book of Daniel*.

69. Nishant Shahani, *Queer Retrosexualities: The Politics of Reparative Return* (Bethlehem, Pa.: Lehigh University Press, 2012), 12.

70. Michael Cadden, "Strange Angel: The Pinklisting of Roy Cohn," in Geis and Kruger, *Approaching the Millennium*, 86.

71. Knabe, "History and AIDS," 222.

72. David Román, "November 1, 1992: AIDS/*Angels in America*," in Geis and Kruger, *Approaching the Millennium*, 40, 41.

73. Román, 48.

74. Kruger, *AIDS Narratives*, 73.

75. Jameson, *Postmodernism*, 368.

76. Jameson, 369.
77. Jameson, 369–70.
78. Jameson.
79. Jameson.
80. Swigger, "New Right, New History," 161.
81. Linda Hutcheon challenges Jameson on this point, arguing in *A Poetics of Postmodernism* that postmodern historical fiction does not simply reflect a condition of ahistoricity but actively responds to it, hence the term "historiographic metafiction." I distinguish *Angels* from Hutcheon's model following her distinction between historical fiction and historiographic metafiction; while Kushner does engage with how history is felt and engaged with, the question of "how we know what we know about the past" is not a central one here. His period detail is used for verisimilitude rather than estrangement; Hutcheon writes that "historical fiction (pace Lukács) usually incorporates and assimilates these data in order to lend a feeling of verifiability (or an air of dense specificity and particularity) to the fictional world. Historiographic metafiction incorporates, but rarely assimilates such data." Hutcheon, *A Poetics of Postmodernism: History, Theory, Fiction* (New York: Routledge, 1988), 114.
82. Jacques Derrida, *Specters of Marx: The State of the Debt, the Work of Mourning, and the New International* (New York: Routledge, 1994); Avery Gordon, *Ghostly Matters: Haunting and the Sociological Imagination*, New University of Minnesota Press ed. (Minneapolis: University of Minnesota Press, 2008). I have written more on the relationship between haunting and historical agency in Jessica Hurley, "Ghostwritten: Kinship and History in *Absalom, Absalom!*," *The Faulkner Journal* 26, no. 2 (2012): 61–80.
83. Carla Freccero, in Carolyn Dinshaw et al., "Theorizing Queer Temporalities: A Roundtable Discussion," *GLQ: A Journal of Lesbian and Gay Studies* 13, no. 2 (2007): 184. Dellamora describes the ways in which "the doubling of mortality and fictional endings are freighted ideologically in ways that gay writers find difficult to manage"; Prior's defiant "More Life" as the last line of the play should certainly be read in this context. See Dellamora, *Apocalyptic Overtures*, 154.
84. Janelle Reinelt, "Notes on *Angels in America* as American Epic Theater," in Geis and Kruger, *Approaching the Millennium*, 242.
85. Bersani, *Is the Rectum a Grave?*, 29.
86. Edelman, *No Future*, 1–31.
87. Tom Boellstorff, "When Marriage Falls: Queer Coincidences in Straight Time," *GLQ: A Journal of Lesbian and Gay Studies* 13, no. 2 (2007): 228.
88. Carla Freccero, *Queer/Early/Modern* (Durham, N.C.: Duke University Press, 2006); Carolyn Dinshaw, *Getting Medieval: Sexualities and Communities, Pre- and Postmodern* (Durham, N.C.: Duke University Press, 1999); Freeman,

Time Binds; Love, *Feeling Backward*; Christopher Nealon, *Foundlings: Lesbian and Gay Historical Emotion before Stonewall* (Durham, N.C.: Duke University Press, 2001); Kate Thomas, "Post Sex: On Being Too Slow, Too Stupid, Too Soon," *The South Atlantic Quarterly* 106, no. 3 (2007): 615–24; Ann Cvetkovich, *An Archive of Feelings: Trauma, Sexuality, and Lesbian Public Cultures* (Durham, N.C.: Duke University Press, 2003).

89. On the side of queerness as antirelational and antifutural are, for example, Jack Halberstam, *In a Queer Time and Place: Transgender Bodies, Subcultural Lives* (New York: New York University Press, 2005); and Jonathan Goldberg and Madhavi Menon, "Queering History," *PMLA* 120, no. 5 (2005): 1608–17. In defense of relationality and optimism are Michael Snediker, *Queer Optimism: Lyric Personhood and Other Felicitous Persuasions* (Minneapolis: University of Minnesota Press, 2009); Muñoz, *Cruising Utopia*; and Sara Ahmed, *Queer Phenomenology: Orientations, Objects, Others* (Durham, N.C.: Duke University Press, 2006).

90. Valerie Rohy, "Busy Dying," in *Sex, Gender, and Time in Fiction and Culture*, ed. Ben Davies and Jana Funke (Houndmills, U.K.: Palgrave Macmillan, 2011), 205. See also Davies and Funke's introduction to the volume, "Sexual Temporalities," 1–16.

91. Davies and Funke, "Sexual Temporalities," 10–11.

92. Christopher Castiglia and Christopher Reed, *If Memory Serves: Gay Men, AIDS, and the Promise of the Queer Past* (Minneapolis: University of Minnesota Press, 2012), 3.

93. Castiglia and Reed.

94. Castiglia and Reed, 8.

95. Abigail Rine, "Jeanette Winterson's Love Intervention: Rethinking the Future," in Davies and Funke, *Sex, Gender, and Time*, 70.

96. Sedgwick lays the groundwork for this when she situates her study of the emergence of the category of the homosexual and its twentieth-century ramifications within the apocalyptic moment in which *Epistemologies* was written.

97. Eve Kosofsky Sedgwick, *Fat Art, Thin Art* (Durham, N.C.: Duke University Press, 1994), 11.

98. Dagmawi Woubshet, *The Calendar of Loss: Race, Sexuality, and Mourning in the Early Era of AIDS* (Baltimore: Johns Hopkins University Press, 2015), 4, 12.

99. Bersani, *Is the Rectum a Grave?*, 5; Peter Baldwin, *Disease and Democracy: The Industrialized World Faces AIDS* (Berkeley: University of California Press, 2005), 26.

100. Steven Bruhm, "Still Here: Choreography, Temporality, AIDS," in

Queer Times, Queer Becomings, ed. E. L. McCallum and Mikko Tuhkanen (Albany: SUNY Press, 2011), 318, 236.

101. Art Borreca, "'Dramaturging' the Dialectic: Brecht, Benjamin, and Declan Donnellan's Production of *Angels in America,*" in Geis and Kruger, *Approaching the Millennium,* 51.

102. Walter Benjamin, "Theses on the Philosophy of History," in *Illuminations,* ed. Hannah Arendt, trans. Harry Zohn (New York: Schocken Books, 2007), 257–58.

103. See Freccero, *Queer/Early/Modern*; Love, *Feeling Backward.*

104. This is particularly visible in the HBO miniseries adaptation, which is not limited by the technical concerns of theaters, which limit the amount of rubble that can fall onto an actor from above.

4. Nuclear Waste, Native America, Narrative Form

1. See Paul Boyer's analysis of the rises and falls of public nuclear fear in *By the Bomb's Early Light,* 352–55.

2. Churchill and LaDuke, "Native North America," 261.

3. "Ongoing and planned cleanup work at Hanford is expected to address, but not be limited to, more than 50 million gallons of high-level liquid waste in 177 underground storage tanks, 2,300 tons of spent nuclear fuel, 12 tons of plutonium in various forms, approximately 25 million cubic feet of buried or stored solid waste, and approximately 270 billion gallons of groundwater contaminated above drinking water standards, all occurring over an area of approximately 80 square miles, more than 1,700 waste sites, and approximately 500 contaminated facilities." Hanford Natural Resources Trustee Council, "Background Information," *Natural Resources Damage Assessment* (2003), http://www.hanfordnrda.org/?page_id=11.

4. See Joel B. Hagen, *An Entangled Bank: The Origins of Ecosystem Ecology* (New Brunswick, N.J.: Rutgers University Press, 1992).

5. Indeed, the second paragraph of the current Wikipedia entry for the Atomic Energy Commission (the agency set up after World War II to handle all military and nonmilitary applications of nuclear technology) is devoted to the impact of the AEC on ecosystems theory. Bear in mind that during the same period, the AEC developed the hydrogen bomb and nuclear power stations, and this high ranking is striking.

6. Kuletz, *Tainted Desert,* 256–59.

7. Kuletz, 261.

8. These "neutral" applications of nuclear science were by no means limited to radioecology. For the myriad of other uses to which radionuclides were

put to work in the experimental life sciences after World War II, see Angela N. H. Creager, *Life Atomic: A History of Radioisotopes in Science and Medicine* (Chicago: University of Chicago Press, 2013).

9. Kuletz, *Tainted Desert,* 262.

10. E. P. Odum, 1958, quoted in Betty Jean Craige, *Eugene Odum: Ecosystem Ecologist and Environmentalist* (Athens: University of Georgia Press, 2001), 71.

11. Lawrence Buell, *Writing for an Endangered World: Literature, Culture, and Environment in the U.S. and Beyond* (Cambridge, Mass.: Belknap Press of Harvard University Press, 2001), 39.

12. Heather Houser, *Ecosickness in Contemporary U.S. Fiction: Environment and Affect* (New York: Columbia University Press, 2014), 10.

13. Here I offer a reversal of Molly Wallace's *Risk Criticism* (2016), which is aligned with this project in their shared commitment to "bringing nuclear criticism and ecocriticism together under the rubric of something like a 'risk criticism'" that analyzes "the risk temporalities of the second nuclear age." Where Wallace brings nuclear criticism to bear on mostly nonnuclear objects, my practice here is the ecocritical/narratological analysis of nuclear infrastructures themselves. See Wallace, *Risk Criticism,* 4.

14. Ulrich Beck, *Risk Society: Towards a New Modernity* (London: Sage, 2010), 72.

15. Susan L. Mizruchi, "Risk Theory and the Contemporary American Novel," *American Literary History* 22, no. 1 (2010): 119.

16. Masco, *Nuclear Borderlands,* 32.

17. Peter C. van Wyck, *Signs of Danger: Waste, Trauma, and Nuclear Threat* (Minneapolis: University of Minnesota Press, 2005), ix, emphasis original.

18. Kosofsky Sedgwick, *Touching Feeling,* 130.

19. This feeling, it must be noted, is a privilege, and not everyone is in a position to experience it. Peter Coviello, in a similar rhetorical moment, writes that "the remarkably comfortable fit of what I would call our nuclear amnesia may well be one of the most puzzling legacies of the Reagan era. Where, one wants almost nostalgically to ask, did the nuclear go?" I don't disagree with Coviello's tracking of nuclear paranoia into the sexual paranoia around AIDS, but the answer to his question still has to be into the air, into the water, into the landscape, into cells. How aware we have to be of that is a function of our location at the intersections of race, class, indigeneity, and gender; for Native communities living in the irradiated ecosystems of the Southwest, for example, the nuclear hasn't gone anywhere. Coviello, "Apocalypse from Now On," in Boone et al., *Queer Frontiers,* 40.

20. Nuclear waste is, along with climate change, one of Timothy Morton's exemplary hyperobjects: "things that are massively distributed in time and space relative to humans"; it also demands the kind of deep-time reading that

Wai Chee Dimock calls for to address "historical phenomena [that] . . . need hundreds, thousands, or even billions of years to be recognized for what they are." As Dipesh Chakrabarty has argued, however, massively distributed temporal objects pose a challenge to such analysis because trying to think beyond human life "can precipitate a sense of the present that disconnects the future from the past by putting such a future beyond the grasp of historical sensibility." See Morton, *Hyperobjects,* 1; Dimock, *Through Other Continents: American Literature across Deep Time* (Princeton, N.J.: Princeton University Press, 2006), 5; and Chakrabarty, "The Climate of History: Four Theses," *Critical Inquiry* 35, no. 2 (2009): 197.

21. Against those who see this challenge to humanism as requiring the return of a beefed-up humanism, Leif Sorensen argues—and I agree—that a nonhumanist apocalypticism is central to the liberatory imaginary of women writers of color who have long been excluded from humanist frameworks. See Sorensen, "The Apocalypse Is a Nonhuman Story," *ASAP/Journal* 3, no. 3 (2018): 523–46.

22. Woodward, *Statistical Panic,* 205, emphasis added.

23. Frederick Buell, *From Apocalypse to Way of Life: Environmental Crisis in the American Century* (New York: Routledge, 2003), 112, 78.

24. Buell, 202–3.

25. Mizruchi, for example, doubles down in favor of our existing realism-based Enlightenment rationalism when she argues that "while modern history is the source of the narrative of risk, it also holds the possibility of a social order founded on more rational, more benevolent principles." Mizruchi, "Risk Theory," 129.

26. Ursula K. Heise, *Sense of Place and Sense of Planet: The Environmental Imagination of the Global* (Oxford: Oxford University Press, 2008), 141.

27. The work of SNL's second panel, the Markers Panel, has received much more attention than that of the Futures Panel (as in van Wyck's excellent psychoanalytic reading in *Signs of Danger*). The task of the Markers Panel, to design the markers and passive institutional controls that would communicate the same message over ten thousand years, caught the attention of the press, and the *Expert Judgment on Markers to Deter Inadvertent Human Intrusion into the Waste Isolation Pilot Plant* contains both theories of communication and pictures of "Landscapes of Thorns" and "Menacing Earthworks" that are undeniably fascinating. But the work of the Futures Panel, while its graphs are less exciting, evidences strong theories of our relationship to risk, to the future and the real, and the actual and the plausible that are put into crisis by the question of the deep-time management of nuclear waste. See Kathleen M. Trauth, Stephen C. Hora, and R. V. Guzowski, *Expert Judgment on Markers to Deter Inadvertent Human Intrusion into the Waste Isolation Pilot Plant*

(Albuquerque, N.M.: Sandia National Laboratories, 1993). See also Andrew Moisey, "Considering the Desire to Mark Our Buried Nuclear Waste: *Into Eternity* and the Waste Isolation Pilot Plant," *Qui Parle* 20, no. 2 (2012): 101–25; and Julia Bryan-Wilson, "Building a Marker of Nuclear Warning," in *Monuments and Memory: Made and Unmade*, ed. Robert S. Nelson and Margaret Olin, 183–204 (Chicago: University of Chicago Press, 2004). Peter Galison and Robb Moss's 2015 film *Containment* does address the Futures Panel, but its lack of skepticism toward the purpose of the panel, casting it as an act of real care for the future rather than as a legally mandated performance of care that allows the future to be irreparably harmed, leads to a rather more optimistic interpretation than the one I present here.

28. R. V. Guzowski, *Preliminary Identification of Scenarios for the Waste Isolation Pilot Plant, Southeastern New Mexico* (Albuquerque, N.M.: Sandia National Laboratories, 1991), 2.

29. Guzowski.

30. Guzowski, emphasis added.

31. Guzowski.

32. Pierre Simon Laplace, *Philosophical Essay on Probabilities,* quoted in Ian Hacking, *The Taming of Chance* (Cambridge: Cambridge University Press, 1990), 10–11.

33. Stephen C. Hora, Detlof Von Winterfeldt, and Kathleen M. Trauth, *Expert Judgment on Inadvertent Human Intrusion into the Waste Isolation Pilot Plant* (Albuquerque, N.M.: Sandia National Laboratories, 1991), ES-1.

34. Hora et al., II-1.

35. Hora et al., IV-27.

36. Theodore J. Gordon, Michael Baram, Wendell Bell, and Bernard Cohen, "Inadvertent Intrusion into WIPP: Some Potential Futures," in Hora et al., C1–C70, C40.

37. Daniel Grausam, "Imagining Postnuclear Times," *Common Knowledge* 21, no. 3 (2015): 458.

38. For the importance of verisimilitude in determining which representations of the real are believable, see Tzvetan Todorov, "An Introduction to Verisimilitude," in *The Poetics of Prose,* 80–88 (Ithaca, N.Y.: Cornell University Press, 1977). For the twinned emergence of scientific and literary forms of verisimilitude, see John Bender, "Enlightenment Fiction and the Scientific Hypothesis," *Representations* 61 (1998): 6–28.

39. Rüdiger Campe, *The Game of Probability: Literature and Calculation from Pascal to Kleist,* trans. Ellwood H. Wiggins Jr. (Stanford, Calif.: Stanford University Press, 2012), 2.

40. Campe, 9.

41. Campe, 196.

42. György Lukács, *The Theory of the Novel: A Historico-Philosophical Essay on the Forms of Great Epic Literature*, trans. Anna Bostock (Cambridge, Mass.: MIT Press, 1971), 56.

43. György Lukács, "Realism in the Balance," in *Aesthetics and Politics*, ed. Fredric Jameson (London: Verso, 2007), 48.

44. Campe, *Game of Probability*, 395–96.

45. Campe, 202.

46. Johann Christoph Gatterer, quoted in Campe, 354.

47. While my focus here is on struggles over statistical credibility, it is also important to recognize how statistics have been deployed as the only acceptable form of truth in order to shut out other forms of knowledge that have been produced by communities whose bodies, land, and genes have been damaged by atomic production and testing. Kate Brown demonstrates how lived experience and bodily knowledge have been excluded as grounds for claiming compensation under existing legislation in favor of state-produced statistics, while Natasha Zaretzky offers a compelling account of how activist groups from across the political spectrum have mobilized new forms of authority in response to this epistemological disempowerment. See Brown, *Plutopia*, and Zaretsky, "Radiation Suffering."

48. Cram, "Becoming Jane," 811, emphasis added.

49. I take my conception of the temporal horizons of neoliberalism from Lauren Berlant's analysis of the stretched-out present that defines historical consciousness and forecloses a sense of the future as different from the present in the neoliberal age; see Berlant, *Cruel Optimism*. Fredric Jameson also frames the neoliberal present in this way in *Archaeologies of the Future: The Desire Called Utopia and Other Science Fictions* (New York: Verso, 2005).

50. The reality of what happened at the WIPP is itself so unlikely as to seem implausible: after deciding to use cat litter as an inert buffer between layers in the barrels of waste, the wrong kind of litter was ordered due to a typo ("an organic" instead of "inorganic"). The organic litter combined with chemicals in the waste, with the result that what was interred at the site was, essentially, a slow-forming nitrogen bomb. See https://wipp.energy.gov/wipprecovery-accident-desc.asp.

51. Charles Perrow, *Normal Accidents: Living with High-Risk Technologies* (Princeton, N.J.: Princeton University Press, 1999), 12.

52. The term environmental racism was coined in 1987 in a report by the United Church of Christ's Commission for Racial Justice. The report "found race to be the leading factor in the location of commercial hazardous waste facilities. . . . [It] determined that people of color suffered a 'disproportionate risk' to the health of their families and their environments: 60 percent of African Americans and Latinos, and more than 50 percent of Asian/Pacific

Islanders and Native Americans were living in areas with one or more un-controlled toxic waste sites." Joni Adamson, *American Indian Literature, Environmental Justice, and Ecocriticism: The Middle Place* (Tucson: University of Arizona Press, 2001), xv–xvi.

53. Daniel Grausam makes this argument about postmodern fiction in *On Endings.*

54. David Foster Wallace, *Infinite Jest: A Novel,* Back Bay 10th anniversary paperback ed. (New York: Back Bay Books, 2006), 382. Further page citations will be from this edition and will be given in the body of the text.

55. See Kuletz, *Tainted Desert,* 264. The ongoing appeal of such a self-cancellation of nuclear weapons and their waste is also represented in the closing scenes of Don DeLillo's *Underworld* (1996), where nuclear bombs are similarly used to destroy nuclear waste; I would connect this fantasy to the national desire for redemption as a form of salvation that cancels out the original sin rather than providing reparation for it that I analyze in chapter 2.

56. An accurate representation of the post–Cold War nuclear complex; both the Bradbury Science Museum in Los Alamos and the National Museum of Nuclear Science and Industry in Albuquerque have as their last exhibits immense interactive displays about nuclear energy, emphasizing its cleanliness and U.S. produced-ness against the mess and foreign dependence of fossil fuels, all in increasingly lush shades of green. For a trenchant analysis of the "greenwashing" of nuclear remediation sites, see Krupar, *Hot Spotter's Report.*

57. See, e.g., Bradley J. Fest, "The Inverted Nuke in the Garden: Archival Emergence and Anti-Eschatology in David Foster Wallace's *Infinite Jest,*" *Boundary 2* 39, no. 3 (2012): 125–49; and Daniel Grausam, "'It Is Only a Statement of the Power of What Comes After': Atomic Nostalgia and the Ends of Postmodernism," *American Literary History* 24, no. 2 (2012): 308–36.

58. N. Katherine Hayles, "The Illusion of Autonomy and the Fact of Recursivity: Virtual Ecologies, Entertainment, and *Infinite Jest,*" *New Literary History* 30, no. 3 (1999): 695.

59. Houser, *Ecosickness in Contemporary U.S. Fiction,* 137. Paul Giles combines the two positions in "Sentimental Posthumanism: David Foster Wallace," *Twentieth Century Literature* 53, no. 3 (2007): 339–40.

60. See Masco, *Nuclear Borderlands,* 18–27.

61. For the legal history of the federal–Indian relationship up to 1992, see Ward Churchill and Glenn T. Morris's annotated table "Key Indian Laws and Cases," in Jaimes, *State of Native America,* 13–21. Further discussions of the ramifications of this accumulation of outrages for Native sovereignty can be found throughout this volume, which is indispensable for any contemporary work in American studies. Vine Deloria and Clifford M. Lytle use the phrase "the nations within" to describe the Native lands located in the United States

in *The Nations Within: The Past and Future of American Indian Sovereignty* (New York: Pantheon Books, 1984).

62. The Union of Concerned Scientists' briefing document *Got Water?* illustrates the immense volumes of clean water required to cool nuclear reactors, whether in power plants or weapons development. It also makes abundantly clear that these sites are no longer ecologically undamaged by the time the site has been operational for a minute or two. See David Lochbaum, *Got Water?* (Washington, D.C.: Union of Concerned Scientists, 2007), http://www.ucsusa.org/sites/default/files/legacy/assets/documents/nuclear_power/20071204-ucs-brief-got-water.pdf.

63. Johnson et al. tell the story of a uranium mining industry that essentially didn't bother with safety regulations when its workers were members of Native nations; Navajo miners who had been promised jobs in return for allowing uranium mines on their lands were paid at two-thirds of the rate of off-reservation workers and not provided with basic safety equipment, such as masks and fans. The federal government actively colluded in this manifestation of environmental racism; "beginning in 1949, the USPHS monitored the health of uranium miners, conducting epidemiologic studies to determine the health effects of radiation. In exchange for the mining company's list of miners' names, the USPHS agreed that its doctors would not divulge the potential health hazards to the workers, nor would they inform those who became ill that their illnesses were radiation related (*Begay et al. v. United States,* 591 F. Supp. 991 [D. AZ (1985)], court document 84–2462)." Barbara Rose Johnston, Susan E. Dawson, and Gary E. Madsen, "Uranium Mining and Milling: Navajo Experiences in the American Southwest," in Johnston, *Half-Lives and Half-Truths,* 103. See also Susan E. Dawson and Gary E. Madsen, "Uranium Mine Workers, Atomic Downwinders, and the Radiation Exposure Compensation Act (RECA): The Nuclear Legacy" (117–44); and Edward Liebow, "Hanford, Tribal Risks, and Public Health in an Era of Forced Federalism" (145–64), in this excellent essay collection.

64. Nader and Gusterson describe how "in a form of nuclear colonialism, nuclear weapons states have consistently externalized the health and environmental costs associated with nuclear weapons development either to colonies abroad (for example, Australia for the British, the Pacific Islands for the Americans and French) or to victims of internal colonization (the Shoshone Indians of Nevada in the United States, the Kazakhs of the former Soviet Union, the Uighurs of China)." Laura Nader and Hugh Gusterson, "Nuclear Legacies: Arrogance, Secrecy, Ignorance, Lies, Silence, Suffering, Action," in Johnston, *Half-Lives and Half-Truths,* 300–301.

65. Quoted in Terry Tempest Williams, *Refuge: An Unnatural History of Family and Place* (New York: Random House, 1991), 283.

66. Churchill and LaDuke, "Native North America," 242. Dana E. Powell offers a nuanced account of the Navajo nation's shifting relationship to nuclear infrastructures in *Landscapes of Power: Politics of Energy in the Navajo Nation* (Durham, N.C.: Duke University Press, 2018).

67. John Beck, *Dirty Wars: Landscape, Power, and Waste in Western American Literature* (Lincoln: University of Nebraska Press, 2009), 25; Gerald D. Nash, *The Federal Landscape: An Economic History of the Twentieth-Century West* (Tucson: University of Arizona Press, 1999), 52.

68. See Churchill and LaDuke, "Native North America."

69. Traci Brynne Voyles analyzes the long history of how Diné Bikéyah (Navajo Country) came to be seen as such a space in *Wastelanding: Legacies of Uranium Mining in Navajo Country* (Minneapolis: University of Minnesota Press, 2015).

70. Michelle Ty, "Trash and the Ends of Infrastructure," *Modern Fiction Studies* 61, no. 4 (2015): 627.

71. My thinking about the quantum geographies of colonialism is informed by Eric Gary Anderson's analysis of how "American Indian and Euro-American Southwests are both solidly grounded and portable, both physical and textual; at the same time and often in the same space." See Anderson, *American Indian Literature and the Southwest: Contexts and Dispositions* (Austin: University of Texas Press, 1999), 3.

72. Bernard Nietschmann and William Le Bon, "Nuclear States and Fourth World Nations," *Cultural Survival Quarterly* 11, no. 4 (1988): 7.

73. Grausam, "It Is Only a Statement," 326.

74. Cited in Ward Churchill, *Struggle for the Land: Indigenous Resistance to Genocide, Ecocide, and Expropriation in Contemporary North America* (Monroe, Maine: Common Courage Press, 1993), 225.

75. Russell Means, "The Same Old Song," in *Marxism and Native Americans,* ed. Ward Churchill (Boston: South End Press, 1983), 25.

76. Masco, *Nuclear Borderlands*, 151.

77. Rob Nixon, *Slow Violence and the Environmentalism of the Poor* (Cambridge, Mass.: Harvard University Press, 2011), 7.

78. Grausam is the only critic to refer even obliquely to this history; Houser, whose work most directly addresses the novel through an ecotoxicity lens, makes no reference to it. The invisibility of U.S. colonial practices is most strikingly visible in Fabienne Collingnon's work; she describes the wall between the United States and Canada in the novel as a technology of settler colonialism by referring to Wendy Brown's work on Israel, and it is clear that when she describes the "citizen experience as colonized subjects," she is using the language of colonization metaphorically to indicate the circumscribed political subjectivities available in the post–Cold War state of exception rather

than the literally colonized nation-states of North America. See Collignon, "USA Murated Nation; or, The Sublime Spherology of Security Culture," *Journal of American Studies* 49, no. 1 (2015): 103. Even the *Infinite Jest* wiki, a site that provides a crowdsourced page-by-page reader's guide to the novel in obsessive detail, contains no references to the real-world analogues of the novel's national sacrifice zones.

79. Nixon, *Slow Violence*, 150.

80. Nixon.

81. I discuss the narrative structure of the novel's perpetual present more fully in Jessica Hurley, "War as Peace: Afterlives of Nuclear War in David Foster Wallace's *Infinite Jest*," in *The Silence of Fallout: Nuclear Criticism in a Post–Cold War World*, ed. Michael J. Blouin, Morgan Shipley, and Jack Taylor, 192–210 (Newcastle on Tyne, U.K.: Cambridge Scholars, 2013). Samuel S. Cohen positions Wallace as one of a generation of writers who occupied an uneasy relationship to the "end of history" narrative that dominated the 1990s, although he doesn't go as far as I do in thinking of *Infinite Jest* as a historical novel about the recent past as well as a science-fiction-y one about the near-future (he excludes Wallace from his book-length study of 1990s historical novels, for example). See Cohen, "To Wish to Try to Sing to the Next Generation: *Infinite Jest*'s History," in *The Legacy of David Foster Wallace*, ed. Samuel S. Cohen and Lee Konstantinou (Iowa City: University of Iowa Press, 2012), 76–77.

82. It's before.

83. Heather Houser, "Managing Information and Materiality in *Infinite Jest* and *Running the Numbers*," *American Literary History* 26, no. 4 (2014): 742–43.

84. Fest, "Inverted Nuke in the Garden," 149. Daniel Grausam also describes the novel as a kind of training device for relearning how to live with a future in a post–Cold War moment when the threat of imminent atomic annihilation has lifted, arguing that "learning to re-inhabit time in a meaningful way is . . . the problem of how to escape the structure of temporality brought into being by the first nuclear age." While these readings are not necessarily inaccurate—indeed, I have argued similarly in "War as Peace"—their repeated invocation of the nuclear bomb as the only danger produced by the atomic age reiterates the bomb-focused narrowness of definition against which this project positions itself, rendering invisible the hundreds of nuclear weapons that *have* been detonated as well as the ongoing disaster that, in fact, the novel places front and center: that of nuclear waste. See Grausam, "It Is Only a Statement," 325.

85. Sven Birkerts, "Apocalypse Now," *New Republic* 205, no. 19 (1991): 39.

86. See the readings of *Ceremony* in, among others, Kenneth Cooper, "The Whiteness of the Bomb," in *Postmodern Apocalypse: Theory and Cultural*

Practice at the End, ed. Richard Dellamora, 76–106 (Philadelphia: University of Pennsylvania Press, 1995); Rebecca Tillett, "On the Cutting Edge: Leslie Marmon Silko," in *The Native American Renaissance: Literary Imagination and Achievement,* ed. Alan R. Velie and A. Robert Lee, 74–87 (Norman: University of Oklahoma Press, 2013); Krista Comer, *Landscapes of the New West: Gender and Geography in Contemporary Women's Writing* (Chapel Hill: University of North Carolina Press, 1999); Adamson, *American Indian Literature*; and Beck, *Dirty Wars.*

87. Kyoko Matsunaga, "Leslie Marmon Silko and Nuclear Dissent in the American Southwest," *The Japanese Journal of American Studies* 25 (2014): 83.

88. Bridget O'Meara, "The Ecological Politics of Leslie Silko's *Almanac of the Dead,*" *Wicazo Sa Review* 15, no. 2 (2000): 65.

89. Ann Brigham, "Productions of Geographic Scale and Capitalist-Colonialist Enterprise in Leslie Marmon Silko's *Almanac of the Dead,*" *Modern Fiction Studies* 50, no. 2 (2004): 304. Some of the best analyses of temporality in *Almanac of the Dead* are Shari M. Huhndorf, "Picture Revolution: Transnationalism, American Studies, and the Politics of Contemporary Native Culture," *American Quarterly* 61, no. 2 (2009): 359–81; Janet M. Powers, "Mapping the Prophetic Landscape in *Almanac of the Dead,*" in Barnett and Thorson, *Leslie Marmon Silko,* 261–72; Rebecca Tillett, "'The Indian Wars Have Never Ended in the Americas': The Politics of Memory and History in Leslie Marmon Silko's 'Almanac of the Dead,'" *Feminist Review,* no. 85 (2007): 21–39; T. V. Reed, "Toxic Colonialism, Environmental Justice, and Native Resistance in Silko's *Almanac of the Dead,*" *MELUS* 34, no. 2 (2009): 25–42; John Muthyala, "*Almanac of the Dead*: The Dream of the Fifth World in the Borderlands," *LIT* 14, no. 4 (2003): 357–85; and Sharon Patricia Holland, *Raising the Dead: Readings of Death and (Black) Subjectivity* (Durham, N.C.: Duke University Press, 2000).

90. Ami M. Regier, "Material Meeting Points of Self and Other: Fetish Discourses and Leslie Marmon Silko's Evolving Conception of Cross-Cultural Narrative," in Barnett and Thorson, *Leslie Marmon Silko,* 186.

91. While not a diegetic narrator telling a metanarrative story, as Genette defines a traditional frame narrative, the snake does share some of the qualities of the frame narrative: it sets the conditions of possibility of the world being described, establishing its ground rules and practices as possible within the confines of the story.

92. Laura Coltelli, "*Almanac of the Dead*: An Interview with Leslie Marmon Silko (1993)," in *Conversations with Leslie Marmon Silko,* ed. Ellen L. Arnold (Jackson: University Press of Mississippi, 2000), 125–26.

93. Coltelli, 126.

94. Caren Irr, "The Timeliness of *Almanac of the Dead,* or a Postmodern Rewriting of Radical Fiction," in Barnett and Thorson, *Leslie Marmon Silko,* 224.

95. Irr.

96. Birkerts, "Apocalypse Now," 41.

97. City of Sherrill v. Oneida Nation, 1490–92, quoted in Mark Rifkin, *Manifesting America: The Imperial Construction of U.S. National Space* (Oxford: Oxford University Press, 2009), 4.

98. See Rifkin, *Manifesting America*, 4.

99. Judith Revel, "Identity, Nature, Life: Three Biopolitical Deconstructions," *Theory, Culture, and Society* 26, no. 6 (2009): 52.

100. See Michael André Bernstein, *Foregone Conclusions: Against Apocalyptic History* (Berkeley: University of California Press, 1994).

101. See Annie McClanahan, "Future's Shock: Plausibility, Preemption, and the Fiction of 9/11," *symplokē* 17, no. 1 (2009): 41–62; and R. John Williams, "World Futures," *Critical Inquiry* 42, no. 3 (2016): 473–546.

102. See the discussion of Frank Kermode's *The Sense of an Ending* in chapter 2.

103. See Masco, *Nuclear Borderlands*, 119, 122.

104. See, e.g., Dimock, *Through Other Continents*, 175–95. Dimock sees no problem in claims like this one: "Who counts as a 'Native' American? The usual definition is *retrospective*, in terms of ancestry. [Gary] Snyder reverses the arrow of time and makes it *prospective*. We become 'Native Americans' by virtue of the descendants we can imagine, the kinds of people we would like to bequeath the world to, to see flourish in our wake" (178, emphasis original). Or rather, she acknowledges and dismisses the problem by quoting Silko's objection that "although [Snyder] is careful, even reverent with this land he is occupying, it is not 'his' land" in a footnote, without letting it disrupt her thorough agreement with Snyder's colonialist argument (Silko quoted in footnote, 233). Snyder/Dimock's argument here serves only to perpetuate settler colonialism by disavowing the fact that the return of Native land must be the first step in any kind of decolonial praxis. If you want to live more in harmony with the land as Native cultures do, decolonize. If you want to use Indigenous temporalities to oppose Euro-American ones, decolonize. If you want to draw inspiration from Native forms of social organization, decolonize. I do not mean *decolonization* in a metaphorical sense here but rather in the sense of returning land and political sovereignty to Indigenous peoples. See Eve Tuck and K. Wayne Yang, "Decolonization Is Not a Metaphor," *Decolonization: Indigeneity, Education, and Society* 1, no. 1 (2012): 1–40. If you want to champion Native culture in any of its myriad forms, you have first to acknowledge that vast swathes of territory have never been ceded by treaty and do not belong to the United States.

105. Regier, "Material Meeting Points of Self and Other," 191.

106. Regier, 187.

107. Steven Belletto, "The Game Theory Narrative and the Myth of the National Security State," *American Quarterly* 61, no. 2 (2009): 337.

108. As Lord is Eschaton's "God" (333), let's call this a moment of *deus in machina*.

109. Daniel Grausam, "Games People Play: Metafiction, Defense Strategy, and the Cultures of Simulation," *ELH* 78, no. 3 (2011): 518–19.

110. Houser, "Managing Information and Materiality," 751.

111. Morton, *Hyperobjects*, 122.

112. Remember when we had analogue TVs, and when you lost the signal, the screen would fill with what we called, in Britain at least, snow? I'm hoping we're not too removed in time and space for the reference to read. Houser describes the work of materialist description in the novel as an attempt to differentiate between information and noise and ascribes this effort to recent ecocriticism as it works to convey the complexities of the material world through language or data visualization. Here, I suggest, we see the breakdown of our attempted mastery. See Houser, "Managing Information and Materiality," 744.

113. Gregory Benford, Craig W. Kirkwood, Harry Otway, and Martin J. Pasqualetti, *Ten Thousand Years of Solitude?* (Washington, D.C.: U.S. Department of Energy, 1991), iii.

114. Benford et al., 17.

115. Martin J. Pasqualetti, "Landscape Permanence and Nuclear Warnings," *Geographical Review* 87, no. 1 (1997): 81.

116. Perrow, *Normal Accidents*, 5.

117. Van Wyck, *Signs of Danger*, xx.

118. Perrow, *Normal Accidents*, 5. The way that probability shades into certainty from a different perspective in time can also be thought on a smaller, more intimate scale. In *Statistical Panic*, Kathleen Woodward details the ways in which we structure our lives and our fears through discourses of probability: "statistics are probabilities cast into possible and alternative futures that for the most part take on a dark dimension. These statistical probabilities seem to implicate us as individuals in scenarios of financial ruin and of disaster by disease and weather. . . . A statistic often seems to contain a complete narrative in and of itself: I have an 80 percent chance . . . you have a 10 percent risk." Even in medical discourse, however, expanding the time frame only slightly leaves us with a 100 percent chance of death. Sooner or later. Woodward, *Statistical Panic*, 209.

119. Adam, *Timescapes of Modernity*, 198.

120. Van Wyck, *Signs of Danger*, 6.

121. Benford et al., *Ten Thousand Years of Solitude?*, 19.

122. Theodor W. Adorno, *Minima Moralia: Reflections from Damaged Life,* trans. E. F. N. Jephcott (London: Verso, 2005), 247.

Coda

1. See Peter Kuznick, "Japan's Nuclear History in Perspective: Eisenhower and Atoms for War and Peace," *Bulletin of the Atomic Scientists,* April 13, 2011, https://thebulletin.org/japans-nuclear-history-perspective-eisenhower-and-atoms-war-and-peace-0.

2. See Christopher F. Jones, Shi-Lin Loh, and Kyoko Satō, "Narrating Fukushima: Scales of a Nuclear Meltdown," *East Asian Science, Technology, and Society* 7, no. 4 (2013): 601–23.

3. For a detailed account of Eisenhower's context and reasoning, including the role of the Korean War in the development of Atoms for Peace, see Matthew Jones, *After Hiroshima: The United States, Race, and Nuclear Weapons in Asia, 1945–1965* (Cambridge: Cambridge University Press, 2010).

4. Quoted in Kenneth Osgood, *Total Cold War: Eisenhower's Secret Propaganda Battle at Home and Abroad* (Lawrence: University Press of Kansas, 2006), 156.

5. Osgood, 156.

6. Dwight D. Eisenhower, "Address by Mr. Dwight D. Eisenhower, President of the United States of America, to the 470th Plenary Meeting of the United Nations General Assembly," International Atomic Energy Agency, https://www.iaea.org/about/history/atoms-for-peace-speech.

7. Eisenhower.

8. Eisenhower.

9. See Muto Ichiyo, "The Buildup of a Nuclear Armament Capability and the Postwar Statehood of Japan: Fukushima and the Genealogy of Nuclear Bombs and Power Plants," *Inter-Asia Cultural Studies* 14, no. 2 (2013): 171–212.

10. For a critique of the flawed ways in which Atoms for Peace even managed to function as restitution, see Lisa Yoneyama, *Cold War Ruins: Transpacific Critiques of American Justice and Japanese War Crimes* (Durham, N.C.: Duke University Press, 2016), 210–14.

11. "A Reactor for Japan," *Washington Post,* September 23, 1954, 18.

12. "A Reactor for Japan."

13. Erich Auerbach, *Scenes from the Drama of European Literature* (Minneapolis: University of Minnesota Press, 1984), 59, 72.

14. Muto, "Buildup," 172.

15. Alexis Shotwell, *Against Purity: Living Ethically in Compromised Times* (Minneapolis: University of Minnesota Press, 2016), 204, emphasis original.

16. Ruth Ozeki, *A Tale for the Time Being* (New York: Penguin Books, 2013), 31, emphasis original. Further page references are given in text.

17. Karen Barad, "No Small Matter: Mushroom Clouds, Ecologies of Nothingness, and Strange Topologies of Spacetimemattering," in *Arts of Living on a Damaged Planet*, ed. Anna Lowenhaupt Tsing, Heather Anne Swanson, Elaine Gan, and Nils Bubandt (Minneapolis: University of Minnesota Press, 2017), 110.

18. Karen Barad, *Meeting the Universe Halfway: Quantum Physics and the Entanglement of Matter and Meaning* (Durham, N.C.: Duke University Press, 2007), 335.

19. Barad, 315.

20. Stacy Alaimo, *Exposed: Environmental Politics and Pleasures in Posthuman Times* (Minneapolis: University of Minnesota Press, 2016), 114.

21. See Barad, *Meeting the Universe Halfway*; Jane Bennett, *Vibrant Matter: A Political Ecology of Things* (Durham, N.C.: Duke University Press, 2010); Donna J. Haraway, *Staying with the Trouble: Making Kin in the Chthulucene* (Durham, N.C.: Duke University Press, 2016); Catherine Keller, *Cloud of the Impossible: Negative Theology and Planetary Entanglement* (New York: Columbia University Press, 2015); Shotwell, *Against Purity*.

22. Michelle M. Wright, *Physics of Blackness: Beyond the Middle Passage Epistemology* (Minneapolis: University of Minnesota Press, 2015), 37, emphasis original.

23. Barad, "No Small Matter," 106.

24. Rebekah Sheldon, *The Child to Come: Life after the Human Catastrophe* (Minneapolis: University of Minnesota Press, 2016), 179.

25. Claire Colebrook, *Sex after Life: Essays on Extinction* (Ann Arbor: Open Humanities Press, 2014), 2:75, emphasis original.

26. Jodi Byrd, *The Transit of Empire: Indigenous Critiques of Colonialism* (Minneapolis: University of Minnesota Press, 2011), 13.

27. Byrd, 18.

28. Jean-Luc Nancy, *After Fukushima: The Equivalence of Catastrophes,* trans. Charlotte Mandell (New York: Fordham University Press, 2015), 36–37.

29. Nancy, 59.

Index

JESSICA HURLEY is assistant professor of English at George Mason University.

Made in the USA
Middletown, DE
23 October 2021